Strategic Partnerships

Strategic Partnerships

States, Firms and International Competition

edited by

Lynn Krieger Mytelka

Rutherford • Madison • Teaneck
Fairleigh Dickinson University Press

Associated University Presses
440 Forsgate Drive
Cranbury, NJ 08512

Library of Congress Cataloging-in-Publication Data

Strategic partnerships: states, firms, and international competition
/edited by Lynn Krieger Mytelka.
p. cm.
'First published in Great Britain in 1991 by Pinter Publishers Limited' – T.p. verso.
Includes index.
ISBN 0-8386-3445-1
1. International business enterprises. 2. Joint ventures.
3. Industry and state. 4. Competition, International. I. Mytelka.
Lynn Krieger.
HD2755.5.S846 1991
658′.049—dc20 90-49475
CIP

Manufactured in the USA

Contents

List of figures

List of tables

List of contributors

John Alic has been a member of the staff of the Office of Technology Assessment, United States Congress since 1979.
Claudio Ciborra Associate Professor of Information Systems, School of Economics and Business Administration, University of Trent, Italy.
Michel Delapierre, head of Centre des Etudes et de Recherches sur les Entreprises Multinationales (CEREM) Université Paris-X, and former Director of the Laboratoire de Recherche en Economie Appliquee (LAREA).
Barbara Jenkins is assistant professor in the Department of Political Science at Carleton University, Ottawa.
Jonah Levy is a graduate student in political science at the Massachusetts Institute of Technology. His research in France has been funded by the Fulbright Foundation and the Social Science Research Council.
Charles-Albert Michalet is Professor, Université de Paris-X and founding director of (CEREM). He is currently on secondment at the World Bank.
David Mowery is Associate Professor of Business and Public Policy at the School of Business of the University of California, Berkeley.
Lynn Krieger Mytelka is a Professor in the Department of Political Science at Carleton University, Ottawa and a senior research associate of the LAREA/CEREM, Université Paris-X.
Richard Samuels is associate professor, in the Department of Political Science Massachusetts Institute of Technology.
Jean-Benoit Zimmermann, economist Centre National de Recherche Scientifique (CNRS), is a member of Groupe de Recherche en Economie Quantitative at Econometrie (GREQE) of the Universités d'Aix–Marseille II et III.

Preface

This book examines a number of important subjects: the growth of inter-firm agreements bearing on technology which is the book's main theme, but also the new mix of competition and cooperation now characterizing the relationships between rival enterprises and the range of government policy instruments aimed at achieving international competitiveness in conditions where scientific and technical knowledge has become a strategic competitive asset. These phenomena all stem from two important contemporary developments: namely the emergence from the mid-1970s onwards of global or world oligopoly as a decisive form of supply structure and the major transformations in the key technologies lying at the basis of production which occured during the same period.

Inter-firm agreements or 'alliances' as they are called in this book have, of course, always existed to some degree or another. International cross-licensing between large corporations, which remains a fairly basic form of technical cooperation agreement in some industries, was already a significant feature of the chemical and heavy electrical equipment industries in the 1920s and 1930s. Similarly, joint ventures have existed for a long time and become increasingly important from the late 1960s onwards. However, the current wave of inter-firm agreements involves a much wider and more flexible range of arrangements which has rightly led a growing number of authors to refer to these agreements as 'new'.

The 'new' forms of agreements provide firms with responses to the particular set of phenomena which has characterized the world economy since the late 1970s. The opportunities created by agreements are different from, and in given circumstances superior to, those associated with the 'internalization' of activities through domestic vertical or horizontal integration or foreign direct investment. In the face of financial and economic uncertainty and turbulence in the world economy and of parallel rapid and radical technological change, the new forms of agreements offer firms a way of ensuring, in a wide variety of situations, a high degree of flexibility in their operations. When technology is moving rapidly, the flexible and risk-sharing (or indeed risk-displacing) features of inter-firm agreements offer firms a wide range of possibilities for acquiring key scientific and technical assets from outside their own walls. In other, somewhat more strictly defined circumstances inter-firm agreements can likewise provide firms with a possibility of pooling limited resources in the face of rising R & D costs.

The novelty and considerable interest of the volume lies in the fact that it examines the data and issues from a number of different angles and with the help of the wide range of analytical approaches adopted by the authors of different chapters. The multi-faceted character of the contributions can be noted in the 'triad' focus of the studies — inter-firm agreements and government–industry relationships in technology are examined in the particular contexts of the United States, Europe and Japan — as well as their cross-industry emphasis: there are two chapters dealing specifically with commercial aircraft and telecommunications, but a number of other industries are also examined in other contributions. More important still, is the fact that the phenomena examined are studied jointly and in a multidisciplinary approach by industrial economists, business management specialists and political scientists. A noteworthy expression can be found in the fact that throughout the book, governments — for example states or in the case of the European Community, the Commission — are considered as being, alongside firms, major forces and actors within the overall context of internationalization–globalization and the search for technology-based international competitiveness by firms and countries.

Of the two major developments which have set the scene for the strong increase in inter-firm agreements, the rise of international or global oligopoly has on the whole received much less attention than technological change and the increasing complexity of technology. Consequently, it may be appropriate to say something about this aspect here with the hope of encouraging researchers to take up the issue seriously.

In one of the last essays, Stephen Hymer predicted in the early 1970s that the economic recovery of Europe and Japan and their re-establishment as major powers would lead to the emergence of international oligopoly as distinct from the extension abroad of American domestic oligopoly which had prevailed as the main international form of supply structure during the 1950s and 1960s, as studied by Caves, Knickerbocker and of course Hymer himself. The 1980s witness the full realization of this forecast. International oligopoly *stricto senso* is now the dominant form of supply structure.

International or world oligopoly is of course not, in any way, a totally new form of supply structure. In the petroleum industry (see the 'Seven Sisters') and in several non-ferrous mining and processing industries (for example aluminium), world oligopoly has long been a key feature of supply. What is relatively new is the *extension* of global oligopoly and the fact that it now constitutes the dominant form of supply structure in most R & D-intensive or high-technology industries as well as in many scale-intensive manufacturing industries (to use Keith Pavitt's terminology). In R & D-intensive industries, the only exceptions are those industries where supply structures are *even more highly concentrated* with only two main manufacturers (as in the case of space launchers) or three (as in the case of the long-range civil aircraft examined by David Mowery in this volume) competing in the market.

World oligopoly and the 'global competition' which accompanies it, is the outcome of two related but none the less distinct processes, that of internationalization and that of industrial concentration and financial centralization. It occurs when:

1. in a given industry, industrial and technological development has created extremely strong constraints on firms (notably in the form of large R & D costs which must be recouped) to produce for world markets as distinct from even the largest domestic markets, as well as important opportunities for world-wide sourcing of key inputs to production, notably in the form of scientific and technological advances made in foreign countries (we have argued and documented this point in other recent work);
2. foreign direct investment by multinational or transnational corporations, after a phase in which investment was principally of American origin, has increasingly developed on a tri-polar (or 'triad' basis) and taken the form of 'mutual invasion' between Transnational Corporations (TNCs) belonging to the three main poles of the world capitalist economy, and
3. concentration after developing principally on a *domestic* basis, has evolved as an *international* process and led to a situation where the number of oligopolistic rivals in the strict sense of the term, that is those *effectively* capable of waging world or global competition has dropped *pari passu* to levels corresponding at the world level to those previously associated with oligopoly as calculated on the basis of earlier domestic criteria.

Research on concentration at an international level has fallen seriously behind the vast changes in the world economy which have taken place as a result of the overall process of internationalization. Measures of concentration (for example market shares by the first four, eight and twenty firms) are still being carried out mostly on a purely domestic basis at a time when the most significant indicator of concentration probably now pertains to global that is world market shares. Such measures have begun to be employed in industrial-sector studies (for instance in some carried out recently by the UNCTC and OECD). These diffuse efforts now require to be centralized and related to the appropriate theoretical underpinning in a way which would contribute to establishing international oligopoly as a recognized and academically 'respectable' concept.

Oligopoly has generally been studied principally in relation to 'fewness' and with special emphasis on price theory. In the case of international oligopoly at the point where it has developed today, taken alone, this is an inadequate approach. As pointed out by Caves long ago the essence of oligopoly is the recognition by a set of firms of their 'mutual market dependence', or again their 'interdependence'. Resulting 'mutual recognition' can take many forms. In the present context, where technology has become a decisive competitive asset, is moving fast and is expensive, it will represent an obvious priority area for cooperation between rivals.

The suggestions made here, substantiated by circumstancial, albeit incomplete case-study evidence, is that once certain thresholds of world concentration are crossed, the surviving firms can take steps to start re-establishing the entry barriers dismantled during the transition period from one form of oligopoly to the next, as well as by the radical technological change which has occurred. One way of doing this would be to organize not simply the *individual* but also the *collective* protection of their technological advances, through inter firm alliances, technology swaps and common action for the setting of standards.

Such situations do not preclude strong or even 'cut-throat' oligopolistic rivalry. The international economy has often recently bordered on such situations, as with the confrontation between Japanese and American oligopolists in a number of high-technology industries. Strong rivalry could, however, represent essentially a transitory phenomenon, the outcome of which could be to increase concentration over the long term as some firms are driven out of business and those remaining prefer to work out arrangements permitting some kind of co-existence with the leaders of the world oligopoly (this has occurred in colour TV manufacture for instance).

Finally, in the case of high-technology industries in particular, the type of competition engaged in today among OECD firms, in which Japanese firms have been particularly successful during the whole of the 1980s, generally involves the participation of governments. As noted quite early by A. Cotta, governments are parties to global oligopolistic competition, thus making world oligopoly 'mixed' 'that is public and private). This point has recently been made with considerable emphasis in D. Ernst and D. O'Connor's study, 'Technology and Global competition, the Challenge for Newly Industrializing Economies' published at the OECD Development Centre, by Sylvia Ostry in her recent book 'Governments and Corporations in a Shrinking World', and in the main papers for the 1990 OECD Tokyo Colloquium on 'Techno-globalism'. Placing special emphasis on R & D cooperation and the use of inter-firm agreements as an instrument of technological policy, the same point is of course made by several of the authors in the present volume. Professor Mytelka and the distinguished group of scholars she has invited to contribute, must consequently be congratulated for having produced a timely and useful book, which is sure to find its place in the thinking and discussions of the early 1990s.

François Chesnais
April 1990

Acknowledgements

The chapters composing this volume are the product of a series of meetings among members of the working group on 'oligopolies and hierarchies in the world economy'. The participants are most grateful to the German Marshall Fund of the United States which provided funding for the working group over a two-year period.

A debt of gratitude is also owing to the many people who gave so generously of their time to help us develop our ideas. The overall approach taken in this project, for example, was refined through discussions with Alain Lipietz, Jonathan Aronson, Daniel Chudnovsky and Dieter Ernst who attended the first meeting of the working group. The chapters themselves benefited from detailed comments provided by François Chesnais, John Hagedoorn, Jon Sigurdson, Fabio Arcangeli and Peter Buckley, all of whom participated in our second meeting.

In addition, a special thanks is due to Tom Hartley who served as rapporteur at our first meeting and to Susan Ship for editorial assistance. Manuscript typing and editorial assistance were made possible by a grant from Carleton University.

Acknowledgments

1 Introduction

In the 1970s, as the protective boundaries between industrial sectors and among national economies broke down under the pressures of rapid technological change and increased internationalization of capital, production and knowledge, the world economy entered a period of turbulence and change. Competition intensified for both firms and states and yet uncertainty made strategic planning for the one and policymaking for the other, more difficult.

The chapters in this book explore the changing role of states and firms in coping with these uncertainties, most notably through their impact on the pattern of international competition and internationalization via the formation of strategic partnerships. By analysing the dynamics behind and some of the consequences of this new form of collaboration between firms both within and across national boundaries, the authors of these chapters shed light on a number of fundamental changes in the relationship of knowledge to production and of states to firms within contemporary capitalism. Because these partnerships are situated at the nexus of the national and international political economy and are particularly prominent in the most dynamic, knowledge-intensive sectors of the economy, they also serve as a vehicle to address several of the more important issues raised in the theoretical literature on the firm and its growth strategies, on the role of states in preserving the international competitiveness of 'national' economic spaces and on the shifting configuration of power in the international system.

But what exactly are strategic partnerships? While there is no single definition for strategic alliances or 'interfirm technology cooperation agreements' as they have also been called, nor any one factor that motivates them, the contributors in this volume share two common elements in their approach to this phenomenon. First, they focus on those agreements among independent firms which involve knowledge-production or sharing activities, whether these are orientated towards the development of new products, new production processes or new routines within the firm or in its management of inter-firm contractual relationships. Strategic partnerships are thus not about the statics of allocative choices but about the dynamics of innovation and competition. Second, alliances are regarded as strategic when they seek to improve the future competitive position of the firm. Because of the emphasis on positioning, strategic partnering activity tends to assume greater importance in the longer-term planning objectives of a firm than it does as an *ad hoc* response to the opportunities for short-term gain.

Although these two criteria enable us to provide some rough boundaries to this phenomenon, the institutional forms that strategic partnering activity takes none the less, remain numerous and varied. Knowledge production and sharing, for example, may or may not be accompanied by other joint activities or by equity participation. But when joint ventures are, in Michael Porter's sense of the term, strategic investments, that is investments which may affect the underlying structural traits that determine profitability in an industry (Porter,1980; Porter and Fuller, 1986), they have been included here. Mergers and takeovers aimed at gaining market access or co-production arrangements that do not involve knowledge production or sharing do not meet the criteria for inclusion as strategic partnerships. Under many market configurations, however, acquisitions and alliances have emerged as complementary strategies.

Because the paradox of joint knowledge production and sharing activities lies in the problem it generates for appropriability at the level of the firm, the one-way transfer of existing technology (as in licensing or second-sourcing agreements, cross-licensing with a strictly marketing or market organizing objective and research contracts between a firm and a university or research institute), frequently included in other taxonomies of partnering activity (Chesnais, 1988: 58; Hagedoorn and Schakenraad, 1988; Haklisch, 1986, 92; Pisano, Russo and Teece, 1988), is not included here. Similarly, arms length purchases of technology that characterize traditional supplier-client relationships (Mariti and Smiley, 1983; 437) are excluded, but newer forms of such relationships which do involve knowledge production and sharing (Lundvall, 1988) fall within the boundaries of the phenomenon as we have defined it. Their inclusion, moreover, serves to illustrate the way in which older institutions may retain their form but with a subtantially altered content. The range of strategic partnering activity (covered in this volume thus extends from pre-competitive R & D consortia promoted by governments or privately initiated — as in the Japanese Key Technology Centres, the ESPRIT programme and SEMATECH — to a variety of technological cooperation agreements: AIRBUS, the AT&T–Olivetti venture, JESSI, Intesa or Safa that involve shared equity arrangements or go beyond the core – knowledge-production and sharing component to include production and marketing cooperation.

Furthermore, the dynamic conception of stratégic partnering activity adopted here leads the authors to part company with those who extend 'strategic' to include opportunism and deception in the Machiavellian sense of the term later adopted by many game theorists beginning with Thomas Schelling (1960), and by proponents of transaction cost analysis from Oliver Williamson (1975) on. Following their logic, the risk of opportunistic behaviour is reduced if alliances are concluded only between partners of similar size, having complementary assets but operating in different markets or market segments. Yet many of the strategic partnerships discussed in this volume are not restricted to links among complementary firms operating at different phases of the value chain: Mowery's work on agreements in the aircraft industry, Mytelka's analysis of inter-firm technological cooperation within the European ESPRIT programme, Levy and Samuels' examination of R & D consortia in Japan and Delapierre and Zimmermann's analysis of partnering activity by French firms point to the emergence of new forms of supplier–client relationships and to the growing importance of strategic partnerships among direct competitors and firms of disparate size. Moreover, as Ciborra and Levy and Samuels argue, opportunistic behaviour is itself antithetical to the kind of collaboration that underlies the successful strategic partnership. Lengthening the time horizon to increase the likelihood of multiple alliances among the same partners and ensuring a careful division of labour among them — or what the Japanese have called 'distributed collaboration' — are becoming important mechanisms for building trust among partners.

But the story does not end there. Why strategic partnering has emerged alongside takeovers, mergers and other more traditional strategies of the firm still needs to be explained and new criteria elaborated to evaluate its success and its significance.

Part I of this volume begins this process by looking at issues that underlie the emergence of strategic partnering activity from a systemic perspective. A number of key factors are highlighted: the growing knowledge-intensity of production, the rise in uncertainty and in the need for flexibility, shifts in demand and in the mode of competition and changes in the process of internationalization within the emerging world economy — whose dynamic interaction provides the basis for understanding why strategic partnerships have recently become prominent features of the competitive landscape. Part II moves from the systemic level to that of the firm and its industry. The authors of the chapters in this section analyse some of the specific conditions under which externalization, as opposed to internalization, becomes a preferred strategy of the firm, the functions it fulfils and its likely durability. Part III carries forward this firm-level analysis and complements it with an examination of the role that states and quasi-states are playing in structuring the environment within which strategic partnering activity takes place.

Strategic partnering activity proliferated both nationally and internationally in the 1980s and proved particularly useful in reducing the costs, risks and uncertainties of knowledge production. But strategic partnerships also made important contributions to change within the firm — in its approach to R & D, its ability to accumulate knowledge, its openness to new routines, its flexibility and its awareness of new markets and potential partners.

Going beyond the strategic behaviour of individual firms, the chapters in Parts II and III also point to the wider impact that strategic alliances are having on global patterns of competition among firms and on hierarchies among countries in the world economy. An analysis of the European ESPRIT programme (Chapter 9), for example, illustrates the way in which networks, formed through repeated partnerships, can give rise to oligopolistic structures through which barriers to entry are created. Close ties between suppliers and clients (Chapter 3) and between firms and home governments, particularly where markets (have become politicized

(Chapter 8) also shape competition within specific industries and across national boundaries. States have thus become involved in the process of shifting the competitive advantage of firms, and implicitly of national economies, through the promotion of strategic partnerships or the conditions that facilitate them.

Among the first to engage in R & D collaboration were Japanese firms. They did so, however, not spontaneously but, as Levy and Samuels point out, through a process of iteration between the state and firms that led to the targeting of key sectors and the formation of R & D consortia. Since then, promoting strategic partnerships has become an active vocation of states and quasi-states in Europe. Delapierre and Zimmermann, for example, point to the springboard effect of alliances in the European market for the international competitiveness of French firms. Similarly, with regard to the European Community, the ESPRIT chapter provides evidence of the way in which 'technology policy' — including R & D funding, the promotion of strategic partnering activity and standard-setting — can substitute for 'industrial policy' in knowledge intensive industries, much as 'trade policy' had earlier substituted for an 'industrial policy' in the restructuring of traditional industries. The critical role that home governments continue to play in a company's ability to compete world-wide also emerges from Jenkins' discussion of the telecommunications industry. If, for historic and economic reasons, as Alic argues, American companies have been reluctant to engage in strategic partnerships among themselves and the (American government has not provided much encouragement, it is nevertheless the case, as other chapters show, that American firms are the most sought-after partner by both Japanese and European firms. The extent to which American firms have become adept at 'learning' through such alliances, however, remains unclear.

Strategic partnerships can give rise to problems of appropriability at the level of the firm, and the problem is compounded by international partnering activity which transposes it to the level of the nation–state. Charles-Albert Michalet, for example, stresses this point when he argues that the growing internationalization of production and capital is further weakening the already tenuous link between the success of domestic firms and the competitiveness of national economies. To encourage such activity thus places in conflict many of the traditional roles that governments have played in strengthening national productive and technological systems (Bienefeld and Godfrey, 1982; Chesnais, 1986; Freeman,1988; Nelson and Winter, 1977) and in altering the country's competitive position within the global hierarchy of nation–states. Challenged, for example, are the views ranging from Alexander Hamilton to Frederick List and including contemporary advocates of strategic trade policy (Krugman, 1986; Milner and Yoffie, 1989, Stegemann, 1989) which, in considering the state's multiple roles in strengthening national enterprise, have looked to tariff and non-tariff barriers to protect national markets. Uncertain is the balance to be drawn between intellectual property laws, anti-trust regulations and financial incentives as means to stimulate innovation (Ouchi and

Bolton, 1987) in a period in which innovation is the key to shifts in a firm's competitive advantage. Under pressure are government procurement, regulatory and industrial policies that in the past secured economic space for the emergence of domestic firms (Ozawa,1980; Mytelka,1979). Despite these challenges to traditional policy instruments, in the uncertain world of the 1990s it is none the less clear that large multinational enterprises cannot regulate international competition on their own, nor can each multinational acting individually ensure the coherence of the whole. As the chapters in this book illustrate, a new role for the state in collaboration with the firm is already in the making and the strategic partnership figures importantly in this process.

References

Bienefeld, M.N. and Godfrey, M. (eds) (1982), *The Struggle for Development: National Strategies in an International Context*, New York, John Wiley.

Chesnais, F. (1986), 'Science, Technology and Competitiveness', *STI Review*, No. 1, pp. 86–129.

— (1988), 'Technical Co-operation Agreements Between Firms', *STI Review*, No.4, pp. 51–119.

Freeman, C. (1988), 'Japan, a new national system of innovation?' in G.Dosi, C. Freeman, R. Nelson, G. Silverberg and L. Soete (eds), *Technical Change and Economic Theory*, London, Pinter Publishers, pp. 330–48.

Haklisch, C. (1986), *Technical Alliances in the Semiconductor Industry*, New York, New York University, Center for Science and Technology Policy, February.

Hagedoorn, J. and Schakenraad, J., (1988), 'Strategic Partnering and Technological Co-operation' paper presented at the EARIE conference in Rotterdam, 31 August–2 September.

Krugman, P. (ed.), (1986), *Strategic Trade Policy and the New International Economics*, Cambridge, Mass., MIT Press.

Lundvall, B.A., (1988), 'Innovation as an interactive process, from user–producer interaction to the national system of innovation' in G. Dosi *et al.*, (eds), *Technical Change and Economic Theory*, London, Pinter Publishers, pp. 349–69.

Mariti, P. and Smiley, R.H., (1983), 'Co-operative Agreements and the Organization of Industry', *The Journal of Industrial Economics*, **XXXI**, No. 4, pp. 437–51.

Milner, H. and Yoffie, D., (1989), 'Strategic Trade Policy and Corporate Trade Demands' *International Organization*, **43**, No.2, pp. 239–72.

Pisano, G., Russo M., and Teece, D, (1988), 'Joint Ventures and Collaborative Arrangements in the Telecommunications Equipment Industry' in D. Mowery, (ed.), *International Collaborative Ventures in U.S. Manufacturing*, Cambridge, Mass., Ballinger, pp. 23–70.

Mytelka, L.K., (1979), *Regional Development in a Global Economy: The Multinational Corporation, Technology and Andean Integration*, New Haven, Yale University Press.

Nelson, R.R. and Winter, S.G., (1977), 'In Search of a Useful Theory of Innovation' *Research Policy*, No.6, pp. 36–76.

Ouchi, M.G. and Bolton M.K., (1987), 'The Logic of Joint Research and Development', University of California, Los Angeles, Graduate School of Management, published in the *California Management Review* Spring, 1988.

Ozawa, T., (1980), 'Government control over technology acquisition and firms' entry into new sectors, the experience of Japan's synthetic fibre industry', in *Cambridge Journal of Economics*, No. 4, pp.133–146.

Porter, M.E., (1980), *Competitive Strategy, Techniques for Analyzing Industries and Competitors*, New York, Free Press.

— and Fuller M.B., (1986), 'Coalitions and Global Strategies' in Michael E. Porter, (ed.), *Competition in Global Industries*, Boston, Harvard Business School Press.

Schelling, T., (1960), *The Strategy of Conflict*, Cambridge, Mass., Harvard University Press.

Stegemann, K. , (1989), 'Policy rivalry among industrial states: what can we learn from models of strategic trade policy' in *International Organization*, **43**, No.1, pp. 73–100.

Williamson, O.E., (1975), *Markets and Hierarchies, Analysis and Trust Implications*, New York, Free Press.

1 Crisis, technological change and the strategic alliance

Lynn Krieger Mytelka

Over the past several decades, the growing knowledge intensity of production gave rise to a set of contradictory dynamics that increased the costs, risks and uncertainties of knowledge production and intensified competition over market shares. These contradictions, by creating a tension between the need for flexibility and the need for critical mass, pitted economies of scale against economies of scope in research and development, in production and in distribution. For the investor this implied a new calculus that involved not only tradeoffs between 'internalisation', which increases the inertia of the firm, and the higher transaction costs of arms length relationships, but between short term financial gain and longer term positional advantages; between older governance structures which set uncertainty reduction in opposition to increased flexibility and new institutional forms through which these twin needs could both be met.

To assess the role of strategic partnering activity within this new context, the first part of this chapter differentiates these partnerships from other more conventional forms of inter-firm relationships and maps the principal sectoral and directional axes along which they concentrate. The second part analyses some of the dynamics behind the formation of strategic partnerships, focusing upon the knowledge-production and sharing component that has emerged as one of the more notable features of this phenomenon. It offers an alternative to those who hold that strategic partnerships can best be understood as a form of internationalization or as a short-lived grey area between 'markets and hierarchies' (Williamson, 1975). It argues instead for a dynamic approach to strategic partnering activity, one that situates this phenomenon more broadly within the context of uncertainty produced by changes in production, notably in the centrality of non-material (knowledge-related) investment, in demand, particularly as it is reflected in the size, shape and growth rates of national and international markets and in the pattern of global competition to which these changes have given rise. The third part relates these changes to the shift from industrial to technology policies that underlies the continuing support by states and quasi-states for strategic partnering activity.

The emergence of strategic partnering activity

Most contemporary theorizing stresses that multinational corporations (MNCs) favour internalized hierarchies and prefer wholly owned subsidiaries to joint ventures (JVs). These preferences, it is argued, stem from the potential that hierarchies afford for a reduction in transaction costs and, in a context of market imperfections, an enhancement of the ability to appropriate rents from tangible or intangible assets (Hymer, 1976; Kindleberger, 1979; Teece, 1981; Dunning, 1979; Buckley & Casson, 1988).[1] Nevertheless, because of factors such as increased risks, higher financial and managerial costs or the restrictions of national regulatory policies that rendered the wholly owned subsidiary impracticable or undesirable, the number of joint ventures and their proportion relative to the wholly owned subsidiary has risen in all sectors of the economy (Curhan *et al.*, 1977; Hladik, 1985). In manufacturing, for example, 'the yearly share of joint ventures in new manufacturing subsidiaries grew from about 10 per cent in the first decade of this century to over 50 per cent in the early 1960s' (Gomes-Casseres, 1988:112).[2] Despite this increase, the joint venture has not replaced the wholly owned subsidiary as the dominant form of direct foreign investment.[3]

While the internalization hypothesis suggests that ownership is the critical means by which firms control access to economic rents, it stops short of considering the possibility that such rents can be appropriated without ownership at all. It deals only in passing, moreover, with changes in the source of such rents over time and in the conditions governing their appropriability, both of which have a bearing on the emergence of strategic partnering activity in research and development.

Coexisting with these more traditional forms of investment are licensing arrangements as well as Original Equipment Manufacturers (OEM) and several types of subcontracting relationships that fall under what is now called 'new forms' of investment (Oman, 1984,1989). Although patents and trademarks provide a basis in ownership, these contractual arrangements, like many strategic partnerships, create arms-length relationships that can exist independently of an equity involvement. Such relationships, therefore, separate ownership from questions of appropriability and they focus attention more on function, particularly market penetration and/or production.

Licensing agreements are a case in point. Two forms of licensing arrangements are common, cross-licensing, as in the international electrical industry (Lean, *et al.*, 1982; Newfarmer, 1980), and simple licensing. The former is a production and marketing device through which the market power of each of the parties — and collectively of the oligopoly to which extensive cross-licensing can give rise — is reinforced. The latter is an asymetrical relationship through which the licensor seeks to incorporate the licensee within its strategic planning parameters. It does so by offering the use of brandnames or process technology subject to a set of negotiated conditions. In both cases technology enters into the relationship, but primarily as a one way transfer.

Through licensing, the licensor accesses a new market, reduces the risks of investing in plant and equipment there and commercializes its particular technological assets. For the licensee, a licence is a means to more rapid production and perhaps to higher market shares and economic rents than the firm could have secured had it invested in the development of the particular product or process technology on its own. But such immediate benefits are often gained at the expense of future technological dynamism, particularly if the licensee substitutes licensing for in-house research and development (R & D) (Mytelka, 1979). Yet, when a licensee does attempt to master the licensed technology and go beyond it, as the Japanese have consistently done, the relationship may become unstable, even conflictual (Hamel *et al*, 1986; Reich and Mankin, 1986).

One might expect a similar pattern to characterize the strategic partnership. But there are grounds for suggesting that this will not be the case, particularly where the relationship is more confederal than hierarchical (Henderson and Castells, 1987; Leborgne, 1987; Piore and Sable, 1985; Scott and Storper, 1986), where relationships are iterative and where distributed cooperation ensures a division of labour among the participants (see Chapters 3, 6 and 9). Moreover, unlike licensing agreements or earlier forms of joint venturing in which production or commercialization activities were dominant, knowledge production and sharing is an increasingly important component in the strategic partnership. Gains from partnering thus derive more from *learning* and the future *positional advantages* that innovation in products, processes or internal routines (see Chapter 3) brings, than from static allocative efficiency.

Decentralizing knowledge production

Arms-length collaboration in research and development reverses a fairly long tradition of directly appropriating knowledge through in-house research and development that dates back to the development of science-based industries in nineteenth century Europe and North America (Freeman, 1974). The absence of references to R & D activities in studies dealing with joint-venture activity since the turn of the century (Curhan *et al.*, 1977; Stopford and Wells, 1972) illustrates how uncommon collaborative R & D was in foreign subsidiaries. More recent research has confirmed this tendency through the 1980s. Thus Hladik found in a study of 420 American overseas joint ventures in the manufacturing sector over the period 1974–1982 that only 15 per cent of the JVs engaged in R & D, although she had broadly defined this to include minor product modifications as well as more collaborative R & D activities (Hladik, 1985;64).

The relatively limited amount of R & D done in overseas joint ventures or wholly owned subsidiaries was also noted in a large number of studies critical of the way MNCs centralized R & D facilities in the parent firm (Britton and Gilmour, 1978; Hymer, 1976; Mytelka, 1979; Vaitsos, 1974). In 1965, for example, only 6.5 per cent of total R & D expenditures by American MNCs was undertaken abroad (US Tariff Commission, 1973). Seven years later this had risen to barely 8 per cent (Creamer, 1976:35).

By the 1980s, however, a rupture in these well established patterns had occurred. A good example of this is the radical change at GLAXO, a major

British pharmaceutical firm, in both the size and geographical distribution of its R & D staff. In 1968, GLAXO employed 750 personnel in R & D, 97 per cent based at two research centres in the United Kingdom. Ten years later, although the number of R & D personnel had doubled, there was little change in their geograhical distribution. By 1988, however, GLAXO's R & D staff had soared to 5,000 and only 63 per cent of these (were located in the United Kingdom (Howells, 1989:, 19–22).

Decentralization of R & D to overseas subsidiaries,[4] has not been limited to large MNCs. Dynamic middle-sized American firms, such as Analog Devices, Cray Research, Dynatech and Loctite, have also internationalized with a view to mobilizing and appropriating R & D assets. One result of this was a dramatic rise in 'reverse transfers' of technology during the 1980s (McKinsey & Co., 1987).

Knowledge production and sharing through strategic partnerships

Paralleling this development, a number of studies also began to report a rise in inter-firm cooperative agreements and in the role of knowledge production and sharing within them. Data collected by the LAREA/CEREM on 1,086 inter-firm agreements in biotechnology, information technology, civil aeronautics and the auto industry, involving at least one European based partner, are typical. Classified into four types by function, these data show a steady upward trend in the growth of reported agreements since 1982, with the average number of agreements per year rising from sixty seven in the period 1980–2 to 133 in 1983–5 and 243 in 1986–7 (see Table 1.1). Of the 1,086 agreements, 27 per cent involved the commercialization of goods or services, whether jointly produced or not, 29 percent the production of goods (including licensing, sub-contracting and joint ventures) and despite the earlier rarity of joint R & D, 29 per cent the production and sharing of knowledge (choice of research priorities, joint pre-competitive research, joint engineering or development activities). In addition, 40 per cent were global agreements involving all three of these functions and frequently an exchange of equity as well. Global agreements are not regarded as strategic partnerships when they lead to the an exchange of shares or the creation of a joint venture that involves the whole range of a firm's activities and constrains the strategic autonomy of the participants (see Chapter 5).

The number of corporate strategic investments (defined by venture economics as investments in research and development activities in venture capital backed companies), show a similar rise. From thirty per year in the first three years of their survey, 1978–80, the figure doubles in 1981 and doubles again two years later. In 1985, the last year for which these data were available, 245 corporate strategic investments had been made (Venture Economics, n.d.).

Other data suggest the same trends. The Studiecentrum voor Technologie en Beleid TNO TASC data base codes 2,279 technological co-operation agreements (in information technology and biotechnology into a number of discrete categories. Two are particularly relevant for an analysis of strategic partnering activity: 'joint ventures and research corporations' which

Table 1.1: Distribution of inter-firm agreements by function, 1980–7 (biotechnology, information technology, civil aeronautics, automobiles)

Year	Knowledge	Production	Commercial.	Global	Total
1980	13	14	8	8	37
1981	29	33	25	25	91
1982	19	19	20	20	74
1983	20	24	28	28	100
1984	36	45	35	35	137
1985	55	58	52	52	162
1986	75	62	55	82	219
1987	70	60	68	126	266
Total	317	315	291	436	1,086
%	29%	29%	27%	40%	100%

Source: LAREA/CEREM data base

collectively account for 26.9 per cent of the agreements and 'technology exchange' agreements which constitute 47.2 per cent of the total. Since the former includes only companies 'which have shared R & D as a particular company objective besides production, marketing, sales, etc.' (Hagedoorn and Schot, 1988:26), it implicitly recognizes the distinction drawn above between joint ventures that are and those that are not strategic partnerships. Unlike the LAREA/CEREM data base, the latter category covers technology sharing and joint development agreements as well as customer–supplier partnerships that involve subcontracting and co-production. The rising number of such technology exchange agreements, however, suggests that customer–supplier partnerships may be evolving from one way to joint technology production and sharing relationships. Further evidence of this change can be found in Mowery's analysis of alliances in the aircraft industry (see Chapter 4).

Table 1.2, which presents data for these two types of technological cooperation agreements, confirms the growth of knowledge-production and -sharing activities in these two industries over the 1980s as compared to the previous decade. From a low of 6.5 in the 1970–5 period, the average number of agreements reported per year rose dramatically to 26.5 in the years 1976–9, quadrupling in 1980–3 to 110.8 and doubling once more in the 1984–7 period to reach a high of 271.3.

The role knowledge production and sharing is playing in strategic partnering activity also emerges from an analysis of the motives partners give for entering into such alliances. Using data from the FOR data base, Mariti and Smiley found that although many agreements were motivated by more than one concern, giving rise to some double counting, technological complementarity, defined as a long-term transaction involving an exchange or sharing of technology between the parties, was a primary motive for many of these agreements (see Table 1.3).

Table 1.2: Technological cooperation agreements* in biotechnology and information technology 1970–87 (in number of agreements)

	before 1970	1970–5	1976–9	1980	1981	1982
Biotechnology	3	5	63	48	55	68
Information technology	12	34	122	68	110	128
Total	15	39	185	116	165	196

	1983	1984	1985	1986	1987	Total
Biotechnology	43	55	123	124	108	695
Information technology	161	206	242	252	249	1584
Total	204	261	365	376	357	2279

*Includes joint ventures/research corporations and technology exchange arrangements

Source: Hagedoorn and Schot, 1988: 21, 27 and 29

Table 1.3: Motivations for inter-firm cooperative agreements

Motivations for the agreement	reported motivations (%)
Technology transfer (a one-way flow of information generally in the form of a licence)	29
Technological complementarity (long-term transactions involving an exchange or sharing of technology between the parties)	41
Marketing agreements (often between a producer and a distributor)	21
Economies of scale in production and/or distribution (including the rationalization of production through specialization in the production of components)	16
Risk sharing (agreements which involve none of the above motivations but provide for the management of the operation by one partner while the other contributes capital and absorbs some of the risks of failure)	14

NB: More than one motivation could be given for an agreement.
Source: Data from the FOR data base as reported in Mariti and Smiley, 1983: 442

Considerable variation in the importance of knowledge production and sharing in strategic partnering activity appears, however, when the data are broken down by partner/country and by industrial sector. Data from the

Table 1.4: Agreements by function* and by region/country (% of total number)

Region/country	Development	Production	Marketing	Total number
Intra–EC	74.4	51.2	15.9	195
EC–USA	65.0	49.1	24.2	169
EC–Japan	49.3	55.0	27.5	69
USA–Japan	42.4	62.7	42.4	59
Intra–USA	71.4	33.9	17.9	56
Intra–Japan	57.1	28.6	14.3	14

*Functions are not exclusive in this table

Source: Adapted from Hergert and Morris, 1988: 108

LAREA/CEREM data base show a concentration on knowledge production and sharing in intra-EC agreement (LAREA/CEREM, 1986b:30), and this is particularly notable in the case of agreements by French firms (see Chapter 5). Data from the INSEAD data base also points to the very high proportion of agreements involving knowledge production and sharing, or what they classify as 'development', among the 195 intra-EC agreements and in the 169 EC–United States agreements and fifty-six intra- United States, agreements they surveyed (see Table 1.4). In contrast, 'development' is of far lesser importance in international agreements involving Japanese firms, most of which emphasize production over development or marketing.

These findings with respect to Japanese firms are confirmed by data on the trend in Japanese international partnerships compiled by Professor Hirotaka Takeuchi. From 1982 to 1986 the number of 'international coalitions' involving Japanese firms rose from 1,009 to a high of 1,436 in 1985, declining to 1,202 in 1986. Japanese–North American coalitions accounted for over 40 per cent of the total throughout this period, but coalitions with European partners fell from roughly a third to a quarter of the total, while those with Asian partners rose from less than one-fifth to nearly one-third (Imai, 1988:9a). Of the 4,709 international coalitions for which a breakdown by function and industry was provided, fully 30.3 per cent were in marketing and sales, including brand licensing, and a further 26 per cent in production, including OEM and parts supply. Twenty per cent of these coalitions involved technology transfer or development (Ibid).

The pattern of competition and product life cycles differs across sectors and thus one would expect some variation in the timing and importance of specific strategic options. Taking this into consideration, it is none the less interesting to note that a sector-by-sector review shows a rising trend in strategic partnering activity across all knowledge-intensive sectors and a focus on knowledge production and sharing in these agreements. Of the 300 international coalitions by Japanese firms that focused on 'technology development', for example, 33 per cent were in the electrical-machinery sector, 28 per cent in basic materials, 12 per cent in machinery, 9 per cent in the transport sector and 5 per cent in precision instruments (Ibid).

Although Fusfeld and Haklisch have argued that the biotechnology industry is still 'in an early and highly competitive stage, in which patentable processes and know-how are of great importance (and where even basic research can lead to commercial concepts that companies can quickly connect to practice' (Fusfeld and Haklisch, 1985:9), other data suggest that biotechnology firms are increasingly able to identify opportunities for collaborative activity. The TASC data base, for example, shows a steep rise in the number of agreements in both the biotechnology and information-technology industries in the mid-1980s (see Table 1.2). The more intensive partnering activity among information technology companies may thus only reflect the relative newness of biotechnology firms and hence their non-availability for strategic partnering activity until the 1980s.

In their work on the machine-tool industry Haklish and Vonortas emphasise the growing importance of inter-firm cooperative agreements in this sector as well. Differentiating inter-firm cooperative agreements in R & D from licences, commercial agreements and traditional joint ventures, their study shows a steep rise in the former for the period 1980 through 1984. This is followed, however, by a small decline from a high of twenty-two agreements in 1984 to eighteen in the first three-quarters of 1985 (Haklisch and Vonortas, 1987, p.35). Thus the question arises as to whether strategic partnering activity has not already peaked.

Data from the LAREA/CEREM and the TASC data bases presented in Tables 1.1 and 1.2, however, show an intensification in the number of technological cooperation agreements in the sectors they cover, with a sharp increase in the number of reported agreements in 1985–6, precisely the period in which the Haklisch and Vonortas data show a downturn for the machine-tool industry. Although Table 1.2 shows a small decline in the number of agreements reported in 1987 in the information and biotechnology sectors, the data in Table 1.1 show a continued increase.

A number of factors suggest that the latter tendency is likely to continue during the 1990s. First, the emergence of new intra-European, intra-Japanese and intra-American collaborative research programmes has provided a further stimulus to strategic partnering activities. Second, as the analysis of the European Strategic Programme for Research and Development on Information Technology ESPRIT illustrates (see Chapter 9), within the context of these collaborative research programmes, large firms are both developing their linkages with each other and with smaller firms. Were it not for these broader collaborative research programmes, many of the agreements with small firms would not have been reported in the professional or business press that serve as the principal source of information in the construction of these data bases. Third, inter-firm cooperative agreements among smaller firms comprise roughly a third of the projects undertaken within the context of the ESPRIT programme. This, too, suggests that the phenomenon will continue to grow at least in the short term.

To the above, however, are counterposed two other tendencies. First, to the extent that a new wave of takeovers and mergers is accompanying this upsurge in collaborative R & D activity, the number of partners available for collaboration will decline. Bigger firms, however, have a wider reach in their search for partners and can cover a larger range of possible technological bases and product categories. While the number of partnerships may thus remain stable or grow more slowly, the number of partners may rise. Second, participation in existing uncompleted projects may slow down the rate at which new collaborative agreements between firms can be undertaken. There is some evidence for this in the lower participation rate of Italian firms in the second-year call for projects in the European ESPRIT programme. Once again, however, by opening EC programmes to firms based in EFTA countries, the base from which partners can be drawn is widened.

While the physical limits on partnering may retard the rate at which new agreements are concluded, such findings tell us little about the importance of the phenomenon itself and its likely persistence over the medium and long term. In the final analysis, interpreting these data will require a deeper understanding of strategic partnering and above all of the conditions that brought it about.

The dynamics of strategy partnering activity

Two broad changes underlie the development of inter-firm cooperative agreements as a major corporate strategy in the 1980s. The first concerns the changing nature of the production process in advanced industrial countries. Some have described this change as a shift from an industrial to a service economy. I think this misses a more fundamental transformation — the growing knowledge intensity of production across all sectors of the economy, where knowledge is understood to include not only the classical components of research and development but also design, engineering, advertising, marketing and management. The second has to do with the impact that slow growth associated with the economic downturn of the late 1960s and 1970s had on both markets and on the strategy of firms. Although these two factors are treated sequentially in the analysis that follows, it is important to stress their interactive nature. Indeed it is the growing knowledge intensity of production within the context of shifts in demand and slower overall growth that, by heightening uncertainty and a need for flexibility, provided the stimulus for new forms of competition and collaboration among firms in the world economy.

Uncertainty as a consequence of the growing knowledge intensity of production

In its narrowest sense of (R & D) activities, the growing knowledge intensity of production is evident as much in agriculture, forestry, fishing and mining as it is in the manufacturing sector and, within that sector, across industries from textiles to telecommunications. It is reflected in the large and increasing number of scientists and engineers engaged in R & D (see Figure 1.1), especially in countries such as Japan and Germany that are currently pursuing strategies of international competitiveness based on technological innovation and diffusion.

It is also evident in the increased gross expenditures on research and development as a percentage of Gross Domestic Product (GDP) in all of the major advanced industrial countries except the United Kingdom (see Figure 1.2). In the industrial sector, the volume of industrial R & D rose 70 per cent in Japan over the period 1980–5, 36 per cent in the United States, 30 per cent in France, 20 per cent in Germany but only 2 per cent in the United Kingdom (Caspar and Afriat, 1988:35).

This indicates a major change in the importance of non-material investment in the competitiveness of firms and more broadly in the competitive advantage of nation–states. Data for 1985 and 1986, for example, show that the ratio of R & D to turnover was greater than that of invested capital to turnover in five of the world's largest information technology firms — AEG (8 per cent and 4.2 per cent), SEL (11.5 per cent and 9.8 per cent), Bull (10.2 per cent and 9.6 per cent), Siemens (11.4 per cent and 5 per cent) and Northern Telecom (10.8 per cent and 8.5 per cent) (von Tunzelmann and Soete, 1987:30). In more aggregated fashion, a recent OECD report similarly noted that

> R & D expenditure has grown at three times the rate of tangible investment over the past 20 years or so in manufacturing industry...The tendency for increasing R & D intensity and decreasing tangible investment intensity is clear. In the OECD area as a whole, expenditure on R & D came to about one-quarter of that on fixed investment, rising high as three-quarters in some countries. Thus international comparisons of fixed investment alone gives an increasingly incomplete picture of the total investment effort. [OECD, 1987:15]

Going beyond the classical notion of R & D, Credit National aggregated expenditures on R & D, training, patents, purchases of software and advertising to arrive at an estimate of non-material investment in GDP. Although seriously underestimating training and other costs, their study none the less shows that over the period 1974–84, the share of non-material investments in GDP has risen in all of the five advanced industrial countries — Japan, the United States, United Kingdom, West Germany and France — for which such data were available (see Figure 1.3). Detailed work on the French economy confirms not only the rising cost of non-material investment by firms but also its increasing share in total investment (physical and non-material) (Kaplan and Burcklen, 1986).

The changing relationship of knowledge to production had a number of important consequences for the nature of competition among knowledge-intensive firms. In intermediate and capital goods industries, where economies of scale were important, the wedding of science and technology to

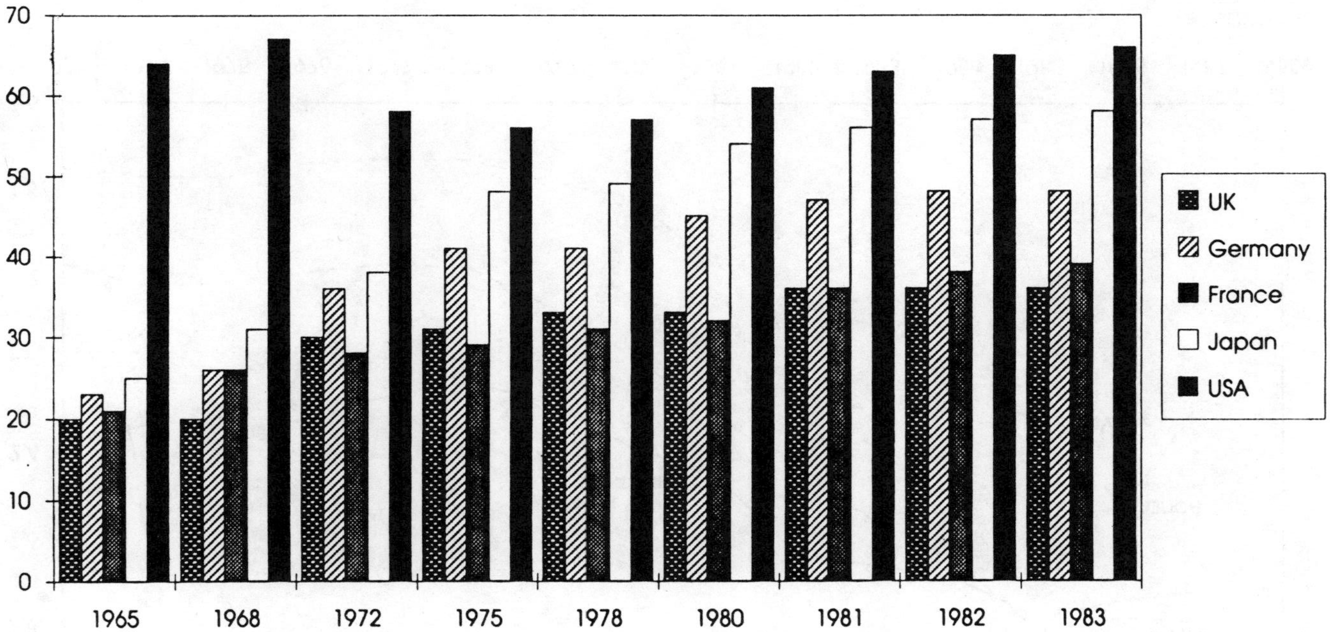

Figure 1.1 Scientists and engineers engaged in R & D (per 10,000 employees), 1965–83

Source: National Science Foundation, Science Indicators, 1981 & 1985

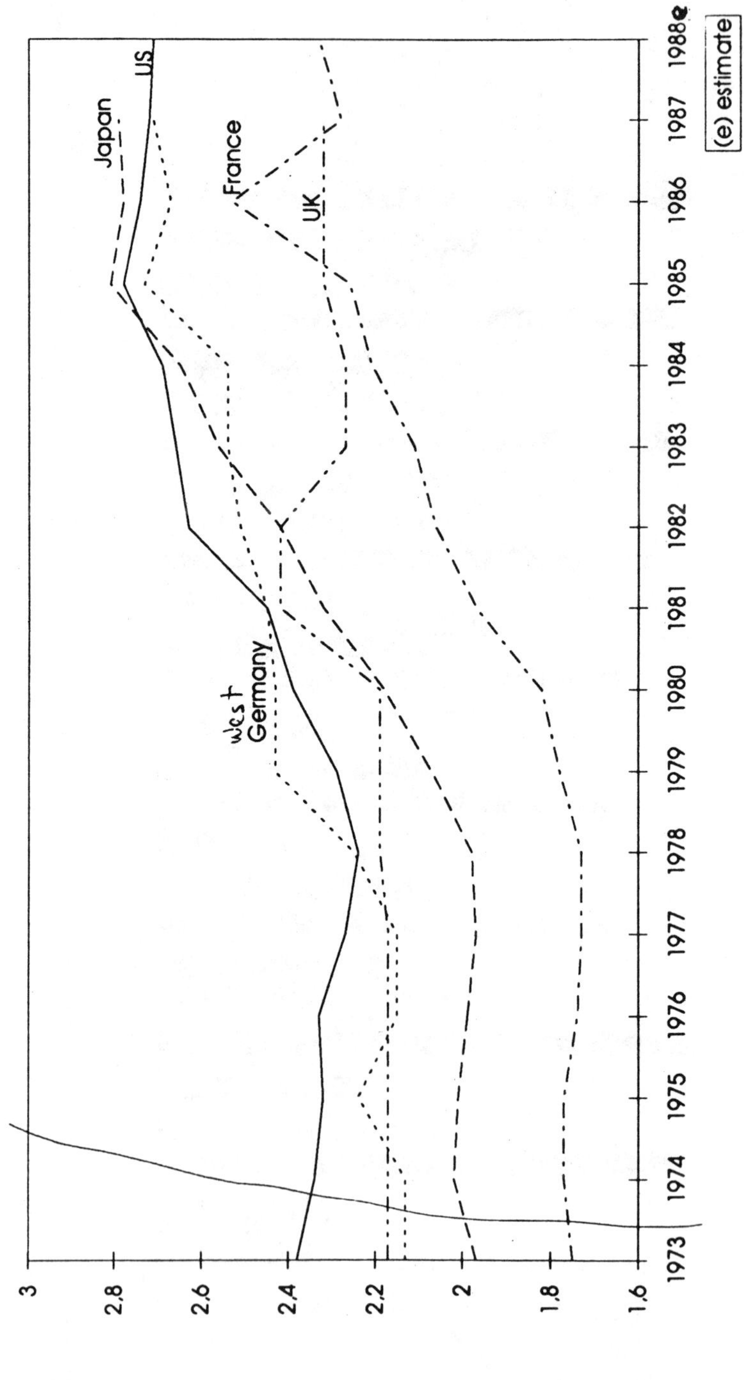

Figure 1.2 Gross Expenditure on R & D as a percentage of GDP, 1973–88

Source: OECD, STIID Data Bank, Nov. 1988

industrial production in the late nineteenth and early twentieth centuries stimulated high levels of concentration, cartelization and patent pooling (Freeman, 1974; Lean, *et al.*, 1982, Newfarmer, 1980). By limiting 'competition, each of these strategies served to reduce the risks in knowledge-intensive industries where research results were not spread evenly over time yet sunken costs were high and where firms were thus induced to secure their markets. In consumer-orientated knowledge-intensive industries, such as pharmaceuticals, risk reduction through concentration and cartelization were complemented by a systematic process of market segmentation through the establishment of brandname loyalty via advertising (Lall, 1975). Ultimately, high research, development and advertising expenditures created barriers to the entry of new firms in knowledge-intensive industries. Small firms, however, did survive in a few of the newer industrial fields or in specialized niches, and some medium-sized firms maintained themselves through state support in the form of procurement policies, R & D funding or export subsidization. Even then, the evolution of the computer and telecommunications industries since the late 1970s suggests that the process of concentration continues to play itself out in successive new knowledge-intensive industries as firms in these industries move beyond their initial innovative entry and into second and third generation products.

In the new knowledge-intensive environment of the 1970s and 1980s, product life cycles in the most dynamic industries began to shorten as the very nature of the products, their uses and the manufacturing techniques required for their production differed substantially from one product generation to the next. In the data processing industry, for example, by the early 1980s, more than half the products were less than five years old (Delapierre and Zimmerman, 1984:12). In the chemical and pharmaceutical industries one out of every two products is less than ten years old (Bellon, 1983:158). Shrinking product life cycles have made it more difficult for firms in these knowledge-intensive industries to justify the high fixed capital costs required for each new product generation.

As product life cycles shorten, firms have also been obliged to spend increasing amounts on R & D to remain at the frontier of technological change in their industry. R & D expenditures of the top ten pharmaceutical companies, for example, averaged 10.6 per cent in 1987–8, having risen dramatically in parallel with a doubling in the number of drugs under development world-wide over the period 1981–6 (*Economist*, February 4, 1989:63). In the telecommunications industry, the top ten firms spent an average of $752.8 million, 7.5 per cent of their turnover, on R & D in 1986. This represented an increase of 9.3 per cent over the previous year (IDATE, 1987:14). For a firm like Siemens that figure straddles several branches of information technology: the share of its products invested within the previous five years rose from 43 per cent in 1976–7 to 52 per cent in 1981–2 and reached 60 per cent in 1986–7 and its R & D budget doubled between 1983–4 and 1986–7 (von Tunzelmann and Soete, 1987:81), suggesting that a process of deceleration has not yet begun.

To amortize the rising costs of knowledge production, firms have come

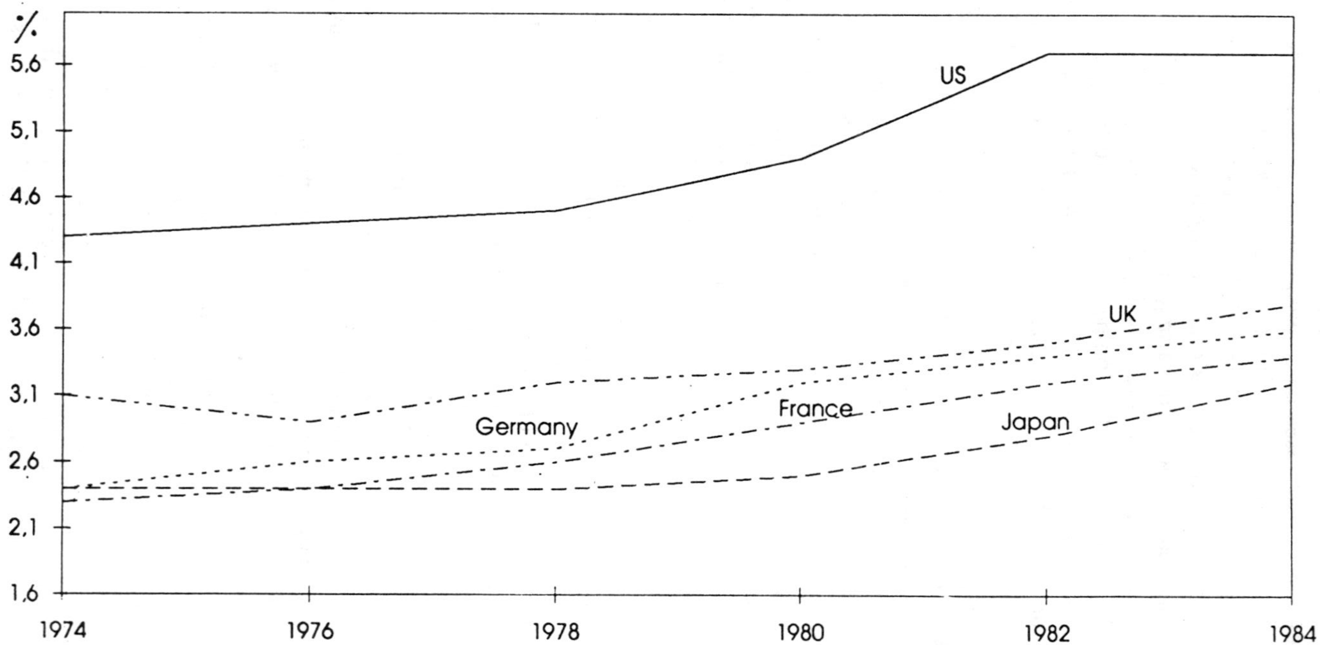

Figure 1.3 Share of non-material investment in GDP [R & D training, patents, purchase of software, marketing)

Source: Credit National, *L'Usine Nouvelle* Paris, 19 Nov. 1987

under pressure to widen their market of sale. Industries that had matured within the context of protected domestic markets and exclusive national procurement policies are thus being forced to internationalize. The development of a new digital switching mechanism in the early 1980s, which cost the world's leading firms approximately $1 billion (*Financial Times*, 6 June 1982), is a good example. For such investments to be profitable, markets of nearly $14 billion in sales over a ten-year period were needed (Dang-Nguyen, 1983,103). Yet the global telecommunications market was already a relatively mature market with growth averaging only 4.8 per cent over the period 1977–87. The expected increase in growth to 5.2 per cent per year over the next decade will not change the essentially zero-sum nature of the competition in this market (IDATE, 1987). Global competition in the telecommunications industry has thus led to pressures for market liberalization (see Chapter 8) and to a surge in mergers and takeovers within the industry.

Matching investment costs to the structure of demand has been problematic for other knowledge-intensive industries as well. In the semiconductor industry, for example, the minimum investment required for a new microelectronics production line, 200 million ecus, is nearly equal to the total value of annual output in a typical plant (Commission, 1986:16). Moving to a system of standardized mass produced integrated circuits as a means of realizing economies of scale, however, merely increased the vulnerability of these large scale plants to fluctations in product demand and to market segmentation. 'Equiped with such high-cost monster plants, Japanese firms didn't have much choice but to flood the market with a limited variety of standard IC commodities. This, in turn, of necessity has produced periodic price collapses' (Ernst, 1987:13) undercutting profit margins and making new investment more difficult.

In this and other industries where the recombination of generic technologies makes it possible to generate a wide variety of products for a multiplicity of markets (GEST, 1986), the boundaries delineating competitors and markets have eroded. As the ability to predict the shape of future markets or identify competitors weakens, traditional strategies of oligopolistic market competition[5] and internalization aimed at securing markets for products with high research and development costs become less efficient and the level of uncertainty rises still further.

Flexibility as a response to uncertainty

Because modern industry, as Gershenkron pointed out, requires large amounts of fixed capital, 'the industrial entrepreneur must look far ahead into the future' (1968,129). This puts a premium on the planning and predictive functions of the enterprise and on the institutional and other mechanisms that affect demand for a company's output. Yet it was precisely a breakdown in the Fordist mode of regulation, the unique postwar pattern of adjusting mass consumption norms, behaviour and institutions at the national level to productivity gains generated by an accelerated pace of technological change that characterized the 1970s (Aglietta, 1976; Boyer, 1985; Lipietz, 1987; Piore and Sabel, 1984; Freeman and Perez, 1988). In the 1950s and 1960s, through the set of social conventions and economic mechanisms put in place to ensure the mutual adjustment of mass consumption and production, a quasi constancy in profit share with respect to value added was maintained. This stimulated investment so long as demand was buoyant. But a crisis was in the making when productivity increases became more difficult to achieve, as began to happen in the 1970s (see Table 1.5).

A number of factors combined to produce this slowdown in productivity growth. On the production side imbalances in capacity utilization between highly specialized mass-production machinery, rigidities in supplier–client relationships and management structures as well as labour problems all played a role in slowing down the diffusion of productivity-enhancing techniques, material and immaterial. On the consumption side, slower growth in domestic purchasing power (see Table 1.6) accompanied by a segmentation of markets into income and product categories within which price and income elasticities of demand differed (Mytelka, 1987a) emerged as early effects of the economic crisis of the 1970s. Market saturation in many of the consumer durables that had been the staple fare of large corporations also occurred in this period and was exacerbated by rising imports of standardized, mass-produced products from low-wage countries (CEPII, 1983; Frobel *et al.*, 1980). Along with radical shifts in the international structure of demand, as the Japanese and European share of the world integrated circuit, telecommunications and aircraft markets rose relative to that of the United States (Ernst, 1986; Mowery, 1988:76–7), demand-side factors contributed to increasing the level of uncertainty that firms now faced.

Table 1.5: Labour productivity growth in five countries: aggregate and manufacturing, 1950–84 (average annual percentage change)

Growth of GDP per hour worked	France	West Germany	Japan	UK	USA
1950–73	5.01	5.83	7.41	3.15	2.44
1973–9	3.83	3.91	3.40	2.18	0.80
1979–84	3.24	1.88	3.06	2.95	1.09
Growth of manufacturing output per hour					
1950–73	5.63	6.31	9.48	3.21	2.62
1973–9	4.90	4.22	5.39	1.15	1.37
1979–84	3.50	2.78	5.46	4.28	3.10

Source: Baily and Chakrabarti, 1988: 5

Table 1.6: Total consumer expenditure in the advanced industrial countries, 1963–6 (avg. annual percentage change in volume)

	1963–73	1973–82	1974	1975	1976	1977	1978	1979	1980	1981	1982
US	4.4	2.6	–0.6	2.1	5.5	5.0	4.5	2.7	0.4	2.7	1.5
Japan	8.7	3.0	–0.7	4.1	3.4	3.8	4.7	6.0	1.3	0.6	4.2
EC (9)	4.5	2.2	1.2	1.7	3.7	2.7	3.9	3.9	1.7	0.3	0.3

	1973–86	1980–6	1980	1981	1982	1983	1984	1985	1986
US	3.0	3.5	0.0	1.0	1.5	4.5	5.0	4.5	4.0
Japan	3.0	3.0	1.5	1.5	4.0	3.0	2.5	2.5	2.5
EC (12)	2.0	1.5	1.5	0.5	1.0	1.5	1.5	2.5	4.0

Source: OECD, *National Accounts of OECD Countries, Vol. 2*; national statistics

A number of consequences for the strategies of firms and states flowed from this crisis of Fordism. First, under an institutional regime marked by monopolistic price fixing by firms and wage bargaining by unions, a fall in the rate of productivity growth during a period of high employment and high capacity utilisation made it more costly for governments to maintain high levels of mass consumption through Keynesian demand-management techniques. Rising inflation in the late 1960s was thus followed by an increase in unemployment, the imposition of credit restricting austerity measures and a resurgence of protectionism in the advanced industrial countries.[6]

Second, these uncertainties made it more difficult for firms to reconcile the growing costs of mechanization with the maintenance of profit levels and wages. Under these conditions, price-cutting strategies became more difficult to sustain and vanishing margins increasingly eroded investment capacity and opportunity thus putting into question earlier growth strategies based exclusively on mass-produced standardized products and exacerbating the pressures for market access noted above.

Global competition heightened uncertainty by transforming 'stabilized national oligopolies into competitive struggles between multinational corporations (at the international level where) the institutional setting is far different from the national one' and not necessarily suited to the stability of a Fordist mode of regulation (Boyer, 1985: 5–6). The revaluation of the yen and the adoption of a floating exchange rate system gave rise to new forms of uncertainty for these export orientated industries because fluctuations in exchange rates now required constant adjustments making macro economic policymaking by states and decisionmaking by firms less predictable.

Paradoxically, new strategies designed to cope with the slow growth in productivity and in demand have only added to the level of uncertainty. This was particularly true of strategies that promoted knowledge-intensive production in the guise of structural adjustment as these gave impetus to the process of innovation and accelerated the diffusion of new technology. In some instances these policies were a product of conscious national reflection — as in the new Japanese industrial strategy developed during the late 1970s and early 1980s (Japan, 1980) or as in France, where state policies were designed to support 'national champions',[7] domestic R & D or modernization. In others it was the outcome of individual corporate responses to the challenge of competition from both low cost suppliers and knowledge-intensive firms.

Pressured to modernize rapidly and compete globally, firms have simultaneously undertaken innovations in product and process development, management and marketing and they have emphasized the individualization of products through increased attention to design, the use of trademarking for standardized goods and the development of customized 'solutions' for clients in technologies as different as lasers (Larue de Tournemine, 1983), computers (Delapierre and Zimmermann, 1986) and integrated circuits (Ernst, 1986, 1987). This, in turn, required greater flexibility in the production system as a whole, permitting shorter production runs, more rapid throughput and model changeovers at lower cost. Whereas industry life-cycle theorists (Vernon, 1966; (Abernathy and Utterback, 1975) had earlier stressed the importance of product innovation and the ability of innovators to reap the economic rents of monopoly pricing in the initial phase of a cycle, with process innovation aimed at lowering costs emerging only once an industry matures, the new form of competition requires the pursuit of product and process innovation simultaneously.

One way to deal with the problem of flexibility is to exploit the systems properties of new technologies and new products. By combining generic technologies, often from hitherto distinct disciplines, a firm is able to position itself on a multitude of existing or potential markets (see Chapter 5). Yet even the largest firms cannot do in house R & D on all such potential generic links (see Chapter 6). Strategic partnering activity plays a central role here.

The state and the strategic alliance

As the changes described above radically altered the relationship of knowledge to production, encouraged the reorganization of production along more flexible, contractual lines and gave rise to new forms of competition in the world economy, they also dramatically changed the parameters within which states could make economic policies that effectively enhanced the competitive advantage of domestic firms and by extension, the national economy as a whole. This was particularly true in Europe where state intervention has traditionally been more pronounced. But its effects have been felt in the United States and Japan as well. One consequence has been to stimulate a variety of new government policies and strategic initiatives.

Liberalization measures such as deregulation at home and pressures to open markets abroad are two of the most salient policy changes to emerge in the 1980s. But these have been accompanied by the development of other policy instruments more evidently in the service of 'national' competitiveness such as strategic trade policies (Krugman, 1988), the commercial use of defence policies (Bellon, 1986; Mowery and Rosenberg, 1989) and the shift away from industrial and towards technology policies in many of the advanced industrial countries. Although there are some common elements to all three policies, particularly their emphasis on the dynamics of innovation and changing comparative advantage, it is the development of technology policies — through defence-related institutions in the United States, through ministries of finance [MOF], industry [MITI] and telecommunications [MPT] in Japan, through ministries of industry and of research and development in the France and DG XIII in the European Communities — that best exemplify the role states are coming to play as promoters of strategic partnerships.

The European experience is illustrative here. During the 1960s and 1970s, as new industrial sectors were created and others lagged behind, industrial policies were developed to stimulate the competitiveness of European industry. Focused exclusively on the national economic space, these policies promoted concentration among national firms, created national champions, supported research in publicly funded institutions and subsidized new capital investment in national firms. In high-technology sectors such as aircraft, telecommunications and nuclear energy, state purchasing provided a protected market for national output. With rising R & D costs, national R & D efforts, however, were less able to fund the move to newer product generations, while national markets became too small to permit national champions to match the scale and scope of production of their American and Japanese rivals.

The contradictory dynamics of costs and markets have thus undermined the use of public procurement policies to protect national markets and accelerated the process of deregulation in industries such as telecommunications. The single European market planned for 1992 will make the protection of 'national' champions politically more difficult as well.

Within that market, moreover, comeptition among 'regions' (Lombardy, Baden–Wurtemburg, Rhône–Alpes, Catalonia, Greater London) has begun in earnest and it is paralleled by the scramble for technology and investment underway globally by the states, provinces and regions that make up the United States, Canada and Japan. A new competitive dimension has thus been added to the global picture.

Many of the changes discussed above, moreover, have rendered industrial policy instruments less effective in the 1990s than in the past. Earlier forms of industrial policymaking, for example, were based on an ability to predict the future shape of the market. Within established technological paradigms (Dosi, 1982) or natural technological trajectories (Nelson and Winter, 1982), technological change was largely incremental. Fixing output goals, as in command economies or targetting products for development, was far easier than in a period of technological change which some have called a technological revolution (Freeman and Perez, 1988). This has contributed to the shift away from industrial policies and towards technology policies in which R & D funding of generic technologies permits a widening of the range of potential applications as the generic technologies themselves develop.

Behind earlier national policies was also the belief that higher rates of innovation and gains in productivity would result from increases in the size of firms or in fixed capital formation within them. In a knowledge-intensive production system, non-material investment and changes in the organization and in the management of the innovation, production and marketing processes have become key elements in a firm's competitiveness alongside traditional investment in machinery and equipment. Moreover, in contrast to the Schumpeterian assumption that R & D performance is correlated with firm size, it is possible to conceive of critical mass in a quite different way today, notably, in terms of the size of the 'system' needed to acquire the relevant knowledge rather than the size of the firm itself. This has a number of consequences for supplier–client relations (see Chapter 4), for the knowledge accumulation possibilities of small firms through strategic partnering activity (see Chapter 9) and for the ability of small and medium sized enterprises to move from the status of sub-contractors to value-added firms in their own right.[8]

Finally, the broad range of capabilities upon which a knowledge-intensive system of production is based also suggests that the process whereby R & D expenditures are translated into productivity gains is neither automatic nor linear. The institutional environment within which new knowledge is generated and diffused is now more widely acknowledged to be a factor in shaping industrial competitiveness. In this new knowledge-intensive environment with its requirements for flexibility and greater market access, strategic partnerships that span national frontiers and link firms to research organizations thus have a potentially important role to play in stimulating both innovation and, even more importantly, its wider diffusion throughout the economy.

But there are dangers in the adoption of a 'springboard' strategy (see Chapter 5). These come from at least two sources. First, problems may arise when, as frequently occurs in the development of 'technology' policies, the R & D system is abstracted from the economic and social systems in which it is embedded. The health of a 'national system of innovation' to use terminology introduced by Richard Nelson (1988) and Christopher Freeman (1988), depends not only upon the number of patents it generates but upon the interface between the supply of new knowledge and the demand for it. Where, as in the United Kingdom, government programmes promote the supply of R & D in universities and in smaller knowledge-based firms (Alvey, 1987), but the health of the overall economy diminishes the incentive for national firms to commercialize new technology, the likelihood is great that such firms will become targets for takeover and as in much of the Third World, scientists and engineers will, if not physically, then by the exclusive research contracts they sign with foreign firms, become part of a national outflow of innovation — a new brain drain.

Second, there is a danger that 'strategic' trade, defence and technology policies will collectively constitute a neomercantalist strategy whose rationale is based on the assumed positive relationship between the health of local firms and national competitiveness and economic growth. The globalization of competition with its attendant internationalization of production sites for goods and knowledge, however, make this relationship problematic at best.[9]

Conclusions

In sum, the emergence of strategic partnerships between firms and the encouragement they are currently receiving on the part of states reflect a number of fundamental changes in the process of production and in the form that competition now takes in the world economy. Among the most important such changes are the growing knowledge intensity of production, the need for flexibility, the development of competition on the basis of both price and innovation and the heightened uncertainty that has resulted from the coming together in the present conjuncture of these changes. Contradictory forces, however, are also at work. Concentration, for example, may over time partially restore the kind of conditions that made traditional oligopolistic forebearance techniques efficient means for reducing uncertainty and maintaining profits. Neomercantilist technology and trade policies which limit the internationalization of R & D may do little to reinforce national systems of innovation but much to create new barriers to entry for small firms and for small countries.

Despite these countervailing forces, changes in consumption and production and in the institutions required to maintain a continuous process of adjustment between them are likely to keep strategic partnering activity alive as a vital complement to other growth and competitive strategies of the firm. This is particularly true where size of the individual firms is no longer as much of a determinant of competitiveness as is the scope and composition of the network of firms and other institutions in which it is a participant. To the extent that strategic partnering activity persists, windows of opportunity, moreover, will remain open for knowledge accumulation by small and medium-sized firms in the advanced industrial countries while simultaneously enabling dominant firms in a market to set the research agenda for the future.

NOTES

1. The exception is an interesting attempt by Gomes-Casseres to demonstrate the existence of cycles in joint venture formation and to explain those cycles in terms of oligopolistic competition (Knickerbocker, 1973). These cycles, he argues, are

driven by the interplay of changes in the nature of global competition and in the organizational capabilities of firms. Thus

> ...there comes a point when the opportunity costs of not exploiting fully the capabilities that firms have built begin to exceed the benefits of further expansion of these capabilities. The basis of competition then shifts to integration and coordination rather than expansion. Again, firms in the oligopoly will be pressed to follow each other's lead in this direction. Because joint ventures are not attractive in this new type of strategy, the rate of joint venture formation will decrease; in addition, the firms will seek to buy out their partners in existing joint ventures [Gomes-Casseres, 1988;122]

2. Across manufacturing sectors there also seem to be some fairly important differences in the propensity to form joint ventures, although the data are sketchy and the trend lines appear to vary with the sample. In a survey of 420 international joint ventures in manufacturing formed during the period 1974–82, for example, Hladik found the highest concentration of joint ventures in the chemical and allied products industry (22.6 per cent), followed by non-electric machinery, (16.7 per cent), electric and electronic equipment (15 per cent), food and tobacco (10.5 per cent) and metals and metal products (10.5 per cent). Over time there was, moreover, a small increase in the intensity of joint venturing activity in the non-electric machinery and the electric and electronic equipment sectors (Hladik, 1985:53). The inter-industry pattern that emerges from Kobrin's more recent work, which directly tests differences in the preference for wholly owned subsidiaries over joint ventures by sector for 139 large American multinational corporations with subsidiaries in the Third World, is quite different. His data show a marked preference for wholly owned subsidiaries in the computer, electronics and instruments sector — over 85 per cent of the subsidiaries in each of these sectors fall into this category. Pharmaceuticals (78 per cent) and electrical equipment (72 per cent) also rank well above the average of 62 per cent for all industrial sectors (Kobrin, 1988,134).
3. This is true even in Latin America where restrictions on foreign investment were common in the late 1960s and early 1970s (Mytelka, 1979). Whereas 59.6% of the Latin American subsidiaries of American MNCs were wholly owned in 1975, that figure had actually risen to 69.7% in 1985 (Kobrin, 1988: 132).
4. Elsewhere I have discussed the delocalization of R & D to research institutes and universities (Mytelka, 1987). See also Delapierre *et al.*, 1988.
5. See Chamberlain (1965) and Newfarmer (1980) for a discussion of oligopolistic competition.
6. 'Even before the 1973 oil crisis, it was evident that major structural changes were occurring...unemployment was becoming a cause for concern...inflation too began to accelerate after 1969...While the effects of the 1973 [and 1979] oil price rises and their inflationary repercussions should not be underplayed, they should therefore not be seen, despite their high visibility as the sole dominant force underlying poor economic performance.' [OECD, 1983:17–8]
7. See Chapters 5 and 8
8. R & D consortia in the Kooriyama technopolis in Japan, for example, enabled ten electronics firms, all subcontractors to major electronics companies, to make such a transition (M. Sasaki-Smith, 'The Technopolis Concept', Tokyo, unpublished paper, 1989).
9. See Chapter 2 and Chesnais (1990) and Ostrey (1990). Strategic trade policies, moreover, can have the reverse effect to the extent that they induce more

dynamic firms into the market. The effect of these on the automobile industry in the United States, for example, is already being felt (Sachwald, 1990).

REFERENCES

Abernathy, W. and Utterback, J. (1975), 'A Dynamic Model of Process and Product Innovation', *Omega*, **3**, No.6, pp. 639–56.

Aglietta, M. (1976), *Regulation et crise du capitalisme*, Paris, Calmann Levy.

Alic, J. (1986), 'Cooperation in R & D, When Does it Work?' prepared for the colloquium on International Marketing Cooperation between Rival Trading Nations, San Miniato, Italy, 29–31 May.

Alvey, (1987), *Evaluation of the Alvey Programme*, Interim Report, London , Her Majesty's Stationery Office.

Arrow, K.J. (1969), 'The Organization of Economic Activity, Issues Pertinent to the Choice of Market versus Nonmarket Allocation' *The Analysis and Evaluation of Public Expenditures: the PPB System*, **1**, No. 1, Washington, D.C., Joint Economic Committee, pp. 47-64.

Baily, M.N. and Chakrabarti, A.K., (1988), *Innovation and the Productivity Crisis*, Washington, DC, The Brookings Institution.

Bellon, B. (1983) 'La chimie' in B. Bellon and J-M Chevalier (eds). *L'industrie en France*, Paris, Flamarion, pp. 41–43.

Bellon, B. (1983), *L'interventionnisme liberal: la politique industrielle de l'État fédéral americain*, Paris, Economica.

Boyer, R. (1986), *Capitalisme fin de siecle*, Paris, PUF.

— (1985), 'New Technologies and Employment in the Eighties' paper presented to the International Institute of Management/Labour Market Policy Conference, 'Barriers to Full Employment' , West Berlin, 1–3 October.

Britton, J. and Gilmour, J., (1978), *The Weakest Link: A Technological Perspective on Canadian Industrial Underdevelopment*, Background Study 43 Ottawa, Science Council of Canada.

Buckley, P.J. & Casson, M. (1988), 'A Theory of Cooperation in International Business' in F. Contractor and P. Lorange (eds), *Cooperative Strategies in International Business*, Lexington, Lexington Books.

Caspar, P. and Afriat, C. (1988), *L'investissement intellectuel: essai sur l'economie de l'immateriel*, Paris, Economica.

Caves, R. (1982), *Multinational Enterprise and Economic Analysis*, Cambridge, Cambridge University Press.

Caves, R.E. and Porter, M.E., (1976), 'Barriers to exist' in D. P. Qualls and R.T. Masson (eds), *Essays in industrial organization in honor of Joe S. Bain*, Cambridge, Mass., Ballinger.

CEPII, (1983), *Economie mondiale: la montée des tension*, Paris, Economica for the Centre d'Etudes Prospectives et d'Informations Internationales .

Chamberlain, E.H. (1965), *The Theory of Monopolistic Competition*, 8th ed., Cambridge, Mass., Harvard University Press.

Chandler Jr., A.D. (1977), *The visible hand: The Managerial Revolution in American Business*, Cambridge, Mass., Harvard University Press.

Chesnais, F., (1986), 'Science, Technology and Competitiveness' STI Revue, No.1, pp. 85–129.

— (1990), '*Compétitivité internationale et depenses militaires*', Paris, Economica/ CPE.

— (1988), 'Technical Co-operation Agreements between Independent Firms, Novel Issues for Economic Analyses and the Formulation of National Technological Policies' *STI Revue*, No. 4, pp. 51–120.

Coase, R., (1937), 'The Nature of the Firm' *Economica*, **IV**, No.16, pp. 386–405.

Commission of the European Communities, (1986), *Communication from the Commission to the Council the Second Phase of Esprit*, Brussels, 21 May, COM, 86, 269 final.

Creamer, D. (1976), *Overseas Research and Development by United States Multinationals 1966–1975: Estimates of Expenditures and a Statistical Profile*, New York, The Conference Board.

Cuhran, J. Davidson W., and Suri R., (1977), *Tracing the Multinationals: A Source Book on U.S. Based Enterprise*, Cambridge, Mass., Ballinger.

Dang Nguyen, G. (1983), 'Telecommunications, a challenge to the old order' in M. Sharp, (ed.), *Europe and the New Technologies* , London, Frances Pinter, pp. 87–108.

Delapierre, M., Lemettre, J.F., Mytelka, L.K., Vavakova B., and Zimmermann, J.B. (1988), 'R & D cooperation between industry, university and non-academic research organizations, the French case' paper prepared for a EUREKA-sponsored project on R & D collaboration, Milan, Bocconi University, March.

Delapierre, M. and Zimmerman, J-B, (1984), 'L'industrie du traitement de l'information' , note de travail pour GEST, Grappe technologique et strategie industrielle, Paris.

Dosi, G. (1982), 'Technological Paradigms and Technological Trajectories: a suggested interpretation of the determinants and directions of technological change', *Research Policy,* **XI**.

Duncan Jr., J.L. (1982), 'Impacts of new entry and horizontal joint ventures on industrial rates of return', *Review of Economics and Statistics*, No. 64, pp. 120–5.

Dunning, J. (1979). 'Explaining Changing Patterns of International Production: In Defense of the Eclectic Theory', *Oxford Bulletin of Economics and Statistics*, **41**, No.4, pp. 269–96.

Ernst, D. (1986), 'US–Japanese Competition and the Worldwide Restructuring of the Electronics Industry — A European View' paper prepared for the Pacific–Atlantic Interrelations Conference, Berkeley, University of California, Institute of International Relations, 24 April.

Ernst, D. and O'Connor, D. (1989), *Technology and Global Competition*, the Challenge for Newly Industrialising Economies, Paris, OECD.

— (1987), 'Global Competition, Strategic Alliances and the Worldwide Restructuring of the Electronics Industry — A European Perspective' paper presented at a Stanford Center for European Studies Conference 'New Technologies and New Intermediaries' ,Stanford University, 4–6 June.

Freeman, C., (1974), *The Economics of Industrial Innovation*, Harmondsworth, Penguin.

— (1988), 'Japan: a new national system of innovation?' in Dosi *et al.*, (eds), *Technical Change and Economic Theory*, London, Pinter Publishers, pp. 330–48.

— and Perez, C. (1988), 'Structural crises of adjustment: business cycles and investment behaviour' in Dosi *et al.*, *Technical Change and Economic Theory*, London, Pinter Publishers, pp. 38–68.

Frobel, V., Heinrichs J., and Kreye, O., (1980), *The New International Division of Labour: Structural Unemployment in Industrialised Countries and Industrialisation in Developing Countries*, Cambridge, Cambridge University Press.

Fusfeld, H.I. and Haklisch, C., (1985), 'Cooperative R & D for Competitors' *Harvard Business Review*, Nov.–Dec., pp. 60–7.

Gershenkron, A. (1968), *Continuity in History and Other Essays*, Cambridge, Mass., Harvard University Press.

GEST, (1986), *Grappes technologiques Les nouvelles strategies d'entreprise industrielles*, Paris, Centre de prospective et d'évaluation, Etude No. 57 , May.

Gomes-Casseres, B. (1988), 'Joint Venture Cycles: The Evolution of Ownership Strategies of U.S. MNEs, 1945–75' in F. Contractor, and P. Lorange, (eds), *Cooperative Strategies in International Business*, Lexington, Lexington Books, pp. 111–28.

Hagedoorn, J. (1989), '*Organisational Modes of Inter-Firm Cooperation and Technology Transfer*' Maastricht, MERIT, April.

— and Schot, J., (1988), *Co-operation between Companies and Technological Development*, Studiecentrum voor Technologie en Beleid TNO, Apeldoorn, February.

Hakansson, Hakan, (ed.) (1987), *Industrial Technological Development: A Network Approach*, London, Croom Helm.

Haklisch, C. (1986), *Technical Alliances in the Semiconductor Industry*, New York, New York University, Center for Science and Technology Policy.

Haklisch, C. and Vonortas, N.S. (1987), *Export Controls and the International Technical System: The U.S. Machine Tool Industry*, New York, Center for Science and Technology Policy, June.

Hamel, G., Doz, Y., Prahalad, C.K. (1986), 'Strategic Partnerships, Success or Surrender?' paper prepared for the 1986 Conference on Cooperative Strategies in International Business, a joint research colloquium between The Wharton School and Rutgers University, October.

Harrigan, K.R., (1987), 'Joint Ventures, A Mechanism for Creating Strategic Change' presented at the Strategic Management Society meetings , Boston, 14–17 October.

Henderson, J. and Castells, M. (1987), *Global Restructuring and Territorial Development*, Beverly Hills, Sage Publications.

Hergert, M. and Morris, D. (1988), 'Trends in International Collaborative Agreements' in F. Contractor and P. Lorange, (eds), *Cooperative Strategies in International Business*, Lexington, Lexington Books, pp. 99–110.

Hippel, E. von, (1987), 'Cooperation between Rivals, Informal Know-How Trading' *Research Policy*, No. 16, pp. 291–302.

Hladik, K. (1985), *International Joint Ventures: An Economic Analysis of U.S.–Foreign Business Partnerships*, Lexington, Lexington Books.

Howells, J., (1989), 'The Internationalization of R & D and the Development of Global Research Network' paper presented at the Internationalization of Research and Development Workshop, The Six Countries Programme, Ottawa, 16–17 October.

Hymer, S. (1976), *The International Operations of National Firms: A Study of Direct Foreign Investment*, Cambridge, Mass., MIT Press.

Hymer, S., and Rowthorn, R., (1970), Multinational Corporations and International Oligopoly: *the non-American Challenge*, in C.P. Kindelberger, (ed), The International Corporation, Cambridge, MA., M.I.T.

IDATE data, (1987), reported in *Telecoms Magazine*, 1987, No. 8, October.

Imai, Ken-ichi (1988), 'Japanese Corporate Strategies towards International Networking and Product Development' paper presented to the Japanese Corpor-

ate Organisation and International Adjustment Conference, Canberra, Australian National University, September.
Japan, Industrial Structure Council, ed., (1980), *Industrial Policy for the 1980s*, Tokyo, Foreign Press Center.
Kaplan, M.-C. and Burcklen, J.-Ph. (1986), 'La montée de l'investissement intellectuel' *Futuribles*, July-August, pp. 3–25.
Kindleberger, C. (1979), 'The Monopolistic Theory of Direct Foreign Investment', in G. Modelski, (ed.), *Transnational Corporations and World Order: Readings in International Political Economy*, San Francisco, Freeman & Company, pp. 91–107.
Knickerbocker, F.T. (1973), *Oligopolistic Reaction and Multinational Enterprise*, Boston, Harvard Business School Press.
Kobrin, S. (1988), 'Trends in Ownership of U.S. Manufacturing subsidiaries in Developing Countries, An Interindustry Analysis' in F. Contractor, and P. Lorange, (eds), *Cooperative Strategies in International Business*, Lexington, Lexington Books, pp. 129–141.
Krugman, P.R. (ed.) (1988), *Strategic Trade Policy and the New International Economics*, Cambridge, Mass., MIT Press.
Lall, S. (1975), *A Case Study of the Pharmaceutical Industry: Major Issues in Transfer of Technology to Developing Countries*, Geneva, UNCTAD, Doc. No.TD/B/C.6/4, 8 October.
Lancaster, K. (1979), *Variety, Equity and Efficiency*, New York, Columbia University Press.
LAREA/CEREM (1986a), 'Le traitement de l'information', Nanterre, Universite de Paris-X.
— (1986b), 'Les strategies d'accords des groupes européens entre la cohesion et l'éclatement', Nanterre, Université de Paris-X.
Larue de Tournemine, R. (1983), 'Activites publiques dans le secteur télécommunications', in *L'innovation vers une nouvelle revolution technologique*, Paris, La documentation française, pp. 225–38.
Lean, D., Ogur, J.G. and Rogers, R. (1982), *Competition and Collusion in Electrical Equipment Markets: An Economic Assessment*, Washington, DC, Federal Trade Commission, Bureau of Economics.
Leborgne, D. (1987), 'Equipements flexibles et organisation productive' in R. Boyer, (ed.), *Aspects de la crise: les economies au milieu du gue*, Paris, Commissariat General du Plan et CEPREMAP, February.
Lipietz, A. (1979), *Crise et inflation: pourquoi?*, Paris, Maspero.
— (1987), 'The Globalization of the General Crisis of Fordism 1967–84' in J. Holmes and C. Leys, (eds.), *Frontyard Backyard: The Americas in the Global Crisis*, Toronto, Between the Lines, pp. 23–6.
Mariti, P. and Smiley, R.H., (1983), 'Co-operative Agreements and the Organization of Industry', *The Journal of Industrial Economics*, **XXXI**, No. 4 , pp. 437–51.
Mariotti, S. and Ricotta, E. (1986), 'Diversification, Agreements among Firms and Innovative Behaviour' paper presented at the 'Conference on Innovation Diffusion', Venice, 17–21 March.
McKinsey & Co, Inc. (1987), *Winning in the World Market*, American Business Conference, November.
Michalet, C.-A. (1985), *Le capitalisme mondial*, Paris, Presses Universitaires de France, 2nd edition.
Mowery, D.C. (ed.) (1988), *International Collaborative Ventures in U.S. Manufacturing*, Cambridge, Mass., Ballinger.

Mowery D. and Rosenberg. N. (1980), 'New Developments in U.S. Technology Policy: Implications for Competitiveness and International Trade Policy' Palo Alto, Stanford University Center for Economic Policy Research, Publication No. 166.

Mytelka, L.K. (1979), *Regional Development in a Global Economy: The Multinational Corporation, Technology and Andean Integration*, New Haven, Yale University Press.

— (1987a), 'Changements technologiques et nouvelles formes de la concurrence dans l'industrie textile et de l'habillement' in *Economie, Prospective, Internationale*, revue du CEPII No. 31. pp.5–28.

— (1987b), 'Knowledge-Intensive Production and the Changing Internationalization Strategies of Multinational Firms' in J. Caporaso, (ed.), *A Changing International Division of Labor*, Boulder, Lynne Reiner, pp.43–70.

Nelson, R. (1988), 'Institutions supporting technical change in the United States' in Dosi *et al.*, *Technical Change and Economic Theory*, London, Pinter Publishers, pp. 312–29.

— and Winter, S. (1982), *An Evolutionary Theory of Economic Change*, Cambridge, Mass. The Belknap Press of Harvard University.

Newfarmer, R. (1980), *Transnational Conglomerates and the Economics of Dependent Development: A Case Study of the International Electrical Oligopoly and Brazil's Electrical Industry*, Greenwich, Conn., Jai Press.

OECD (1983), *Multinational Enterprises and the Structural Adjustment Process*, Paris, OECD Committee on International Investment and Multinational Enterprises, 23 September.

— (1986a), *Technical Co-operation Agreements between Firms: Some Initial Data and Analysis*, Paris, OECD, Directorate for Science, Technology and Industry, DSTI/SPR/86.20- Part 1, 21 May.

— (1986b), *Technical Co-operation Agreements Between Firms: Some Initial Data and Analysis*, Paris, OECD, DSTI, DSTI/ SPR/86.20-Part II, 30 May.

Oman, C. (1984), *New Forms of International Investment in Developing Countries*, Paris, OECD Development Centre.

— (1989), *New Forms of Investment in Developing Country Industries: Mining, Petrochemicals, Automobiles, Textiles, Food*, Paris, OECD.

Ostrey, S. (1990), *Governments and Corporations in a Shrinking World;* N.Y., Council on Foreign Relations Press.

Piore M.J. and Sable, C. (1984), *The Second Industrial Divide*, New York, Basic Books.

Porter, M.E. (1980), *Competitive Strategy: Techniques for Analyzing Industries and Competitors*, New York, Free Press.

Reich, R. and Mankin. E. (1986), 'Joint Ventures with Japan Give Away our Future', *Harvard Business Review*, No. 2, pp. 78–86.

Sachwald, F. (1990), 'Les accords dans l'industrie automobile' *Economie Prospective Internationale*, No. 41, pp. 45–68.

Scott, A.J. and Storper, M. (eds.), (1986), *Production, Work, Territory: The Geographical Anatomy of Industrial Capitalism*, London and Boston, Allen & Unwin.

Stopford, J.M. and Wells Jr., L.T. (1972) Managing the Multinationale Enterprise: Organisation of the Firm and Ownership of the Subsidiaries, New York, Basic Books.

Teece, D. (1981), 'The Multinational Enterprise, Market Failure and Market Power Consideration' *Sloan Management Review*, Spring, pp. 3–17.

von Tunzelmann, N. von and Soete, Luc, (1987), 'Diffusion and Market Structure with Converging Technologies', paper prepared for the Conference on Technology and Government Policy in Computers and Communications at the Brookings Institution, Washington DC 4–5June.

US Tariff Commission, (1973), *Implications of Multinational Firms for World Trade and Investment and for US Trade and Labor*, Washington, DC, GPO.

Vaitsos, C. (1974), *Intercountry Income Distribution and Transnational Enterprises*, Oxford, Clarendon Press.

Venture Economics, Inc. (n.d.), *Corporate Partnering in the 1980s*, Wellesley, Venture Economics, Inc.

Vernon, R. (1966), 'International Investment and International Trade in the product Cycle', *Quarterly Journal of Economics*, **80**, pp. 190–207.

Vickery, G. (1987), 'Diffusing New Technologies Micro-electronics' *STI Review*, No. 2, pp. 41–80.

Viesti, G. (1988), 'International Cooperative Agreements, New Strategies for International Growth and Technological Learning?', paper presented at the 14th annual meeting of the European International Business Association, Berlin, 11–13 December.

Walsh, V. (1987), 'Technology Competitiveness and the Special Problems of Small Countries' *STI Review*, No.2, pp. 81–133.

(1988), 'Desperately Seeking Solvency, or External Linkages of Small UK Biotechnology Firms', paper prepared for the Workshop on Inter-firm Technological Co-operation Agreements, Nanterre, Université Paris-X, 21–22 November.

Williamson, O.E. (1975), *Markets and Hierarchies: Analysis and Antitrust Implications*, New York, The Free Press.

2 Strategic partnerships and the changing internationalization process

Charles-Albert Michalet

Over the past three decades the internationalization process has undergone considerable change, yet the models developed to deal with these successive realities have been far from adequate. Equally deficient is the literature on strategic partnering, much of which confounds the treatment of networking and alliances under a single banner. These, however, are two distinct strategies: the former, corresponding to the breakup of an existing firm and its transformation into a multinational network-firm; the latter, signifying an agreement between two or more firms to engage in joint activities, all the while preserving their separate identities.

Although these two strategies can be analytically differentiated, both reflect a number of major changes in the process of internationalization within the emerging 'world economy'.[1] These changes put into question the status of direct foreign investment as the privileged vector for the internationalization process and they challenge the logic of situating alliances as intermediary forms between markets and hierarchies. By undermining the validity of earlier models of the internationalization process, these changes thus render the search for a new paradigm ever more critical.

This chapter contributes to this search by examining four models that seek to explain changes in the process of internationalization. The first part deals with the traditional model of international trade and its counterpart, the model of multinational production. The key issue here is the difficulty encountered in integrating the activities of multinational corporations (MNCs) into the Ricardian and neoclassical theory of international specialization. The second part contrasts the model of a global economy with that of a contractual economy based on the development of different types of strategic partnerships. Once again the problem of dealing simultaneously with national economies and internationalization processes is evoked but in a changed context, one in which finance has become particularly important. In analysing each of these models the chapter focuses on three main characteristics: the dominant actors, the dominant forms of the internationalization process and the dominant mode of economic regulation within the world system that results from the dialectical interplay of changing forces in the world economy.

From international trade to multinational production

In the period since World War II, the activities of MNCs fundamentally altered the process of internationalization, giving rise to new realities that remained unexplainable within established theories. Two new approaches were thus developed to deal with this change: one by mainstream economists attempting to adapt the neoclassical theory of international trade, the other by international business management analysts centred on the growth in direct foreign investment. In this fashion multinational production and international trade came to be treated as two separate and conflicting levels of economic reality and the nation–states and MNCs were perceived to be in constant opposition. Such dichotomies are hardly warranted today, when it has become increasingly clear that both are components of a single reality — the emerging world economy.

Nation–state versus multinational corporation

The paradigm of the international division of labour that underlies the theory of international economics is concerned exclusively with trade among nations. Its basic objective is to explain why a country exports a certain basket of goods and imports another. Country specialization based on comparative advantage is the well-known answer. Comparative advantages defined either in Ricardian terms as labour productivity differences, or in neoclassical terms as endowments of factors of production are strictly determined by the characteristics of each nation–state.

In an attempt to render the theory more dynamic, the Heckscher–Ohlin–Samuelson model introduced technology as a variable. This addition, however, did not change the cornerstone of the neoclassical approach to international specialization the concept of the nation–state. Within this version of the model, therefore, only goods circulate among nations. The circulation of factors of production such as capital, labour and land remain strictly limited to the area within national frontiers for were these factors to cross national borders, a country's comparative advantage would undergo constant modification and the basis for an international division of labour would be unspecified.

As the multinationalization of production accelerated in the 1960s and 1970s, the inadequacy of this approach became increasingly evident. Countries no longer exported only goods, but also factories to manufacture products which, in some cases, had previously been exported. The neoclassical premise that trade was the sole form of international economic activity could no longer be sustained. To cope with the delocation of manufacturing activities generated by the growth in foreign direct investment, neoclassical economists like R.A. Mundell (Mundell, 1957) reduced the internationalization process to the international movement of capital. With capital mobility replacing for the mobility of goods, it became possible to argue that open economies and the free movement of factors, were prerequisites for an optimal allocation of resources.

The core of the neoclassical international paradigm was thus preserved, but the price paid for such an heroic integration of the international production phenomenon into the international trade paradigm was high. First, if international capital is mobile, then trade flows can no longer be said to exist as an analytically distinct phenomonon, since the one can effectively substitute for the other. In its modified form, the neoclassical paradigm thus had difficulty accommodating both of these realities simultaneously. One consequence of this was seriously to weaken the utility of this paradigm during the 1960s and 1970s when international trade and international production were expanding together.

Second, once the assumption of factor immobility is relaxed, the endowment of factors of production that previously defined a nation–state are transformed into a variable, thus making it impossible to define a nation–state according to the H–O–S model. In an effort to overcome this theoretical difficulty, Mucchielli (1987) introduced a ' factor-specific' concept, for example, a 'capital specific' that circulates internationally but only within a given sector. By confounding the specificity of the 'capital specific' with the competitive advantages of the MNCs, the argument, however, became circular.

Like Lenin, in his theory of imperialism[2], neoclassical economists have thus erred in their attempt to reduce the internationalization process to the international movement of capital. Several empirical studies also put into question this revision of the neoclassical paradigm. It has been shown, for example, that foreign investments by American MNCs involved the export of only a small percentage of capital from their home country — less than 20 per cent on average during the past several decades. With the increasing role of eurocapital markets, moreover, outward flows of capital from one country to another as a share in total foreign direct investment have declined. New forms of direct investment (Oman 1984) also enable foreign firms to acquire a stake in a local firm's equity through joint venture agreements, transfer of technology and know-how, management contracts and leasing. These developments indicate a growing disconnection between the process of internationalizing production and the export of capital, and they suggest that the concept of foreign direct investment must be taken beyond its financial dimension. One promising innovation was to stress the management control exercised by a foreign firm over a local company[3]. Whatever the degree of equity control, therefore, a foreign direct investment was distinguishable by a firm's strategic decision to produce products or services abroad instead of exporting them.

A great number of theories were subequently developed to explain the jump from exports to production abroad. But the basic strategic choice may be reduced to a set of two options: to produce for the local market through the establishment of a 'relay affiliate' or to produce for the international market through the creation of a 'workshop affiliate' (Delapierre and Michalet, 1975). In the first option, the decision to invest abroad is an extension of the rationale for exporting. It is taken, for the most part, because increased tariff and non-tariff barriers, changes in consumer preferences or in government constraints made it more and more difficult for a firm to export to a given country. The second option[4], involves export-orientated manufacturing, with the bulk of a subsidiary's output directed towards the international market. The main reason for investing in a 'workshop affiliate' is to take advantage of the lower costs of production resulting from cheap energy sources or low wages. In both cases, it is important to recognize that the decision to produce a specific good in a specific country is made by the foreign firm. It no longer results from the spontaneous opening of the national economy to free trade as the neoclassical paradigm assumes. To be sure, MNCs do take a country's comparative advantages into consideration when they scrutinize investment locations. But in the end, the decision to produce or not to produce abroad is theirs alone. This is why the old paradigm, focused exclusively on the nation-state, has lost its relevance.

The emerging world economy is thus characterized by two majors actors, nation-states and MNCs, and two coexisting forms of internationalization, international trade and international production. In such a world economy, however, the problem of 'regulation' looms large.

Changes in the regulation of the world economy

If we accept the neoclassical theory of the international division of labour, it is to market forces that we turn to guarantee the smooth regulation of the international system. Thus, specialization among countries ensures an optimal allocation of resources through the free trade in goods. In this approach, the gains from trade are equitably shared among the different countries, notwithstanding their size or the nature of the products exported and imported. Nor does money change this, in keeping with the usual formula 'money is a veil'.

If, however, we take the process of international production and the activities of multinational corporations into consideration along with trade, then the whole system becomes much more complex. At least two important changes differentiate the new system from the traditional model. First, in the international trade model a country's specialization is determined *ex-ante*, that is on the basis of comparative advantages the country had before it opened its economy. In the internationalization of production models, the existing comparative advantages of a country are turned into locational advantages for the firm. With the introduction of the MNC, then, the *ex-ante* international specialization of a country becomes *ex-post*. In an increasing number of activities, foreign direct investments thus determine the host-country's specialization. Obviously, as noted above, the existence of some comparative advantage is a prerequisite for attracting MNCs. But the effective exploitation of existing comparative advantages is no longer the result of a change from a closed economy to an open economy; it is now the result of the firm's decision to invest in a specific activity, even if — often because of — protectionism.

The reversal of the classical form of regulation is particularly spectacular in the case of export-orientated investments, which correspond even more closely to one of the central elements in the activities of the MNC, its 'internalization' of the world market. As a consequence of the growth of MNCs and of the subsequent increase in the number of their subsidiaries, a noticeable proportion of the international flows of goods, technology, high-skilled labour and financial funds has been transformed into internal flows between the MNCs' subsidiaries and the parent-company. Rough estimates by the United Nations Centre on Transnational Corporations (1983, 1988), suggest that well over one-third of world trade consists of intracorporate flows.

In a seminal paper, Coase (1937) argued that the very nature of the firm is to substitute its internal market for the external market, that is the market described in textbooks. It does so, he maintained, in order to reduce the transaction costs inherent in imperfect markets of which international markets are a particularly good example. Internalization most often takes the form of vertical economic integration with the result that the prices, royalties, interest rates and wages paid by these firms for goods and services, technology, capital funds and labour circulating within their own framework are not determined by market forces, but by the firms themselves on the basis of discretionary computational methods.

Although the hierarchical model of the multinational firm is at odds with the market model of international trade theory, there are authors who argue that the final results obtained through the working of internalized structures will be identical to those which would have occurred in a competitive market. A. Rugman (1981), for example, sees the MNC as a perfect substitute for the Smithian 'invisible hand'. His argument rests on the assumption that world production will be rationally organized and planned by MNCs and that this would lead to an allocation of resources similar to that which could have been obtained through the market. Rugman's argument, however, repeats the same mistake that Kautsky made in his ultra-imperialism theory (1914). In both cases the authors forget that world monopolies are very rare and that the current situation faced by MNCs is rather one of competition. Obviously, what is at stake is oligopoly competition, not pure and perfect competition. As a number of economists have demonstrated since the 1930s, oligopolistic markets can not be counted upon to guarantee an optimal allocation of resources. Indeed hierarchies cannot lead to a situation of general equilibrium precisely because they generate imperfect markets and are the product of such markets, a point that O. Williamson (1981) also missed in his now classical dichotomy between market and hierarchy. Substituting MNCs for nation–states as the modern supporters of the ultra-imperialism theory have done thus leads ultimately to a world of uncertainty, where the rules of the game resemble those of Clausewitz far more than those of Adam Smith.

In sum, unidimensional approaches that substitute capital movements for the trade in goods or MNCs for nation–states are no longer adequate. To understand the emerging world economy better it is necessary to deal simultaneously with both dominant actors and dominant forms of the internationalization process.

The dialectics of the world economy

Despite several interesting attempts within both Marxist (Palloix, 1973; Andreff, 1976) and more orthodox, if eclectic frameworks (Dunning, 1981), to cope with the emerging world economy, no general model able to compete with the still dominant, though obsolete, neoclassical paradigm has emerged. To some extent, this can be explained by the fact that the world economy is still in process and cannot be described in a comprehensive model, as was the case for international trade. Following Fayerabend (1980: 273), theoreticians are thus forced to adopt a 'metaphysical approach'. They can point out 'something' new, but they are unable to define its nature with precision.

But more importantly, the absence of a new paradigm is due to the very dialectical nature of the internationalization process that characterizes the emergence of the world economy — a process whose components, nations–states and MNCs, are transcended by the dynamism of the change itself. Neither theoretical approaches centred on the nation–state, nor those centred on the firm can encompass this dynamic since both provide only a partial view of the whole. Thus, on the one hand the neoclassical approach to trade leads us to focus on well-defined national territories, characterized by a stable stock of production factors, managing their own money, their own interest rates, their own labour force, their own macroeconomic policies and regulations, with their own history, culture and language. This patchwork of nation–states is linked together solely by trading relationships. Diversity, heterogeneity, specificity, nationalism are key words to describe this approach. On the other hand there is the realm of the MNCs. It consists of internalized flows, world-wide strategic planning and sourcing, off-shore facilities, transnational marketing, funding and technology that cut across these national territories. Within their economic space, moreover, MNCs are generating undifferenciation, homogenization and deregulation.

Clearly the concept of a world economy cannot be reduced to one or the other of these simple alternatives : the multinational model versus the nation–state model — or devils against angels. Take the MNC model, for example. Were MNCs to substitute for nation–states, a unified world market without obstacles to the internationalization of manufacturing and sales activities would be created. Yet, the very basis for foreign direct investment lies in the existence of international disparities. The superior profitability of MNCs largely results from their ability to play with international differences in wages, interest rates, income per capita, business cycles, inflation rates, consumer preferences, taxation systems, economic policies and political regimes. But the real secret of multinational management is to be in a position simultaneously to exploit and to erase the existing differences across countries.[5]

The dialectical interplay between homogenization and differentiation is also being played out in the relationship between integration and accumulation in the emerging world economy. Since the 1950s, an economic movement of accumulation on a world scale has accompanied the process of internationalization. The geographical dimension of this phenomenon was particularly central, especially in so far as the developing countries were concerned. Thus trade was considered to be an engine of their transformation, and foreign direct investment strengthened the integrative process through which this would occur. Over time, the development of manufacturing plants, a working class, entrepreneurs and bankers — largely as a result of the establishment of foreign firms — would condemn the pre-capitalist structures of the host countries to disappear.

The central argument, then, was that the internationalization process, through the geographical extension of a capitalist mode of production, would be a leading force in the progressive disappearance of the existing diversity among the different national economic systems. In light of developments that took place during the 1980s, such an apparently irreversible trend, however, must be questioned. 'Globalization', the newly fashionable way to describe the internationalization process in this period is not, it will be argued below, an extension of this earlier dynamic.

From globalization to networking

Let us begin by looking at some of the trends that correspond to this new label (Michalet, 1989). With 'globalization', both the dominant actors and the dominant forms of the internationalization process have changed. Since the early 1980s, it is the financial dimension that has become central. This has been the era of the mergers and acquisition mania and of the 'casino-economy'.

MNCs are still there; their number has even increased. But the multinationalisation of the firm has become commonplace. Firms in all the developed countries and even those from a small group of newly industrialized countries (NICs) such as Korea, Singapore, Hong Kong, Taiwan and Brazil are going abroad. As a consequence, the relative importance of American MNCs and of American direct investment abroad has declined when compared with its position in the sixties. An even more striking change, however, is the emergence of the United States as the most important host country in the world. Foreign direct investment flows towards the developing countries, in contrast, have fallen and in some countries, notably in sub-Saharan Africa and Latin America, considerable disinvestment has occurred since 1982–3. New flows of capital to the third world, moreover, have been concentrated in a smaller group of countries than before — mainly the NICs and China, a newcomer.

Several explanations can be given for these trends. First, the economic crisis in most of the developing countries coupled with their indebtedness has changed the investment climate deterring in particular foreign direct investments orientated towards the local market. Second, the comparative advantage in cheap labour that many developing countries enjoyed is less and less relevant for export orientated foreign direct investments as a result of the accelerated introduction of automated and flexible techniques of production in the more industrialized countries. Third, the powerful attraction exercised by the United States market is largely due, in the case of European firms, to the poor economic performance in the South and to the recession in the EEC which persisted well into the 1980s. For Japanese investors, American threats of retaliation against Japanese exports in the form of increased protection has played a major role.

As a growing number of MNCs focused their activities in the same market, competition intensified. The easiest and quickest way for firms to expand their activities and to increase their market share was to take over their main competitors. This is the reason why mergers and acquisitions have become the most frequent form taken by foreign direct investment in the United States. The new strategy of the global firm, however, is very different from the multinational strategy of the previous decades. Previously the multinationalization process began with exports, moved on to the creation of a local distribution subsidiary and then a manufacturing plant. This sequence is no longer relevant. Instead, the global firm first identifies carefully its specific competitive advantage *vis-à-vis* all of its current and potential competitors world-wide. Second, it tries to eliminate most of them through takeovers and mergers so as to become the world leader in a specific world market. Competition being more intense, the key factor of success is to be faster than the others. As a result, the global multinational can be called an 'instant' multinational on the model of 'instant' coffee.'

If buying a competitor is the more efficient way to capture market share, there is, however, a prerequisite: the financial capacity to support such a strategy. Finance is thus a crucial dimension in the globalization process and the most successful firms are those that are able to mobilize huge amounts of money in a very short period of time. To meet this precondition, firms build up a large cash flow. Frequently the firm's liquidity is enhanced by the sale of parts of its portfolio — assets which no longer fit the new focus on a select number of competitive activities.

The volume of merger and acquisition activity that began to take place, however, would have been impossible without new financial tools — innovations which have given firms direct access to financial markets. Junk bonds are the most spectacular and controversial result of the financial revolution of the 1980s.

The 'securitization' process has modified the traditional frontiers between banks and nonbanks. Financial departments of big corporations now look like banks. As a matter of fact, new corporate managers would like to be able to manage their companies the way bankers manage their financial portfolios, reacting instantaneously to new profit opportunities by buying or selling industrial and services activities world-wide and taking advantage of fluctuations in foreign exchange and interest rates around the globe. By the late 1980s, the financial divisions of some of the larger MNCs had acquired so much expertise in the field and had made such substantial profits that they were able to develop their activities on a quasi-autonomous basis, independently of the current activities of their own company. Extending this process further, it would not be hard to conceive the organization of an international inter-firm market for industrial assets as the final stage of such a trend. Such a development would coincide with the eclipse of the public corporation celebrated by M.C. Jensen (1989).

Paralleling the above transformation of the large industrial corporation, investment banks as well as commercial banks have developed specialized departments to deal with the growing demand for information, advice and financing resulting from the increase in mergers and acquisitions. In many instances, banks are multiplying their equity stakes in the new companies emerging from these operations. In spite of Nicholas Brady's exhortations to supply endebted countries with fresh money, the major international banks, like the MNCs before them, have reduced their exposure in the developing countries and concentrated the bulk of their operations within the so-called 'triad' — the United States, the EEC and Japan.

In sum, the globalization process is quite different from the multinational process described in the previous section. First, with globalization, the world is shrinking. MNCs and international banks are focusing their activities within the 'triad' and a small group of NICs. The extension of MNC manufacturing plants around the world has slowed down and in some cases receeded, thus reversing a major trend of the sixties and seventies. Within the 'triad', economic integration is very high. Homogenization, largely a result of the multinationalization process, is predominant. Disparities having been greatly reduced, time and speed have replaced geographical space in the competitive strategies of the firm.

Second, the reshaping of world industry through mergers and acquisitions is not giving rise to an economic process of capital accumulation. In contrast to the previous period, foreign direct investment mainly constitutes a shift in the ownership and control of existing companies. As newcomers in the multinational game, Japanese firms are still pursuing an export-substituting strategy through the delocation of their manufacturing capacity. As a result they tend to create more new productive capacities than European and American firms. Nevertheless, like European firms in the United States and American firms in Europe, a majority of their investments have been devoted to takeovers. If in the sixties and seventies the internationalization process through trade and the delocation of manufacturing activity had a 'real' basis, in the eighties the predominant form taken by the internationalization process was not conducive to the creation of new physical investments or new productive capacities. Rather, globalization was chiefly a process whereby financial assets were redistributed among members of an international oligopoly. As a result, the link between the 'fundamentals' and these global activities loosened. In the worst case scenario, the latter represented little more than pure financial speculation.

Third, the logic of globalization gave to private agents and to market forces a central role. It appeared moreover to require the greatest possible mobility and flexibility on the part of major global actors. This has led to pressures for a reduction in state intervention. Globalization and neoliberalism are thus two faces of the same coin. It is not easy, however, to make privatization programmes and deregulation policies compatible with a Keynesian concept of the role of the state.

Finally, if we return to the Manichean opposition between MNCs and nation-states that marked many of the debates in the earlier period, then the former seems to have totally won and with its victory to have imposed its own rules of the game. If homogenization has triumphed, then the dialectic movement, that we argued earlier is a constitutive element of the world economy, has ceased to exist and we must join with F. Fukuyama (1989) in heralding the eighties as the end of history. If globalization, however, is merely a transitory phenomenon, such a conclusion would not be warranted. It is thus important to examine other processes also at work in the emerging world economy.

Deregulation at stake

From the viewpoint of the arch-rivalry between MNCs and the State, there is no doubt that globalization has changed the equilibrium in favour of the firms. There are many reasons why such a 'revolution' took place at this time. The persistent economic recession certainly played a major part in the reconsideration of Keynesian economic policy. Although this is beyond the scope of the present chapter, it is important to stress that the internationalization process has played an important role in weakening the state's ability to manage macroeconomic variables. Nevertheless, and in a paradoxical way, it is not impossible to imagine that the consequences of the globalization process will in turn trigger a reappraisal of the role of the state and of multilateral organizations.

After the Mexican alert in August 1982, private international banks re-evaluated the risks involved in further lending to the developing countries and drastically revised their policies. But the whole story cannot be reduced to a simple exercise in cost-benefit analysis. The Mexican crisis, in fact, introduced a basic change in the international financial system. If a major financial crisis was successfully avoided after the Mexican announcement of its inability to fulfil its obligation towards foreign banks, this was largely due to the quick reaction of the Federal Reserve and the support extended by the IMF and of the European central banks through the International Bank for Settlements. Later, the Brady report would propose a new framework for the future relationship between the banks and multilateral organizations. What is important here, from the perspective of an emerging world economy, is that this incident demonstrated the inability of the private off-shore banking system to regulate itself. In a non-official manner, it was now recognized that a lender of last resort is needed to ensure that the international monetary and financial system functions well. The structural weakness of a floating exchange rate system, managed for the most part by private international banks uncontrolled by Central Banks or the IMF, was therefore clearly established.

The return to favour of some form of public regulation was illustrated again with the release of the Cooke committee's recommendations at the end of 1988, relative to the prudential ratios that banks will have to respect in the future. These constraints represent another attempt to breach the gaps in the global banking structure constructed upon the ruins of the Bretton Woods system.

The financial crash of October 1987 is still another illustration of the shortcomings of the globalization process and this time of the need for a reregulation of stock exchange operations. According to the Brady report, commissioned by President Reagan after the crash, it might even be necessary to extend the reregulation of financial operations to all international financial markets. In the mean time, the investigative powers of the American Securities and Exchange Commission have been strengthened. France enforced measures of the same type for the Commission des Opérations de Bourse. Some well known corporate raiders have been prosecuted in the United States, in France and elsewhere.[6] The G-7 meetings as well as the repeated summits of the Western heads of state represent other attempts aimed at setting up some kind of informal global regulation through inter-state cooperation.

Because the thorough liberalization of foreign investment regulations in most of the developing countries has not been sufficient to reverse the decline in capital flows to those countries, national agencies and multilateral organizations are multiplying incentives to convince reluctant investors to resume or develop their activities in Africa and Latin America. In this respect the creation of MIGA (Multilateral Investment Guarantee Agency) by the World Bank in mid-1988 constitutes another illustration of a public initiative to promote private foreign investments to developing countries.

By the end of the eighties, the deregulated globalization process was under pressure and it appeared likely that a revival of some kind of state intervention would occur in order to ensure a more stable pattern of growth. But this should not be taken to imply that the classical concept of the nation–state will return. To the contrary, if a reregulation movement is currently underway, it is not national so much as world-wide or at least regional in scope. The continental integration policies followed by the European countries and by the United States and Canada (perhaps, Mexico in a subsequent phase) are opening the way for what might be called a world mixed economy.

The networking economy

For their part, MNCs are also on the verge of transforming their strategies and structures to enter into a postglobalization era. Since the early eighties, a number of studies have pointed to the growth in inter-firm cooperative agreements.[7] This could be a major trend in the next decade.

Inter-firm agreements take two forms: network firms that result from a strategy of 'externalization' and alliances that are based on links between independent firms which have decided to operate jointly in specific activities. Firms chose a strategy of externalization, in large part, because of the growing costs of their internalized structures. This occurs because successful multinational growth increases the size of the firm and the bureaucratic costs of managing it. Ultimately the marginal benefit of internalized structures becomes lower than the marginal bureaucratic cost (Jones and Hill, 1989). In a first stage, the firm's managers may decide to change the organizational structure, eliminating the multidivisional structure and setting up a global matrix with regional or product divisions — or a mix of regions and products. When this decentralization option proves incapable of resolving the problem, management may chose to abandon certain activities or 'strategic segments' (Porter, 1986), originally under the control of the firm, to independent entities outside the company. Like Antonnelli's network firm where independent companies are assembled into confederations (see, Chapter 3) and the kinds of supplier–client relationship that are developing among independent firms in the aircraft industry (see, Chapter 4), the 'network firm' or 'hollow corporation' that emerges from this streamlining exercise is not simply another form of the conventional sub-contracting model. The external entities in the network firm are partners and not mere sub-contractors. As such, they maintain control of their own comparative advantages. While the old internalized structure was based on hierarchy, the network firm thus favours horizontal relationships similar to those developed in Japanese companies (Aoki, 1986).[8]

The advantages expected from an externalization process are twofold: first, a reduction in costs resulting from an improvement in productivity due to more specialized components within the firm; and second, greater flexibility allowing for more rapid and more extensive product differentiation and a more innovative attitude towards changes in the environment. In contrast to the global firm which favoured the homogenization of products and processes world-wide, the network firm is thus able to adapt more easily to an increasingly diversified demand. To achieve these results, however, reciprocal confidence among the different components of the network firm is a major requirement and this, in turn, places greater emphasis on the need for an equitable sharing of both risks and gains among them. The network firm is well adapted to industries in which competitiveness is based on prices, that is mature industries producing consumer goods.

The alliance strategy is of a very different nature. Like the network firm, alliances are concluded between independent entities. But unlike externalization, they do not imply a reshaping of the firm's activities and structures. Their main objective is the pooling of financial, human and knowledge resources in some joint activities among firms that otherwise remain competitors. As we saw in Chapter 1, such agreements frequently involve research and development. But there are also cases where firms jointly manufacture specific components which are then assembled in their own plants into goods that are distributed independently. This is characteristic of production in the aerospace, the electronic and the automotive industries for example. Nevertheless the fact that technology is more than ever a crucial factor in world oligopolistic competition has contributed to the growing importance of alliances between firms of the same size across many industries and between big and small firms, where the latter has a specific technological edge, as in biotechnology or artificial intelligence.

Like network firms, alliances have a number of advantages over other strategies in today's competitive world. They help to reduce the burden of R & D funding and the risk involved in unsuccessful programmes. Moreover, many of the new technological fields require the combination of knowledge bases so diverse that they exceed the resources of a single company. Technological alliances are also relevant for firms looking for ways to apply their accumulated knowledge and experience in sectors others than those in which they originally developed their own specific competence. In this case, alliances are a new tool for expanding a 'technology bunching' strategy.[9] Finally, alliances are a prerequisite for the definition of technological norms, interfaces and gateways for new products and new fields of activities. This last aspect is of crucial importance since it will enable alliances to reshape existing industries. In the future, new frontiers between industries will thus in great part be the result of rules of the game defined within the framework of alliances between the dominant firms of technology-based oligopolies (Mytelka, 1984).

Although network firms and alliances are distinct strategies and derive from different rationales, they are not incompatible. Both may be adopted simultaneously by a single firm. As such relationships proliferate, it is therefore possible to envisage a world economy structured by global networks within which 'contracts' replace the 'market' (Delapierre and Michalet, 1989).

Conclusion

Though still in its inception, there is no doubt that the networking process will introduce dramatic changes in the regulation of the world economy. As a conclusion, and in a very tentative way, therefore, it is important to sketch some of the trends that are likely to emerge from the proliferation of alliances and network firms over the next decade.

First, the dominant form of the internationalization process will no longer be trade, foreign direct investment or financial restructuring. Information flows and especially knowledge and technology will be the core of the new system. Within the 'world mixed economy', technological links will thus supplant the equity and financial relationships between firms that were dominant in the multinationalization and globalization processes.

Second, neither the market, nor the hierarchy will be the structuring force in the world economy. Instead, a 'contractual economy' will emerge based on actors — nation–states and firms — of a very different nature than in the past. The complex structure of network firms and alliances, each network firm belonging to a specific set of alliances, will structure the world economic space. Competition, if any, will shift from firms struggling directly against one another for market shares to a new type of cartel structure based on technology. Henceforth, market access for a firm will be determined, first, by its position as a partner in a network firm and, then, by the network firm's membership in an alliance. Conventional conceptions of the market, of nation–states and of firms, will thus lose their force as descriptions of the future contractual world economy.

Third, since 'national' industry and services, for the most part, will be integrated into a new constellation of network firms and alliances, the temptation will be great to proclaim the death of the nation–state. But a number of developments point to a different conclusion. Governments, for example, are already playing an important role in setting up strategic alliances, as the European programmes in high technology fields like ESPRIT, RACE, EUREKA and the American Strategic Defense Initiative illustrate. In the future, moreover, it is likely that an even greater number of state entities will participate in alliances alongside private firms. As the arguments made earlier with respect to reregulation suggest, it is also likely that states will be called upon to guarantee or supervise the rules of the game developed by the members of alliances and insure a minimal compatibility between the various standards set up by antagonistic business coalitions. In sum, states and public multilateral organisms will be essential components in the regulation of the world contractual economy.

Despite their role in ensuring the smooth functioning of the world contractual economy, it would be a mistake, however, to assume that states and firms will make of the contractual economy an engine for homogenization as in the globalization process. There are grounds for arguing that diversity and differentiation will persist and may be encouraged by the greater ease with which they can be reproduced through networking and alliance strategies than through the hierarchical model and their greater importance as a basis for competition within the new model. In this respect national diversity, at least regional diversity, as well as individual or social group preferences may be better served by the contractual than by the global economy thus generating new contradictions within the world economy.

In sum, we are not entering into a stable, homogeneous world economy but a dynamic one. The time has not yet come, therefore, to accept Fukuyama's view. The end of history is not for tomorrow.

NOTES

1. The concept of a 'world economy' is introduced in order to emphasize its differences from the traditional concept of 'international economy' that remains dominant in the economic literature.
2. It is possible that Lenin made this mistake because Hobson's influence superseded that of Marx when he wrote his *Imperialism* (Michalet, 1985).
3. While control may be based on equity, such as in the wholly owned or a majority–owned subsidiary, for a number of reasons, reliance on equity ownership has declined in recent years.
4. The concept of a 'workshop' affiliate excludes raw materials' production.
5. National industrial policies based on long term planning, subsidies directed to private firms and public funding of research and development programmes by reinforcing the international competitiveness of private firms also stimulate their internationalization.

6. This was the case in Mexico in early 1989, for instance.
7. For a good survey, see Chesnais (1988); Chapter 1 of this volume provides some updates.
8. Though 'Fordism' implies much more than the structure of production, one might conclude that the externalization process is leading towards the substitution of a 'Toyotism' model for a Fordist one.
9. See the Chapter 5 for a more extensive discussion of combinatory and technology-bunching strategies.

REFERENCES

Andreff, W. (1976), *Profits et structures du capitalisme mondial*, Paris, Calmann Lévy.

Aoki M. (1986), 'Horizontal vs vertical information structure of the firm', American Economics Review December, pp. 971–983.

Coase, R.-H. (1937), 'The nature of the firm', *Economica*, November, pp. 386–405.

Chesnais, F. (1988), 'Technical cooperation agreements between firms', *STI REVIEW*, No. 4, pp. 51–119 .

Delapierre, M. and Michalet, C.A. (1975), *Les investissements étrangers en France: stratégies et structures*, Paris, Calmann Lévy.

——— (1989), 'Vers un changement des structures des multinationales: le principe d'internalisation en question', *Revue d'Economie Industrielle*, No 47.

Dunning, J.H. (1981), *International Production and the Multinational Enterprise*, London, Allen and Unwin.

Fayerabend, P. (1980), 'Comment être un bon empiriste. Plaidoyer en faveur de la tolérance en matière épistemologique' in P. Jacob (ed.), *De Vienne à Cambridge*, Paris: Gallimard.

Fukuyama, F. (1989), 'The end of History', *National Interest*, Summer, pp.3–18.

Jensen, M.C. (1989), 'Eclipse of the public corporation', *Harvard Business Review*, September–October, pp.61–74.

Jones G. and Hill, C. (1989), 'Transaction cost analysis of strategy-structure choice', *Strategic Management Journal*, Vol. **9**.

Michalet, C.A., (1985), *Le capitalisme mondial*, Paris, PUF.

——— (1989), *Global competition and its Implications for Firms*, Paris, OECD.

Mucchielli, J.L., 1987, Principes d'économie internationale, Paris,Economica.

Mundell R.A., (1957), 'International trade and factor mobility', *American Economics Review*, No 47, in J.N. Bhagwati (ed.), *International Trade: Selected Readings*, Cambridge, Mass., Massachusetts Institute of Technology Press, 1981, pp. 17–30.

Mytelka, L. (1984), 'La gestion de la connaisance dans les entreprises multinationales', *Economie et Prospective Internationale*, No. 20, pp. 7–33.

Oman C., (1984), *New forms of International Investment in Developing Countries*, Paris, OECD.

Palloix, C. (1973), *Les firmes multinationales et le processus d'internationalisation*, Paris, Maspéro.

Porter, M. (ed) (1986), *Competition in Global Industries*, Boston, Harvard Business School Press.

Rugman, A. (1981), *Inside the Multinationals*, London, Croom Helm.

United Nations Centre on Transnational Corporations (1983), *Transnational Corporations in World Development*, New York, United Nations.

——— (1988), *Transnational Corporations in World Development*, New York, United Nations.

Williamson, O.F. (1975), *Markets and Hierarchies*: Analysis and Antitrust Implications, New York, The Free Press.

3 Alliances as learning experiments: Cooperation, competition and change in hightech industries

Claudio Ciborra

Introduction

Under the heading of cooperative agreements, the economic and business literature regroups a whole array of governance mechanisms: licensing, franchising, subcontracting, consortia sponsored by government agencies, trade agreements, joint ventures, equity and non-equity coalitions and strategic alliances. The current explanations for such a variety of interorganizational relationships are centred on factors such as transaction costs efficiency, market power and appropriability of innovation outcomes.

These explanations have a certain utility when applied to the more clear-cut and constraining forms of interorganizational relationships such as licensing, franchising or subcontracting. For the less well-defined if not ambiguous forms of cooperation, henceforth referred to as alliances, however, the consideration of organizational factors such as mutual trust, learning and other 'invisible assets' (Itami, 1987) that determine the success of many partnerships and justify the superiority of certain companies (namely the Japanese) in 'managing by agreements', invite the suspicion that neither power nor static efficiency are the driving forces behind them.

This chapter, therefore, develops an alternative interpretation of cooperation between firms, based on the idea that many alliances among firms in rapidly changing industries are set up to reduce 'transition costs', that is costs that organizations incur when they seek to undergo a drastic restructuring to meet new challenges and implement new strategies. Along the lines sketched out in Chapter 1, it starts from the proposition that firms in knowledge-intensive industries must cope with higher levels of technological innovation, strive for the rapid accumulation of know-how and the immediate penetration of new markets. Governance structures that are efficient in managing transactions in a steady environment may be ineffective when the velocity of response is at stake. In achieving higher levels of dynamic efficiency, a key competence is organizational learning, consisting of both a capacity for learning by doing which leads to the incremental modification of routines, and for radical learning, when shifts in technological paradigms are required by significantly new contexts of action. Alliances are the institutional arrangement that allows firms to implement strategies for organizational learning and innovation more effectively.

In the first part a number of key weaknesses in conventional analyses of cooperative agreements are analysed. In the second a more dynamic approach to alliances is proposed. Here, both the rivalry and the trust that co-exist in successful partnerships are shown to have a common origin, that is the need for firms in high-tech industries to accumulate and apply new knowledge at a relatively fast pace. This goal can be achieved by acting on two main control variables: on the one hand by regulating the complexity of the environment in which the firm operates and on the other by modifying its repertoire of available skills and invisible assets at hand. From this perspective, alliances are seen as competitive moves to survive and grow in a turbulent environment, for they allow firms simultaneously to simplify their relevant environment and enrich their internal competencies so that the gap between environmental complexity and the firm's capabilities to face it are sensibly reduced. The last part focuses on a selection of case studies involving multinational corporations operating or based primarily in Italy, engaged in strategic alliances and joint ventures with foreign multinationals in the information technology and related industries. These cases exemplify instances of the double and open nature of alliances, illustrate the various implications of cooperation for each of the partners and indicate some unexpected outcomes.

The conventional wisdom

Why do alliances form at an increasing rate, especially in the high-tech industries (Chesnais, 1988; Cainarca *et al.*, 1989)? Five broad explanations are offered in the literature: technical coordination needs, market power, transaction costs, innovation and global competition. In what follows these themes are reviewed and their strengths and inconsistencies assessed.

For G.B. Richardson (1972), cooperation among firms stems from the need to coordinate closely complementary but dissimilar activities. Gaps in knowledge make market arrangements insufficient for that purpose. If an industry carries out a large number of activities, such as research, development and design, production and marketing of goods, different organizations will specialize in subsets of these activities, accumulating idiosyncratic knowledge, experience and skills. Coordination between these different stages can be maintained through hierarchical, market or cooperative arrangements that bind partners through mutually agreed plans and long term obligations. Cooperative coordination, however, would be required when activities are dissimilar but economies of scale or the matching between R & D efforts are required and cannot be left to the vagaries of the market (Richardson, 1972).

In a similar vein, Baligh and Richartz (1967) see vertical cooperative relationships between firms, sellers and buyers as an efficiency device that can improve the functioning of markets when exchange costs are not negligible. The output of a given vertical market structure where cooperation complements competition is a larger number of exchange transactions and this justifies the interest in cooperative behaviour among competing firms.

The 'technical coordination' explanation rightly points out the benefits of cooperation, but it is inconclusive when dealing with the issue of trade-offs. What, for example, are the specific advantages of cooperation over the internalization of transactions? Why isn't cooperation ubiquitous and what is the special nature of alliances between competitors?

Market power theorists, such as A. Phillips (1960) and J.S.Bain (1956), have argued that coalitions are simply types of cartels: the manifestation of collusive behaviour to control prices and reap monopoly rents. In a similar fashion K.J. Blois (1972) describes cooperation in terms of vertical quasi-integration between larger and smaller firms, usually suppliers and clients. Underlying this approach is the belief that the driving force behind agreements is the influence or power large firms seek to exert over the economy. A stable interorganizational arrangement of alliances is thus one that deals successfully with the distribution of two scarce resources: money and authority (Benson, 1975). According to Hamel, *et al.* (1986), however, stability would always elude such alliances because they rarely define relative power clearly between the partners. Alliances are internally unbalanced and this contributes to the tendency for one partner to seek gains at the expense of others. Indeed, Hamel, Doz and Prahalad would go so far as to suggest that success of an alliance is not defined by the longevity of the bond, but by the ability of one partner to erode the other's autonomy. From their perspective it is thus wise to be wary of partnerships that do not look conflictual, for they may merely conceal a collusive move to divest a firm of certain activities. Aggressive partners may also attempt to use allied firms to fight proxy battles for them against dominant competitors, as in the use of Amdhal, ICL, Bull and Siemens as frontline troops by Fujitsu and NEC in their assault on IBM. Finally, dominant firms tend to engage in a network of partnerships, playing a central role that allows them to enter/exit alliances according to their competitive strategies of the moment (for example IBM). When compared to internalization, partnerships are thus a 'second best solution' (Hamel *et al.*, 1986).

Unfortunately this 'conspiracy view' of alliances, although seemingly supported by the evidence of a high failure rate in joint ventures, is internally inconsistent when it comes to managerial prescriptions. Hamel, Doz and Prahalad, for example, acknowledge that the most successful partners are those who possess 'receptivity to learning', that is a superior ability to foster horizontal and vertical communications and to transfer learning from individual projects back to the organization. Japanese firms are thus said to be more skilled at 'managing by agreements' because they are more open to learning.[1] None the less, they advise prospective partners to manage alliances according to the tenets derived not from this insight but from their power perspective:

— deal with alliances as second best solutions, even in ideal circumstances
— beware of encroachment by one's partner

— enforce technology transfer restrictions
— replenish the inventory of one's core skills in order to strengthen the bargaining power within the alliance;
— regulate the flow of the contributions to the partnership.

Note that if both partners apply the principles just listed, cooperation, innovation and growth will never take place, for effective learning requires that control be relinquished and not increased (Argyris, 1982). The more cheating is covert, the harder it is for partners to learn from each other, that is the more difficult it is to build trust and reputation as a good partner.

As a remedy Buckley and Casson (1976) suggest an opposite set of prescriptions whereby an alliance which would give all parties a strong incentive to cheat must involve a great deal of mutual forbearance if it is to be successful. Thus

— in the alliance, decisions must be made in an open and overt way;
— what the agent does when he is observed should be a reflection of the way he behaves when he is not observed.

Unfortunately, such prescriptions contradict the very model of opportunistic economic behaviour that is common both to the power explanation and the transaction costs approach that Buckley and Casson themselves embrace and to which we now turn.

O. E. Williamson (1975, 1985) successfully deals with what the technical coordination school left largely unresolved, the issue of trade-offs between alternative organizational forms. In his framework, the selection of the most appropriate governance mechanism is determined, in a competitive environment, by its efficiency in managing transactions with the lowest possible costs, contingent upon a set of behavioural and environmental factors; these are bounded rationality and opportunism on the one hand and complexity and a small numbers of players on the other. Asset specificity and the complexity of the task and service exchanged favour the internalization of transactions as the mechanism whereby fewer resources would be consumed in coordinating separate activities. The standardization of goods and services and the corresponding large number of producers and buyers suggest that a market arrangement would perform better. Alliances fall somewhere in between. Although the transaction-cost perspective contemplates such an arrangement, it is wary about its stability in the longer term. If alliances are chosen as a governance mechanism for complex exchanges, such as those involving R & D, they are exposed to the dangers of opportunism, while if they merely broaden the scope of internal organization over standardized transactions, they are better superseded by more efficient market arrangements. It follows that, at least in evaluating alliances, because both theories share the same view of the economic agent, the power and the transaction-costs perspectives reach the same pessimistic conclusion (Ciborra, 1989).

A number of recent empirical studies appear to support the transaction-costs approach. Mariti and Smiley (1983), for example, compared a range of interfirm transactions and found that the more complex the exchange and its exposure to the hazards of opportunism, the more elaborated the governance structure of the relationship. Mariotti and Migliarese (1984) demonstrated for the semiconductor industry that the more uncertain the product or service being exchanged and the more specific the assets involved in carrying out interfirm transactions, the higher the rate of internalization of such transactions. In his analysis, Gomes-Casseres (1987) found that multinational enterprises tend to rely on joint ventures, seen as intermediate forms between licensing and full ownership, because of issues sensitive to transaction costs. Joint ventures are thus regarded as the best compromise between internalization that for various reasons (lack of resources, presence of institutional barriers) cannot be implemented and a more arm's length relationship that cannot cope with the complexities of sharing R & D activities. Pisano (1989) reaches similar conclusions for the biotechnology industry. Note finally, that the transaction-costs approach is increasingly adopted as an interpretive tool to analyse the behaviour of the multinational enterprise with regard to foreign direct investment. From this latter perspective, cooperative agreements are looked upon as one of the transactionally efficient options available, contingent upon a set of technological, location specific and institutional factors (Buckley and Casson, 1976; Teece, 1981, 1982).

Two major problems dog the heels of the transaction costs approach. First, it considers trade-offs between institutional arrangements in a static way. However as Langlois (1985) argues, in a turbulent environment an arrangement that has bad transaction costs properties may be far more efficient, that is better able to survive, than an organization with good transaction costs properties in equilibrium. In the high-tech industries, the main trade-off to consider may thus be that between efficiency and flexibility (Klein, 1977). Second, the transaction cost perspective lacks the discriminating power to explain why an alliance is set up in the first place. Straightforward transaction-costs considerations would uniformly recommend internalization of transactions when dealing with technological innovation. But there is a growing convergence of empirical data and theoretical reflection that suggest that alliances are becoming a preferred solution to the problem of acquiring and managing knowledge assets, that is strategic alliances are a primary mechanism by which firms formalize their links to external sources of innovation (Wilson, 1987). Indeed, today alliances differ from interorganizational collaboration of the past precisely because they are endowed with large budgets; they occur in high-tech industries; and partners invest considerable portions of their R & D budget in them.[2]

Only a few authors have pursued an explanation of alliances specifically related to the process of innovation. The nature of technical innovation coupled with the strategic drive to capture the largest share in profits generated by innovation is responsible for defining the firm's boundaries, its degree of integration and its overall configuration. According to Teece

(1986), alliances are a means for the firm to obtain straightforward access to those co-specialized assets which are essential for the efficient commercialization of any innovation. If assets are innovation specific and they are not vested in a stand-alone enterprise, acquisition may be impractical. In these circumstances non-equity coalition arrangements are likely to emerge. For Antonelli (1987) the origin of new organizational forms such as the 'network firm',[3] and the federation of firms can also be traced to technological change. In order to appropriate profit streams stemming from innovation, and given the imperfection of the markets in trading know-how, the firm tends to grow through the internalization of innovative processes. But coordination costs set a limit to such growth and intermediate, cooperative forms are thus the solution to the trade-off between the complexity of coordination and the advantages of continuing integration.

This version of the conventional wisdom remains deficient because it envisages the incremental growth of the firm when adopting an innovation through stepwise, marginal trade-offs between costs of coordination and integration. Unfortunately, in the high-tech industries things do not proceed only incrementally and innovation seems to require a special genre of learning, which differs from the learning-by-doing concept on which most industrial economists base their explanations of innovation and organizational change (Nelson and Winter, 1982). This is due to three factors. First, the urge to increase the stock of knowledge is very compelling, so that competitive advantage in such industries is more a function of the rate of increase in knowledge than of an absolute increment to the stock of knowledge (Mytelka, 1987). Second, R & D costs and risks are much larger; they invite as never before the sharing of resources among different organizations. Third, product life cycles are much shorter. They barely exceed the length of time required to secure patent protection. This diminishes the ability to appropriate technological rents through patenting and incites competitors to cooperate in order to capture R & D results at their source and then to compete in the traditional domains of production, marketing and distribution. In contrast to the innovation approach, alliances are, rather, the outcome of two simultaneous failures: that of markets in transferring knowledge and that of internal organization in accumulating it at a fast pace.

The literature on global competition appears to show a pragmatic concern for both these failures and assigns particular importance to the rate of change. According to Porter and Fuller (1986), for example, long-term alliances, or strategic coalitions, are related to the process of industry and firm globalization. Coalitions permit firms:

- to obtain superior economies of scale, or ride down the experience curve faster;
- to gain more effective access to knowledge;
- to reduce risks of costly projects;
- to shape competition by *inter alia* modifying the number of actual competitors and creating new barriers to entry.

The same authors, however, point out that establishing an alliance can be affected by transaction costs stemming from:

— coordination between the partners, contingent upon their respective strategy and configuration;
— lack of trust between the partners that makes coordination more difficult;
— erosion of competitive position: coalitions can strengthen the position of the allied competitor;
— adverse bargaining position: coalitions can expose one of the partners to extraction of profits by the other because of a weaker bargaining position. (Porter and Fuller: 1986:329).

An alliance is adopted as a result of the trade-off between benefits and costs of alternative arrangements. Market relationships show higher transaction costs when flexibility is required because the environment is uncertain or a technology is difficult to transfer convincingly without disclosing proprietary information. If proper incentives are difficult to define, a long term engagement may obtain including flexible, tailored forms of monitoring and control.

The advantages of alliances over internal development or acquisition boil down to the greater rapidity of change that they permit: 'the time required to build expertise or gain market share internally is likely to exceed the time required with a coalition. As product life cycles have shortened and competitive rivalry has intensified, the timing advantages of coalitions are increasingly important' (Porter and Fuller, 1986:328). At the same time, alliances are easier to dissolve than internal development or a merger, for their sunk costs are smaller, commitments are less irreversible and inertia lower. A degree of flexibility can be preserved as a result. In sum, coalitions will be more frequent during periods of rapid and significant structural change in an industry.

The dynamics of alliances: trust, learning and change

In Figure 3.1 we develop this approach in terms of the following hypothesis: if transaction costs are low, an arm's length relationship between firms would do; however, if transaction costs are higher, change or 'transition' costs discriminate between internal development/acquisition and alliances. The stability and longevity of alliances are thus determined by transaction *and* change costs. If the former are very high, alliances may break up. If the latter are very low, partnerships will be transitional devices that ultimately lead to internalization.

Some theoretical issues none the less remain unresolved despite this more realistic view. How are the routinization required by efficiency (lowering transaction costs) and the creativity required by higher flexibility (lowering transition costs) to be reconciled within an organization? What happens

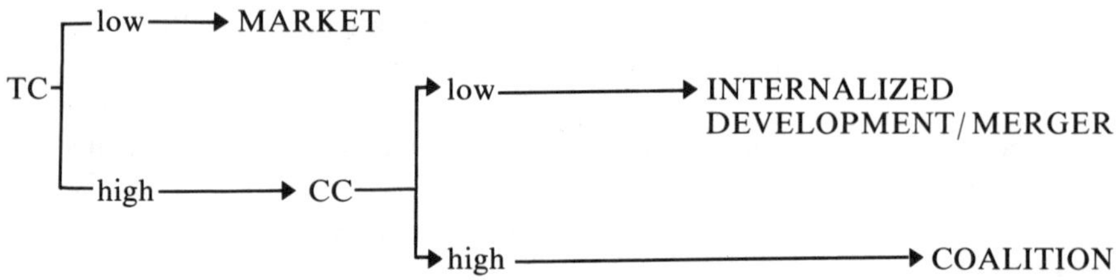

Figure 3.1 Transaction Costs (TC) and Change Costs (CC)

when human resources are required to switch abruptly from one mode of functioning to the other? What are the most effective forms of organization to deal with these problems? Organization theory and the economic literature on change and innovation, by focusing on trust, provide some answers.

A.W. Gouldner (1961), for example, views trust as a future-orientated concept based on the notion of reciprocity emanating from the continuation of a mutually satisfying relationship. Reputation and, more importantly, past performance are the two other essential ingredients of such an invisible asset (Thorelli, 1986; Itami, 1987). In his analysis of research partnerships in Japan, Ouchi (1984) similarly emphasizes the role played by trust in sustaining collaboration among competitors. While the competitive drive of each individual company is central to the success of the Japanese electronics industry, associations create a network of relationships among firms for the common good (Ouchi and Bolton, 1987; see also Chapter 6). Such institutions become the '*loci* of the social memory'. Competitors enter into joint research without the protection of clear patent agreements, 'yet secure in the knowledge that no party will cheat the others, because cheating will surely be detected and punished in the future' (Ouchi, 1984:122). Thus, fears about appropriability of innovation outcomes (von Hippel, 1987; Teece, 1986) can be dealt with by longer term commitments, trust and mechanisms of social memory.

If trust is the lubricant of successful alliances, how is it to be developed, implemented and maintained? After all, trust requires the willingness mutually to adapt; to engage in a reciprocal commitment to a behaviour which is fundamentally at odds, in both its assumptions and daily implementation, with the more normal practice of competitive market behaviour. A second element in the process of developing a better understanding of alliances, therefore, is to consider them as an organizational innovation where practical experiments in non-rivalrous behaviour take place, precisely in order to increase the openness of organizations, to enhance their learning capabilities and to augment their trustworthiness. For the corporation that engages in them seriously, alliances thus represent an instance of radical change, especially when they entail the transition from an autonomous, self-sufficient organization to a relatively stable network of firms within which core businesses are being redefined, boundaries and identities are being modified and conduct and strategy are shifting from competition to cooperation.

Both the transaction-costs and the power approaches are wary of alliances and recommend internalization because they are based on the assumption of opportunism and the need for setting up control mechanisms to curb it. But such theories of control, if put in practice, lead to the design of organizations that block the way to learning, innovation and trust. Instead, effective learning can only take place by practicing a behaviour that is anti-control, that is by successfully denying the reasons for internalization of transactions. Alliances represent one of the few institutional arenas within which to experiment with such innovative behaviour and the only one that can lead to trust and innovation.

If alliances are learning experiments, what are the learning processes that characterize them? To be sure, new knowledge is the product and the goal of the alliance. The alliance brings into the corporation new expertise concerning products marketing strategies, organizational know-how, new tacit and explicit knowledge. New management systems, operating procedures and modifications of products are the typical outcomes of such a process of incremental learning. A firm can learn how to set up and fine tune alliances *per se*. The result of such learning is the institutionalization of the organization's rules and routines aimed at managing alliances. For example, Japanese firms are, in general, more experienced in reaping the benefits from alliances because they are more accustomed to grow on the basis of externally generated technology and to exploit cooperative relationships with other firms in their own country (Ouchi, 1984; Hamel *et al.*, 1986; Westney, 1988).

Economists seem to indulge primarily in the consideration of those kinds of learning processes which are smooth and evolutionary, that is learning by doing. However, there is a utility for firms in high-tech industries to engage in alliances in order to implement a different type of learning, to obtain rapidly quantum leaps in knowledge, as a precondition for further growth (Penrose, 1959). The implementation of radical learning moreover, is certainly one of the main sources of change or transition costs. In this respect, an alliance is a device to reduce such costs by creating the opportunity to access or develop different cognitive frames, work arrangements and cultures so that the firm is able to look at both itself and the environment in which it operates in a fundamentally different way, smashing old frames and overcoming organizational inertia. Alliances thus provide, through new insights and successful restructuring of organizational problems, a shortcut to radical change, by-passing organizational vicious circles and deadlocks (Ciborra, 1989; Lyles, 1988; Louis and Sutton, 1987).

Unfortunately, even when tackling the issue of radical, Schumpeterian innovations, economists consider them to be the result of complex forms of learning-by-doing, that is as successful recombinations of the routines that govern the firm (Nelson and Winter, 1982). The qualitative accounts that Nelson and Winter give of the learning processes surrounding major innovations fail to recognize important aspects of learning as performed by human agents, rather than by routines. First, learning by human agents can be impaired: search routines may not be triggered at all for new events are considered threatening. Second, the link between search, problem solving, development and trial of a new routine is not automatic. Third, and most important, routines aimed at correcting errors lead to the repetition of the performances that were considered faulty in the first place: instead of new routines, vicious circles are unwittingly generated. (Kahneman and Tversky, 1974; Ackerlof and Dickens, 1982; Argyris, 1982).

A realistic account of why firms seek change and growth through alliances must be found, then, in a more thorough investigation of the limitations of individual and organizational learning processes. In this respect, the economic theory of predictable behavior put forward by Heiner (1983) provides a fresher approach. Heiner is concerned with a broader definition of bounded rationality and ultimately limited learning. His theory can enable us to understand strategic partnering as a rational strategy of organizational design and it helps us to develop a new typology of organizational forms based on more realistic cognitive attributes of the economic agents.

Neoclassical economics, including the integrations and variations by Simon and by Williamson, assumes that the agent's competence is always commensurate with the complexity of the problem of choice. Once all the relevant information is available, the agent is able competently to select the best alternative at hand; either an optimal choice according to pure neoclassic economics, or a 'satisficing' one when limits in human information processing capabilities are explicitly factored in. To this Heiner (1983) adds the hypothesis that there is always a gap (called the CD, or competence-difficulty, gap) between the problem of choice and the required competence. This occurs because the agent may hesitate about his true preferences or incorrectly interpret the feedback coming from past actions, and in any case is likely to make mistakes even when all the relevant information is available. Such an hypothesis contains a variety of implications both at the individual and organizational levels. For example, in complex decisionmaking situations, agents may worsen their performance even if they are exposed to new relevant information for they are unable to imitate optimal decisionmaking rules (limited learning). Agents may enhance their performance if they rely on local and circumscribed information and follow rigid, simplified decision rules (reliability theorem). On the other hand, only the reduction of the C-D gap can provide the basis for the effective use of non-local information and the testing of more sophisticated decision rules. Such a reduction cannot occur incrementally through learning-by-doing, if the learning processes are already deficient and biased. Rather, it must rely on higher-order learning that has an impact on the very routines that govern learning-by-doing (Bateson, 1972).

From an organizational point of view the considerations above suggest a new explanation for strategic alliances. Given the higher complexity of the primary task of the firm caused by the continuous development and shifting of technical innovations, alliances are harnessed to reduce the gap between the corporation's competence and the complexity of the environment through two mechanisms: an outbound manoeuvre to control the complexity of the environment and an inbound manoeuvre to augment the organizational capabilities of the firm. In what follows we look at each of these in turn.

Alliances generate a higher rigidity in the environment, thus reducing its complexity and increasing its predictability. The creation of networks of firms stabilizes the environment where new products, services and technologies are continuously introduced. On the one hand, the development of local, proprietary know-how and exclusive control over a core technology is no longer a viable alternative. Stable technologies that can be embedded into a 'core' are exceedingly rare, and unbounded growth aimed at internalizing all types of innovation lies outside the reach of even the largest corporations, as the recent failures of IBM and AT&T to expand through acquisitions into the related fields of telecommunications and data processing respectively demonstrated.

Given the limited capacity to grow and change even for the largest firms, agreements allow the environment to be loosely managed through various forms of weak ties (Granovetter, 1985), thus achieving higher predictability and reliability for the entrepreneurial action. Alliances can be seen as attempts to limit competition and cast an orderly structure on the market place. They are indeed the expression of market power, but in a different way from cartels. In the steel or oil industries agreements are made to control prices and output, while in the high-tech sectors, agreements are aimed at coping with a wider C-D gap due to technological innovation.

If innovation continuously requires the application of new, non-local knowledge, alliances can also be seen as attempts at opening the boundaries of the corporation towards the external environment (for example other corporations, research and government institutions). In order to enhance growth in competence, alliances provide a selective and controlled access to new knowledge coming from the environment. They set the stage where new knowledge can be pre-digested and assimilated. Otherwise, the full and unchecked opening to new information coming from markets and R & D institutions, given the limited stock of competences, may increase the error rate of corporate action and lower performance. Successful alliances generate a texture of shared competences, both in the environment and among the partners, where learning-by-doing is applied to fine tune new ideas, products and innovations.

From this perspective it is possible to generate a typology in which alliances play an independent role analogous to other organizational forms such as markets, hierarchies and clans (Ouchi, 1980) rather than being viewed as hybrid or residual contractual arrangements. In response to the increasing complexity of the primary task of the organization, the following design strategies can be singled out: — (a) as regards the limits in information processing, higher lelels of complexity of the task to be executed are met by (see Table 3.1):

— ignoring new information, by insulating the organization from incoming information, creating slack resources, setting up buffers of various sorts etc.;
— improving the information processing capabilities by increasing the number of vertical and horizontal communication channels, for example introducing management information systems, task forces, teams and matrix arrangements. (Galbraith, 1977)—

(b) as regards the limits to learning, the C-D gap can be reduced by:

— rigid behaviour based mainly on local and reliable information (Heiner, 1983);
— augmenting the competence through effective, higher-order learning, overcoming the obstacles of incremental learning ('learning to learn') (Bateson, 1972) or 'doubleloop learning' (Argyris, 1982).

Table 3.1: A typology of organizational forms

	Decrease learning	Increase learning
Ignore information	Market	Alliances
Increase information processing	Hierarchy	Clan

These design strategies serve to identify a new typology of organizational forms. In a *market* agents have limited processing capabilities and rely solely on local information (Hayek, 1945). The *hierarchy* has a higher capacity to process information for it deals with a more uncertain task (Williamson, 1975; Galbraith, 1977). But it has limited learning capabilities and hence is susceptible to bureaucratic inertia (Williamson, 1985), that is it has less flexibility. The *clan*, a highly cohesive group whose members share the same values, traditions and goals, has a dense texture of communication links and at the same time is highly flexible. Fewer self-defence routines and attempts at opportunistic behaviour impair its performance (Ouchi, 1980). Alliances show some of the features of both the market and the clan. They rely on more limited information processing than does the clan, but they allow for greater learning, flexibility and trust than does the market. They are viable in an environment where the organization needs higher competence but cannot increase the channels of communication and points of access to new knowledge *ad infinitum*. As an organizational form they can be set up more rapidly than a clan or a hierarchy, thus showing superior dynamic efficiency. They represent a decentralized form of organization encompassing high levels of autonomy, market elements and limited opportunism: which is possible because effective alliances invest resources in second-order, as opposed to incremental, learning. Finally, alliances may drift towards markets, if firms do not invest adequately in second-order learning and trust, or towards mergers/acquisitions if higher control is sought at the expense of flexibility and learning. Or, they may become clans, if partners come to accept common values and traditions and a stable, joint set of goals develops over the long run.

Alliances as learning experiments

A few short case studies serve to illustrate the learning and innovation processes in the creation and management of alliances. Seven different partnerships are considered. The strategic alliance between Olivetti and AT&T is treated first and at somewhat greater length because of its particular importance. The remaining six cases are joint ventures recently formed in Italy to sell innovative services and products, create a new, regional market or compete in international ones. Though small in size, they are the *locus* of important learning processes.

The Olivetti AT&T Case

The Olivetti corporation is engaged in hundreds of agreements, acquisitions, joint ventures and alliances, both equity and non-equity (Ciborra, 1986). At least six forms of partnerships are systematically initiated by Olivetti's Strategy Department. These include

(i) licensing of technologies and components;
(ii) use of venture capital as a means to window on the development of new products and processes at start up companies, especially those in Silicon Valley;
(iii) establishment of joint ventures for sharing markets, technologies or production processes;
(iv) participation in precompetitive research consortia, especially within EEC programs;[4]
(v) formation of alliances involving equity participation in order to acquire or set in motion new strategies;
(vi) use of acquisitions to rapidly increase market share.

The choice between these various forms of partnership depends upon a number of factors of which Olivetti's management point out the following in particular: internal resources available; relative strength in the technology; maturity of the product; size of the partner; amount of capital involved and profitability of the investment. While each agreement cannot be the object of a thorough investigation, some interesting and yet puzzling evidence seems to emerge from a closer look at several of them.

Consider first the general reasons why alliances are sought by Olivetti. Two of the most frequently mentioned by the company's management are access to capital and access to know-how in order to achieve rapid growth. Growth is needed to survive during the present computer industry shakeout (McClellan, 1984), when a rather fragmented industry structure gives way to an oligopoly with only a few major players remaining.[5] In this scenario, Olivetti must become a global competitor in terms of its volume of sales, geographic scope of operations and range of products. Internal growth may be the preferred alternative, but the required speed of transformation is so high compared to the resources available, that alliances are often sought instead. It is not the efficient management of pre-existing governance structures but the economics of organizational change that is at stake.

This is particularly important in assessing the main strategic alliance in which Olivetti has been involved during the past decade, its partnership with AT&T. Established in 1983, the AT&T – Olivetti alliance was a very asymmetric partnership, given the size of the companies (AT&T is roughly ten times larger than Olivetti), type of core technology (telecom vs. office equipment), type of culture, history, location and markets served. As part of this agreement, AT&T took a 24 per cent share in Olivetti. The scope of their partnership, however, was far broader than might be concluded from the size of this equity investment. It included goals related to controlling the environment such as the formation of an alliance against IBM; imposing a new operating system standard (UNIX) in Europe as well as in the United States; easing access of both companies to each other's markets; enriching the organizational capabilities of the partners such as mastering the convergence between telecommunication and computer technologies; transferring different managerial skills (AT&T's public monopoly savvy for Olivetti's strong marketing orientation); sharing R & D projects and results; and perhaps, most importantly, enabling each corporation to become a global competitor both geographically and technologically.[6] The global agreement thus opened the possibility for collaboration in a variety of activities — R & D, reciprocal sales of each other's products, joint development of new ones and the exchange of personnel.

The AT&T–Olivetti alliance is now history. In 1989 AT&T transferred its participation in Olivetti to the De Benedetti family's holding, CIR. Before reaching the point of breakdown, at which AT&T abandoned its attempt to develop a joint strategy with Olivetti, the alliance had already passed through hard times. Only a few of the alliance's stated goals had been achieved. But as an exercise in learning, there have been some positive, if unexpected, results. As a supplier to AT&T, Olivetti was transformed almost instantly into a major vendor of PCs. The alliance also placed Olivetti in a particularly advantageous position to develop Unix based systems jointly with Bell Labs. Finally, the transfer of managers reached its peak when the head of Olivetti of America, Vittorio Cassoni, went to manage the troubled AT&T information systems division. From a financial perspective, AT&T's investment in Olivetti's capital can also be counted a success, since the value of Olivetti's stock almost quadrupled. To be sure, there were disappointments on both sides, joint R & D never went beyond the UNIX area, where AT&T maintained its leadership. The delivery of PCs was later discontinued because AT&T was unable to market them. More importantly AT&T management rethought its goal of becoming an 'information company' and retrenched to its core business, telecommunications.

The AT&T–Olivetti alliance was a general framework, a declaration of common intent whose content was to be fleshed out through detailed agreements on the development of new products and the formulation of common projects. In the absence of these detailed agreements, the alliance could still be said to have worked as an 'acquisition' if it proved to be a satisfactory investment or lowered transaction costs compared to the market. But it would have to be rated an overall failure, if it did not allow one or both partners to reach their stated goal of rapid growth. In other words, efficient alliances may be ineffective.

Two factors stand out in this regard with respect to the Olivetti—AT&T strategic partnership: the relative unimportance of the appropriability issue and the far greater importance of learning and goal change in the gains from partnering. As the Olivetti—AT&T case shows, interfirm agreements may fail not because of conflicts between partners over the property of know-how, but because know-how and innovation are plainly not generated. The collapse of such partnerships thus results from a lack of skills in exploiting the alliance as a new resource. Organization inertia rather than preoccupation over proprietary knowledge seems to be a key factor in explaining these failures.

In the case of Olivetti, this conclusion is reinforced by comparing its successful acquisition of Acorn — a small, innovative British computer firm — to its problematic relationship with AT&T's Bell Laboratories. In the former case, while preserving the autonomy of Acorn, top researchers from the British firm were transferred to Olivetti's central R & D department. Herman Hauser, one of Acorn's top scientists has since revolutionized Olivetti's corporate R & D. New products based on the Risc technology introduced at the British company have been jointly developed and a new direction of research in multimedia workstations has been established. In accordance with Olivetti's partnering policies, Acorn was originally acquired to gain market share in the United Kingdom and a strong foothold in the education market. After the acquisition, both these objectives lost their importance or failed completely because of the company's very troubled financial situation. However, it came as a surprise that Acorn's labs contained a wealth of people, skills and on-going projects. The possibility thus opened up for Olivetti to become a leader in workstation technology instead of remaining a follower of IBM. To be sure, all this did not happen automatically, but rather resulted from both circumstances and the ability of Olivetti's vice president for strategy to 'read' the weak signals coming from this small, financially troubled British company, interpret them, assign value to the invisible assets found there and take the bold move of bringing in a foreign scientist from a small, newly acquired company to head Olivetti's central R & D facility. Because the central R & D facility reported to and advised the Strategy Department, Hauser's ideas have had a major impact on Olivetti's orientation.

In contrast, the relationship with Bell Laboratories was on the whole disappointing. No real joint development took place, nor any significant exchange of human resources. The only exception of strategic importance for Olivetti was the direct access it acquired to the UNIX operating system developed by Bell Labs. This enabled Olivetti to start building a new minicomputer line.

Although the unsatisfactory relationship with Bell Labs could, at first glance, appear to confirm the hypothesis that internalization is better than an alliance when the transfer of know-how is at stake, the success in the former case and the failure in the latter appears related far more to the different identities of the partners, their culture, internal organization and definition of goals than to the high costs stemming from opportunistic behaviour. In fact one could submit that there cannot be any opportunistic behaviour from the Bell Laboratories given that its sheer size, its lack of precise, coherent identity and its composite structure appear to be far more important obstacles to cooperation with anybody (even AT&T itself!) than power games or managerial shirking.

Finally it should be noted that, although in serendipitous ways, at least two results have been obtained by Olivetti from the various alliances in which it is currently involved. First these alliances enabled Olivetti to be part of the 'club' that set the standards in the PC/workstation market. The relationship with AT&T, in particular, greatly simplified the internal choices for Olivetti regarding the adoption of UNIX as a standard. Second, they accelerated internal learning and the acquisition and absorption of new knowledge through the deprovincialization of management. What seems to be particularly significant here is that in each alliance the elements of surprise and tinkering seems to have played a role in learning at least as important as the specific contractual arrangement selected. Sometimes, as in the Acorn case, an acquisition is carried out to appropriate certain specific, standardized assets that turn out to be volatile or simply not there. Invisible assets are subsequently discovered and appropriated. In this case the specific contractual form was there almost by chance to allow for such transfer of skills and know-how. Similarly, the AT&T Olivetti global strategic agreement paved the way for a simple quasi-market transaction, that is the sale of PCs to AT&T, since it was the new agreement that suggested the choice of Olivetti when AT&T decided to sell PCs. Nor had Olivetti planned for it. The new state of the art automated factory they were building had been designed to produce varying volumes of different types of workstations. This flexible production unit had to be rapidly transformed into a rigid assembly line producing very large volumes of one type of PC to accommodate the new partnership. In sum, the ability to set up alliances of various kinds and to be open to exploit them more for their unexpected outcomes than for the original goals has become a core skill of Olivetti's Strategy department, an asset that other computer companies such as Apple or DEC, now entering a period of dramatic change after years of undisturbed leadership in their own markets, seem eager to imitate.

Table 3.2: The six joint ventures

Company	Parent companies	Main product/service	When created	Number of employees
INTESA	Fiat–IBM	VAS (value-added services in logistics)	1987	100
OCI	Olivetti–Canon	Reprographics	1987	200
SAFA	Apple–Benetton	Financial services	1987	3
SESAM	Fiat–DEC	Factory automation	1987	80
SEVA	Olivetti–SIP–ENI–American–Express–VISA	VAS	1987	90
SINTED	Honeywell Honeywell–Bull-SIRTI	Intelligent buildings	1987	20

Six cases of joint ventures in high-tech industries

In Italy as in other industrialized countries, information technology is cutting across established industries and defining new ones. It is in these overlappings between industries or at their border that new companies are set up by large corporations to probe the existence of a new market or develop new products. This is often done by creating a joint venture (JV) with a partner whose core technology may be merged with computer technology to create a new product or service. The six cases are instances of such industrial moves. Their common characteristic is that at least one partner is a data processing or telecommunication company. The JVs operate in market niches where competitors are very few or non-existent. Their selection is based on their novelty and experimental nature; therefore they should not be regarded as representative of industry-wide traits.

Table 3.2 presents the essential data of the cases listed in alphabetical order. In what follows a short description is given of each JV.

INTESA, a joint venture between Fiat and IBM in the field of value added services (VAS), provides data-processing services for logistics and distribution over a packet-switched network. When fully operational it will have 200 employees. Each of the partners supply half the personnel. Specialists in the systems area and in marketing come from IBM, while the application–problem solvers come from Fiat. The new company was created after a period of preparation that lasted a full year, and during which, in addition to carrying out market analyses and investment plans, groups from the two parent companies worked together on a common project for a third client. IBM initiated the JV as part of a more general policy geared towards the establishment of partnerships with large user companies in Italy and elsewhere. Fiat's interest in forming INTESA stems from a decision by Fiat not to develop an internal telecommunications unit.[7] INTESA also fits into Fiat's overall diversification strategy which is aimed at entering businesses related to its core activity, in this case systems for industrial logistics. After initial negotiations with SIP (the Italian telecom monopoly) were aborted, a decision was made to work with IBM. In turn, when IBM was looking for a qualified partner to enter the value added services market, recently deregulated in Italy, Fiat provided a distinctive competence in logistics.

SEVA is a joint venture between Olivetti, SIP and other companies operating in the financial industry. While Intesa operates in the VAS market for logistics, SEVA manages a network that provides a variety of services, mainly in the credit card business, but also in electronic mail and education. SEVA enables SIP to extend the use of its packet-switched data network and permits Olivetti to enter the VAS market. The SEVA network is also an example of the utilization by Olivetti of AT&T technology (minis and network software) in the Italian context. While credit card services are well established, other value-added services are still looking for customers. Thus SEVA has a very strong marketing orientation that more strongly embodies Olivetti's culture and goals than it does those of SIP. Merging the two cultures of its main partners is one of the major problems in SEVA.

Financial services were also the basis for SAFA, an alliance between the manufacturer of the Mackintosh computers and a fashion knitwear mass producer. Benetton had recently diversified into financial services by creating a separate company. Apple Italy was seeking to provide financial assistance to its sales force, its specialized Apple dealers and its customers, especially professionals and small businesses in order to widen the market for its more advanced and expensive workstations. SAFA sells financial services, such as leasing and loans, provided by Benetton through Applelink, the dedicated network that connects Apple personnel worldwide.[8] Its main office is in Apple Italy's headquarters in Milan and its organization is very 'slim', comprising only a director, an assistant and one secretary.

The OCI joint venture originates in Olivetti's failure to play a significant role in the reprographic market outside Italy. Olivetti, a latecomer to that business, had severe quality problems with its first model that somewhat tainted its reputation. Its low end-product line, moreover, could not compete with Japanese imports. Declining production levels and rapid product obsolescence led to a substantial reduction in operations and to the near phasing out of the plant. In the early 1980's there were attempts to put these operations on a different track through alliances. An initial agreement, signed with Sharp to design medium- to high-range photocopiers, was subsequently terminated by Olivetti when it decided to abandon the highspeed machine market altogether. In 1986 negotiations were begun with Xerox on a global agreement to cover the entire office automation area, including reprographics. These, however, failed. In order to save Olivetti's presence in the business, the Strategy Department decided to seek an alliance with the most dynamic and aggressive Japanese leader in photocopying technology, Canon. Such a move seems paradoxical from a firm accustomed to meeting Canon outside the market place only in the EEC courts, where it acted as the lead European company in bringing Canon to trial for dumping practices. Olivetti is also a major supporter of EEC legislation designed to force Japanese manufacturers to produce at least half of their components in Europe. Despite this conflictual past, it took Olivetti only a short time to persuade its Japanese rival to use the Italian plant to expand its production base in Europe (precisely as a consequence of the EEC regulations). The resulting partnership looks very asymmetrical. Canon is the leader in a technology where Olivetti is weak, yet it has given up its traditional preference for maintaining full control over its subsidiaries. Not only has Canon allied itself with one of its toughest rivals in Europe but it has also created a potential competitor in OCI, whose products are sold in European markets such as West Germany, where a Canon plant and distribution network are already in place. On the other hand, there are complementarities at stake: Olivetti is keen to broaden its partnerships with Japanese companies, while Canon seeks to become one of the most 'cosmopolitan', or Western-like, of the Japanese companies.

SESAM is a system integrator company bringing together Digital Equipment Corporation (DEC), one of the first, and certainly one of the most successful companies to produce minicomputers and Fiat's automation subsidiary, Comau. DEC's main marketing strategy focuses on selling hardware. Because it is too costly to maintain a large sales force specializing in applications, DEC has relied on a network of OEM software houses to design custom applications for its systems. DEC grew rapidly as a monolith, surrounded by a network of loosely connected software houses with which it had a quasi-market relationship. Such a network, however, is too volatile to be an effective knowledge accumulation and transfer mechanism. Establishing alliances and joint ventures, could, moreover, provide DEC with more direct access to large customers. Fiat has been a user of DEC systems for the automation of its assembly lines. There is also a tradition of cooperation between the two companies in designing automated factories. Through its subsidiary, Comau, Fiat designs the equipment, machines and programmable controllers for SESAM, while DEC contributes its production information systems. The market for SESAM consists of large users who require integrated systems and solutions for factory automation. Internal development of a factory automation division had been a possible option for both companies. But Comau lacked a distinctive competence in information systems and their automation division realized it would be difficult for them to keep pace with developments in data processing. As for DEC, it would have been too costly to develop an in-house competence in operations and control systems. Moreover, a similar JV initiated by IBM with a state-owned automation firm pushed both companies to move into this new market at a faster pace than would have been possible through internal growth. Creating SESAM took one year. Its personnel is composed of specialists in systems integration and manufacturing process engineers.

Because of the need to reconcile the very different backgrounds of these two groups of highly skilled employees, SESAM has been innovative in the development of a special internal labour-market structure (incentives, career paths).

Finally, SINTED is the newest of the JVs considered here. It was created through the externalization of various groups of specialists out of their parent companies: Honeywell Control Systems (the subsidiary of the American control systems manufacturer), Bull (a French computer manufacturer) and Sirti (a state-owned company in the cable sector). It operates in the 'smart building' or building automation industry. In Italy this market is still small. Thus the parent companies continue to provide the JV with a steady stream of resources and skills. As in the case of SESAM, SINTED is situated at the interface between several types of technological know-how: process control, telecom services and data-processing systems. Through SINTED these technologies are harnessed to offer customers turn-key solutions. This requires a considerable amount of teamwork between engineers coming from the different companies. Overall, it falls to the data-processing specialists to integrate these three technologies into the kind of complex offer that design of a 'smart building' involves.

These brief descriptions permit us to observe the many ways in which such partnerships foster new forms of learning that augment the internal competences of the JVs themselves and those of their parent firms. (see Table 3.3)

Learning about the technology of the product or service: This is the case of OCI, where Olivetti's goal is to learn the technology of laser printers, of SESAM, where Fiat obtains know-how about factory automation, (especially distributed systems) and SINTED, which is an opportunity for Honeywell Control Systems to learn about telecommunications technology;
Learning about the other firm: SEVA, for example, needs rapid access to the Italian PTT market through SIP; DEC and IBM want to establish a better relationship with their large customers; Olivetti is interested in having an insider's view of Canon's special brand of Japanese management;
Learning about managing an alliance per se: This may no longer be true for Olivetti, already down this particular experience curve, but it is the case for DEC and Apple. These companies see in the small ventures located in Italy, experiments in organizational innovation that, if successful, could be replicated elsewhere. Through SINTED, SIRTI and its parent holding STET are interested in learning about the scope of specialized alliances in order to enter new markets.

The JV's are also a locus for innovative practice:

Internal innovation: All six of the joint ventures examined here, have been designed to enhance internal flexibility. Special provisions in human resource management, which were not present in the parent companies, for

Table 3.3: JVs as learning experiments

Company and goal	Internal innovation	Innovation in the product/service	Innovation for parents	Transaction costs	Learning
INTESA (FIAT–IBM) create a market	Cross-fertilization of skills New career paths	New service in the VAS industry Alternative design of MIS functions	New relationship with users for IBM New design of information systems for FIAT	Development of system for FIAT	New way of designing information systems How to manage alliances with users
OCI (Olivetti–Canon) re-create a company	Higher integration of manufacturing and subcontractors	New design of photocopiers	Closer access to Japanese management (for Olivetti)	Easier access to EEC market (Canon) Access to technical know-how (Oliv.)	How to co-manage with the Japanese How to cooperate with a competitor
SAFA (Apple–Benetton) create a new service	Sale of service through a network High flexibility of operators	New distribution of a traditional service	Experimenting with alliances (Apple)	Lower costs of services to Apple dealers	A new distributive channel How to manage an alliance
SESAM (Fiat–Dec) create an alliance	New careers/rewards Cross fertilization of skills	New systems that incorporate richer knowledge of production systems	New relationship with users (Dec) Experimenting with alliances (Dec)	Develop systems for Fiat	New relationship with software houses (Dec)
SEVA (Olivetti–SIP)	Flexible organization	New services (VAS)	A new marketing approach (SIP)	Lowers transaction costs for delivering services (Olivetti)	Identification of a new market for VAS
SINTED (Honeywell, Honeywell-Bull, Sirti) Create a new service	Cross fertilization of skills Higher flexibility	Integrated systems for building automation	Access to new know how		Integrating know-hows in offers of building automation systems

example, have been introduced to facilitate the sharing of innovative know-how. Interfunctional, intercompetence teams have been set up in INTESA, SESAM and SINTED to integrate different engineering techniques in automation, software and telecommunications. Career paths have been streamlined to increase upward mobility, motivation and creativity. The structure of incentives is also much finer than in the more bureaucratic parent organization. Thus, the internal structure of the JVs provides an appealing setting for the professional and dynamic knowledge workers who operate as if in an independent consulting firm but one which has a captive relation with its parent companies.

Innovation in the product/service: The JVs have been set up to launch a new product or service, either for the domestic or international market. These include value-added services in the financial sector (SAFA), in logistics (INTESA), in banking and education (SEVA); in building automation (SINTED), in factory automation (SESAM) and in new laser printers and photocopiers (OCI).

Innovation for the parent companies: Here alliances are a means for the parent companies to acquire knowledge. Access to know-how in building automation is provided to Bull through SINTED. A new understanding of marketing value-added services is used by SIP via its participation in SEVA. Olivetti acquires access to a major Japanese competitor, while DEC and IBM reach a closer relationship with their large customers.

It is difficult to say whether these learning and innovation processes are radical or incremental and to what extent they are endangered by the hazard of opportunism. They are too new to provide any clear-cut indication. But to appreciate the extent to which they can be the *locus* of radical learning, consider once again the case of INTESA. Being small and selling a new service, at least in Italy Electronic Data and logistics (EDI), INTESA needs a captive market to develop — in this case provided by one of the parent companies, Fiat. To any operating unit of Fiat, for example an assembly plant, INTESA offers a service that in part is exclusive, but more often than not is in direct competition with the traditional online data-processing services provided by the central data processing (DP) department or by the DP unit of the local department itself. In other words, INTESA is selling to Fiat a new way of doing data processing based on value-added networks rather than traditional mainframes or local distributed systems. By creating a JV, Fiat has given up the internal development of telecommunications services, but it has not abandoned the idea of diffusing the VAS innovation internally. Still, INTESA may encounter resistance in such a captive market from the various central and local DP services precisely because it sells a service based on a technological paradigm that may undermine more traditional technological power bases.

That the JVs are never fully cooperative is shown by the case of OCI. This venture is successfully managed through negotiations and bargaining. The existence of the venture has not softened lobbying by Olivetti within the EEC for additional trade barriers against Japan. Olivetti continues to be aggressively 'anti-Japanese' during the hearings of the EEC Commission so as to maintain the very conditions under which Canon remains committed to the JV.

All the JVs, however, provide instances of knowledge sharing between independent companies. In most cases this sharing is complementary, that is it brings together the know-how of different experts. Often, the creation of the JV has entailed the phasing out of internal units or functions in the parent company. The JVs thus represent instances of externalization of idiosyncratic and innovative know-how. This is done in the name of higher dynamic efficiency and in response to potential new market opportunities, such as VAS (INTESA) and building automation (SINTED). In other words, the JVs have not been developed to achieve a higher static efficiency in transacting an established good or service, but to create a new product or service and to create a new market. The risk of missing a market opportunity is reputed to be higher than the hazard of giving up proprietary knowledge. Parent companies are well aware of the experimental nature of the ventures, so they keep them small and sheltered, with turnover and profit goals that are not too ambitious.

Finally, concerning control over the firm's environment, note how these new ventures introduce a certain rigidity in the Italian market — for factory automation, by linking suppliers and customers (for example SESAM and INTESA) more tightly together; by establishing a possible cartel for the photocopier market in Europe (OCI), and by creating a preferred relationship between Olivetti and the state telecommunications monopoly in Italy (SEVA). The JVs examined here thus have a dual impact on market structures. On the one hand they have been created to increase the flexibility of the parent companies, their response to market opportunities, the pace of innovation and, in general, to govern the convergence of different technological trajectories (Dosi *et al.*, 1987). On the other hand, as Mytelka argues in relation to the ESPRIT programme[9], they introduce elements of rigidity into markets along more oligopolistic lines.

Conclusions

Current explanations for alliances contain ambiguities and dilemmas. As an organizational innovation, alliances are a rational response to the special exigencies of firms: to invade new markets, harness new technologies and grow globally at a fast pace. But they are also seen as temporary arrangements, endangered by opportunism, lack of trust and power games. Indeed, they can appear inefficient when viewed from the transaction-costs or power perspectives.

In this chapter, a different tack has been taken. Alliances have not been regarded as oddities or deviations within the neoclassic economic context, but rather as organizational forms with an independent standing, the occurrence, development and decay of which have to be explained *per se*. Such an explanation requires that more attention be paid to the issues of dynamic efficiency and organizational change. How the firm operating in industries with rapidly changing technology can increase its capabilities by effective learning must be taken into consideration in evaluating trade-offs between alternative institutional arrangements.

Alliances, it has been argued, have a twofold impact: on the environment they reduce uncertainty and complexity, while they unfreeze cultures and structures inside the firm, allowing for a sort of controlled openness to new knowledge. To be sure, their management is difficult and always exposed to the danger of high transaction costs. However, their open nature underlines to the fact that corporations, in order to change and grow, must invest resources in organizational learning. Such learning, moreover, does not take place automatically, but requires from the organization and its members special stratagems and quantum leaps. Alliances, then, make sense if considered within this broader trade-off and, surprisingly enough, their efficient management runs against the conventional wisdom based on the static neoclassical models of economic organization.

Notes

1. Indeed participating in a strategic alliance, as one manager of a high-Tech company observed, involves a 'willingness to risk sharing confidential information . . . where one cannot maintain a competitive position without it' (Wilson, 1987).
2. Up to 25 per cent according to Fusfeld and Haklish (1985).
3. For a somewhat different view of the 'network firm' see Chapter 2 in this volume.
4. The European Strategic Programme for Research and Development in Information Technology (ESPRIT) is discussed in detail in Chapter 9.
5. A similar trend is affecting the telecommunications industry as Jenkins and Mytelka point out.
6. After deregulation, AT&T sought to become an 'information company' rather than just a telecom company. Olivetti needed to overcome the narrow boundaries of its European market.
7. Fiat's management argued that there was insufficient internal demand to warrant such a unit.
8. Apple, for example, has also set up partnerships with a small telecommunications software company and with the state-owned telecom equipment manufacturer, Italtel, in Italy.
9. See Chapter 9.

References

Akerlof, G. and Dickens W.T. (1982), 'The Economic Consequences of Cognitive Dissonance', *American Economic Review*, **72**, No. 3, pp. 307–19.

Antonelli, C. (1987), *L'impresa rete: cambiamento technologico, internalizzazione e appropriazione di quasi rendite*, Milan, Annali della Fondazione Assi, 3.

Argyris, C. (1982), *Reasoning, Learning and Action*, San Francisco, Jossey-Bass.

Bain, J.S. (1956), *Barriers to New Competition*, Cambridge, Mass., Harvard University Press.

Baligh, H.H. and Richartz L.E. (1967), *Vertical Market Structures*, Boston, Allyn and Bacon.

Bateson, G. (1972), *Steps to an Ecology of Mind*, New York, Ballantine.

Benson, J.K. (1975), 'The interorganizational network as a political economy', *Administrative Science Quarterly*, 20 June, pp. 229–49.

Blois, K.J. (1972), 'Vertical quasi-integration', *Journal of Industrial Economics*, pp. 253–72.

Buckley, P.J. and Casson M., (1976), *The Future of the Multinational Enterprise*, New York, Holmes and Meier.

Cainarca, G., Colombo M.G., and Mariotti S., (1989), 'Accordi tra impreso nel sistema industriale dell'informazione e della comunicazione' in Fondazione Olivetti, *Tecnologie dell'Informazione e Accordi tra Imprese*, Milano, Edizione Comunita.

Chesnais, F. (1988), 'Technical Co-Operation Agreements between Firms', *STI Review*, December, pp. 51–119.

Ciborra, C.U. (1986), *Le Affinita a Asimmetriche. Il Caso Olivetti–AT&T*, Milan, Franco Angeli Editore.

— (1989), 'Transitions vs transactions: the nature of firms' change', *Annali di Storia dell'Impresa*.

Dosi, G., Teece D.J., and Winter S., (1987), *Technology and the Changing (Horizontal) Boundaries of the Firm*, Il Settimana Internazionale di Storia e Studi sull'Impresa 'Tecnologia e impresa in une prospettiva storica', Milan, Fondazione Assi, Fondazione Adriano Olivetti.

Fiol, C.M. and Lyles M.A., (1985),'Organizational Learning', *Academy of Management Review*, **X**, No. 4, pp. 203–13.

Fusfeld, H.I. and Haklish C.S., (1985), 'Cooperative R&D for Competitors', *Harvard Business Review*, **63**, No. 6, pp. 60–67.

Galbraith, J.R. (1977), *Organization Design*, Reading, Mass., Addison–Wesley.

Gomes-Casseres, B. (1987), *Ownership Structures of Foreign Subsidiaries: Theory and Evidence*, working paper, Harvard Business School.

Gouldner, A.W. (1961) 'The Norm of Reciprocity', *American Sociological Review*, **25**, pp. 161–79.

Granovetter, M. (1985), 'Economic Action and Social Structure: A Theory of Embeddedness', *American Journal of Sociology*, **l**, No. 3, pp. 481–510.

Hamel, G., Doz Y. and Prahalad, C.K., (1986), 'Strategic Partnerships: Success or Surrender', colloquium on Cooperative Strategies in International Business, New Brunswick, NJ, October.

Harrigan, K.R. (1986), *Managing for Joint Venture Success*, Lexington, Lexington Books.

Hayek, F.A. (1945), 'The Use of Knowledge in Society', *American Economic Review*, **35**, pp. 519–30.

Heiner, R.A. (1983), 'The Origin of Predictable Behavior', *American Economic Review*, **35**, pp. 519–30.

von Hippel (1987), 'Cooperation between Rivals: Informal Know-How Trading' *Research Policy*, vol. 16, pp. 291–302.

Hladik, K.J., (1985), *International Joint Ventures on Economic Analysis of U.S.Foreign Business Partnerships*, Lexington, Lexington Books.

Itami, H. (1987), *Mobilizing Invisible Assets*, Cambridge, Mass., Harvard University Press.

Kahnemann, D. and Tversky, A., (1974), 'On the Psychology of Prediction', *Psychological Reviews*, **80**, No. 4, pp. 237–51.

Klein, B.H. (1977), *Dynamic Economics*, Cambridge, Mass., Harvard University Press.

Langlois, R.N. (ed.), (1985), *Economics as a Process: Essays in the New Institutional Economics*, Cambridge, Cambridge University Press.

Louis, M.R. and Sutton, K.I., (1987), *Switching Cognitive Gears: From Habits of Mind to Active Thinking*, working paper, Center for Applied Social Science, Boston, Boston University.

Lyles, M.A., (1988), 'Learning Among Joint Venture Sophisticated Firms' in F.J. Contractor and P. Lorange (eds), *Cooperative Strategies in International Business*, Lexington, Lexington Books, pp. 301–16.

Mariotti, S. and Migliarese, P., (1984), 'Organizzazione industriale e rapporti fra imprese in un settore ad alto tasso innovative', *L'Industria*, **1**, pp. 47–62.

Mariti, P. and Smiley, R.H., (1983), 'Cooperative Agreements and the Organization of Industry', *Journal of Industrial Economics*, **31**, pp. 437–51.

McClellan, S.T. (1984), *The Coming Computer Industry Shakeout Winners, Losers and Survivors*, New York, Wiley and Sons.

Mowery, D.C. (ed.) (1988), *International Collaborative Ventures in U.S. Manufacturing*, Cambridge, Mass., Ballinger Publications.

Mytelka, L.K., (1987), 'Knowledge-Intensive Production and the Changing Internationalization Strategies of Multinational Firms' in J.A. Caporaso (ed.), *A Changing International Division of Labor*, Boulder, Lynne Rienner, pp. 43–70.

Nelson. R.R. and Winter, S.G., (1982), *An Evolutionary Theory of Economic Change*, Cambridge, Mass., Harvard University Press.

Ouchi, W.G., (1980), 'Markets, Bureaucracies and Clan', *Administrative Science Quarterly*, **25**, pp. 129–41.

——— (1984), *The Reform Society*, Reading, Mass., Addison-Wesley.

——— and Bolton, M.R., (1987), *The Logic of Joint Research and Development*, mimeo, Graduate School of Management (GSM) University of California, Los Angeles (September).

Penrose, B.T. (1959), *The Theory of the Growth of the Firm*, Oxford, Basil Blackwell.

Phillips, A. (1960) 'A Theory of Interfirm Organization', *Quarterly Journal of Economics*, **74** November, pp. 602–13.

Pisano, G.P. (1989), *The Governance of Innovation: Vertical Integration, Joint Ventures, and Licensing in the Biotechnology Industry*, Boston, MA. Harvard Business School.

Porter, M.E. and Fuller, M.B., (1986), 'Coalitions and Global Strategy', in M.E. Porter (ed.), *Competition in Global Industries*, Boston, Harvard Business School Press.

Richardson, G.B. (1972), 'The Organization of Industry', *Economic Journal*, September, pp. 882–96.

Teece, D. (1981), 'The Market in Know-how and the Efficient International Transfer of Technology', *Annals of the American Academy of Political and Social Science* (November): 81–96.

Teece, D. (1986) 'Profiting from Technological Innovation: Implications for Integration, Collaboration, Licensing and Public Policy', *Research Policy* **15**, No. 6 (December) pp. 285–305.

Westney, E. (1988), 'Domestic and Foreign Learning Curves in Managing Cooper-

ative Strategies' in F.J. Contractor and P. Lorange, (eds), *Cooperative Strategies in International Business*, Lexington, Lexington Books, pp. 339–46.
Williamson, O.E. (1975), *Markets and Hierarchies: Analysis and Anti Trust Implications*, New York, The Free Press.
——— (1985), *The Economic Institutions of Capitalism*, New York, The Free Press.
Wilson, D.D. (1987), 'The Effects of Organizational Structures and Technology Transfer as Strategic Alliance Success', Cambridge, Mass., Sloan School of Management, Massachusetts Institute of Technology.

4 International collaboration in the commercial aircraft industry

David Mowery[1]

Introduction

The international aircraft industry now contains a complex system of collaborative agreements involving links among the major 'prime contractor' firms and an extensive set of cooperative relationships between these firms and suppliers and subcontractors. The innovation process was different prior to the early 1970s, when both airframe and engine producers largely developed and manufactured their products independently of other firms. Since then, however, virtually no large commercial transport or engine has been developed and produced by an American firm without significant foreign involvement. This chapter analyses international collaboration in the aircraft industry, including the following recent examples[2]:

— Boeing and the Japan Commercial Aircraft Corporation (JCAC—a consortium of Mitsubishi Heavy Industries, Kawasaki Heavy Industries and Fuji Heavy Industries), a venture that is producing the Boeing 767 in collaboration with Aeritalia.
— The 7J7 venture, now cancelled, between Boeing and the Japanese consortium.
— General Electric and the Société Nationale d'Etude et de Construction de Moteurs d'Aviation (SNECMA), producers of the CFM56 engine.
— International Aero Engines, a venture that involves Pratt and Whitney, Rolls Royce, Fiat, MTU, Ishikawajima-Harima Heavy Industries, Mitsubishi Heavy Industries and Kawasaki Heavy Industries in the development of the V2500 engine.
— Airbus Industrie, involving governments and firms from France, Great Britain, Spain, West Germany and the Netherlands.

Both governments and private firms are important actors in many of these joint ventures. Government involvement includes direct ownership of the firms or negotiation of the agreement, as was the case in Airbus Industrie in its early period, provision of risk capital, which is done for the non-American firms in virtually all of these ventures, or approval of the transfer of 'dual-use' technologies, which is necessary for the participation of American firms in many of these undertakings.

As has been noted in other chapters in this book, there are many different forms of international collaboration, as well as a wide range of diverse motives and actors. The commercial-aircraft industry is no exception, and there are at least three different groups of actors within these collaborative ventures. American firms primarily, pursue collaborative ventures for purely commercial motives, as we shall see below, in order to retain their dominance within the global commercial-aircraft industry. Despite their significant presence as military suppliers, the United States' government has played a very modest role in these firms' decisions to seek foreign risk-sharing partners in development projects.

A second group includes a number of firms in Western Europe, many of whom produce both civilian and military aircraft or components. Many of these firms are government owned or are subject to extensive influence by government agencies through such policies as military and civilian procurement or the provision by public agencies of partial funding for development projects. In many cases (most notably, Airbus Industrie) these firms have chosen to pursue international collaborative ventures with the strong support and encouragement of their national governments in order to remain viable within the international industry, and thereby maintain their domestic employment, and because they represent an important national security asset for their national governments. These firms are largely concerned with maintaining their status as important producers and sources of technology rather than attempting to enter the aircraft industry through collaborative ventures.

A third group includes the nascent Japanese aerospace firms as well as firms in such newly industrializing economies as Indonesia or Brazil. These firms have pursued international collaborative ventures (for example the Embraer–Aeritalia venture; CASA–Nurtanio; the Boeing–JCAC venture) as a way of learning the necessary skills to enter the global commercial-aircraft industry. As is the case with the second group, these firms often have substantial backing (largely financial, but occasionally political) from their national governments to support their participation in international collaborative ventures. Firms in each of these groups seek different objectives from international collaboration. The mix of firms from each group within a specific collaborative venture will influence the financing, structure and operation of the venture. Nevertheless, as the discussion below suggests, there are strong similarities among all international collaborative ventures in this industry that reflect the realities of the technology of commercial aircraft and the markets for the products of this industry.

The Structure and Performance of the Global Commerical-Aircraft Industry

The manufacture of aircraft engines requires considerable expertise in aeronautical engineering and airframe design and the converse is true of airframe manufacture. Nevertheless, engine producers do not manufacture airframes, and vice versa, due in part to differences in the cost structure and minimum efficient volume of production of these goods. Selective withdrawal during the 1970s by each of the three engine manufacturers, General Electric, Pratt and Whitney and Rolls Royce, from one or more market segments meant that only one segment of the engine market now has more than two producers. This withdrawal was aided in one case (the V2500 venture between Rolls Royce and Pratt and Whitney) and attempted in another (a collaborative agreement between General Electric and Rolls Royce concerning the CF6-80 and the RB211–525 dissolved in late 1986) through collaboration between two of the three firms.

A number of airframe producers also have exited from the industry. Boeing now dominates the global commercial-aircraft market as thoroughly as Douglas dominated the market of the 1930s, although Airbus Industrie recently has increased its share of the large transport market to more than 25 per cent. The other major American producer of large commercial aircraft is McDonnell Douglas, presently manufacturing one aircraft design (the MD80 and its various derivatives), although the MD11, a derivative of the DC10, now is being developed for introduction in 1990.

Both the commercial-aircraft and engine industries also contain a large population of vendor and subcontractor firms, engaged in the production of assemblies and components for the much smaller group of major contractors. This group of supplier firms within the United States includes as many as 15,000 firms, many of which produce components for both military and civilian aircraft. These firms now are exposed to greater competition from foreign producers as a result of international collaborative ventures in commercial aircraft and increased foreign involvement in the production of American military aircraft.

Product development in aircraft and engines is a design-intensive process (Steiner, 1982). Firms produce dozens of 'paper airplanes' prior to the decision to launch the development of a specific design in an effort to accommodate the varied requirements and desires of airline customers.[3] Although the design phase is lengthy, once the decision is made to introduce an airframe or engine, it is essential to bring the product to market rapidly. American producers historically have been able to move from design commitment to production more rapidly than European firms.[4] Design capabilities, as well as the ability to manage the transition from design to production, are among the most important influences on commercial success and failure in this industry.

Another important competitive asset is a world-wide product support and service network. Following the introduction of a new aircraft or engine, incremental modifications are made throughout the life of the design, relying on information gained from close monitoring of operating experience. This monitoring function, as well as the importance of world-wide spare parts supplies and field service, means that a global marketing and product support organization is critical to the commercial success of a new aircraft or engine design. The requirement for product support and marketing networks acts as a major barrier to entry into the aircraft industry. The high fixed costs of supporting these networks also create a strong incentive for producers to market a number of different aircraft or engine models. The ability to supply a full line, covering all segments of the aircraft or engine market for a given customer class, enables producers to utilize their marketing network more effectively. This factor has played an important role in the decisions of American manufacturers of airframes and engines to seek alliances with other firms.

The high cost of new product development within the aircraft industry is another source of entry barriers. Development of the Boeing 767 is estimated to have cost nearly £1.5 billion, while estimates of the development costs for a 150-seat transport range up to and beyond £2 billion. The V2500 high-bypass engine required nearly £2 billion for development. Rising development costs have increased the risks of new product development in the aircraft industry. An important motive for American firms' participation in multinational collaborations is their desire to reduce the financial risks of new product development. High development costs have also been an important motivation for much of the trans-European collaboration in military and commercial aircraft.

The Policy and Technological Environment of the Global Commerical Aircraft Industry

The recent growth of international collaboration in the commercial-aircraft industry reflects change in the competitive environment faced by firms in the United States, Western Europe and Japan. These changes were most pronounced and important for American firms, whose decision to invite foreign firms to collaborate in new product development ventures largely created the opportunities that Japanese and some European firms have exploited. Western European aerospace firms also experienced significant erosion in their viability as independent producers during the 1960s which led to the formation of the Airbus Industrie consortium. Within Japan, the most important developments were the identification of the commercial-aircraft industry by MITI as an important sector for future development, combined with the failure of efforts to develop passenger aircraft independently (Mowery and Rosenberg, 1985).

Change in the structure of federal policy toward the American commercial aircraft industry and changes in other aspects of the domestic and international environment have contributed to increased international collaboration since the 1960s. These changes included deregulation of domestic air transportation in 1978, a decline in the commonality of military and civilian aircraft technology and some erosion in the aeronautics research and technology budget within NASA. Combined with steady growth in development costs, these changes made market demand more uncertain and increased the financial risks borne by American airframe and engine producers. The American aircraft industry also was affected during the 1970s and 1980s by a reduction in the American share of world airline traffic. Although the American market for commercial aircraft still represents the largest single market in the world, it no longer constitutes an absolute majority of world demand.[5]

Decline in the relative size of the American market for commercial aircraft, coupled with steady growth in development costs, means that penetration of foreign markets, always important to American and aircraft firms, now is essential. Access to foreign markets by American firms often is facilitated by enlisting a foreign firm as a partner in the development and production of an airframe or engine. The larger size of the American market also means that penetration of this market is important to the commercial success of foreign aircraft.

Foreign markets also have become more important for firms in the second tier of the American aircraft industry. American components accounted for as much as 35 per cent of the value of the early versions of the Airbus A300, for example,[6] and estimates of the U.S. content of the Embraer Bandeirante, produced in Brazil, range above 40 per cent. Producers of components and other firms in the second tier have a stake in open international markets for aircraft and components that is no less significant than that of the major American firms.

The principal motives for American firms in seeking out foreign partners in aircraft development projects are access to foreign markets, access to lower-cost capital, and risk-sharing. Government ownership or control of the customers for aircraft in many foreign markets means that market access often is improved by providing foreign firms with a share of the development or production of an airframe or engine. Such partnerships also spread risk and can lower the cost of capital, since many foreign governments provide loans or other subsidies for a portion of the development costs incurred by their domestic aircraft firms.

Collaboration that focuses on development and production, rather than licensing or direct foreign investment, is necessary because of the nature of the key competitive assets and the political obstacles to market access that pervade this industry . The corporate assets that are essential to success in this industry include design and system integration capabilities, the capacity to manage the transition from paper design to actual aircraft on schedule, the ability to deal with wide swings in production volume without incurring major cost penalties and the marketing and support networks which will facilitate the incorporation of information from aircraft operations into design modifications. Since these are, for the most part, intangible assets they are difficult to transfer through licensing agreements. Yet direct foreign investment, one alternative strategy for foreign market access, provides little possibility for reductions in the size of the capital investment necessary for product development and no reduction in the risks faced by investing firms. Moreover, the cost structures of airframe production and, to a lesser extent, engine production, make multiplant production undesirable (Mowery, 1987, 1988).

The major Western European industrial economies had developed significant aerospace industries during and after World War II, although West Germany's aerospace industry recovered only very slowly from its destruction during the global conflict. Great Britain, for example, introduced the first jet-powered passenger transport. By the 1960s, however, domestic military and civilian aircraft markets appeared to be too small to support independent product development and manufacture. Competition from American producers of military and commercial aircraft, as well as the growth in 'tied' military aid from the United States and the Soviet Union to potential military aircraft purchasers in the Third World, reduced military export markets. As a result, a number of trans-european consortia for the development of military and commercial aircraft began to develop during the 1980s. Participation in aircraft development and production consortia became major issues of public policy within the industrial European democracies. Partly because of the elevation of these ventures to 'high politics', they produced some notable commercial disasters, such as the Concorde (Henderson, 1977), and a number of extremely costly military aircraft such as the Tornado (Hayward, 1986; Lorell, 1970). Stabilization of domestic employment, the preservation of a defence industrial base, and the strengthening or retention of certain technological capabilities were the central governmental motives for trans-european collaboration. These motives contrast with those of American firms, which were primarily commercial, as well as those of Japanese firms, which centred on the expansion of a tiny domestic industry by acquiring critical skills and technologies through international collaboration.

In its 'Vision of Industrial Structure for the 1980s', MITI indentified commercial large transports as a key industry for the future development of the Japanese economy.[7] The attributes of this industry that rendered it attractive, according to MITI, included the high value-added characteristics of aircraft, a high world income elasticity of demand for its products, minimal environmental pollution and high knowledge intensity. Two other characteristics of the industry cited by MITI deserve particular attention. The first concerns the important links between aircraft and other high-technology industries.[8] In addition, the technology of commercial aircraft was described as one in which a Japanese comparative advantage would not be undercut by such Asian competitors as South Korea or Taiwan as rapidly as had been true of other industries (for example steel). Obviously, this argument is a two-edged sword—the prospective difficulty faced by South Korea or Taiwan in acquiring aircraft production and design skills also will hamper Japanese efforts to acquire such skills from American or European producers.

The YS-11 project, in which a Japanese consortium developed a commercially unsuccessful commuter transport for the domestic market, demonstrated that the small Japanese domestic market limited the possibilities for a conventional 'catchup' strategy in commercial aircraft, just as the impact of the co-production of military aircraft was limited by the small size of the market for military aircraft. In view of the deficiencies in the infant-industry strategy for encouraging the development of the aircraft industry, participation in international collaborative ventures seemed to offer opportunities for the acquisition of expertise in all phases of commercial aircraft design, manufacture and sales.

Case Studies in International Collaboration

Boeing–JCAC

During the 1970s Boeing began the development of successor aircraft to the 727 and 707. Simultaneous development of successors to each of these aircraft was necessary for Boeing to remain a producer of a full line of aircraft. The costs of such an ambitious development programme, however, were £1.5–2.5 billion. The participation of risk-sharing partners would provide capital and reduce the firm's financial risks. Such an arrangement would continue the trend of greater reliance by the firm on domestic and foreign subcontractors and suppliers for development funding and risk-sharing that had accelerated in the development of the 747.[9]

Foreign aircraft firms were especially attractive candidates for collaboration, however, because of the availability of government funds to support development and production start-up costs for these firms. The importance of foreign markets for the commercial success of the 757 and 767 further enhanced the attractiveness of foreign firms as partners in the development and production of these aircraft. None the less, Boeing discussed participation as risk-sharing subcontractors in the 757 and 767 projects with several American firms during this period, without success.[10]

Negotiations between Boeing and the Japan Commercial Transport Development Corporation (JCTDC, the predecessor of the Japan Commercial Aircraft Corporation, JCAC, a consortium made up of Mitsubishi, Kawasaki and Fuji Heavy Industries) and Aeritalia, an Italian producer, were concluded in 1978 with the signing of a memorandum of understanding for the production of the Boeing 767. As 'risk-sharing subcontractors', Aeritalia and the JCTDC each assumed the costs of development and production tooling for 15 per cent of the total value of the aircraft, the overall design of which was largely fixed at that point, for the first 500 aircraft.[11] The JCTDC was responsible for several sections of the fuselage and wing, as well as rudder flaps, a component employing new composite (nonmetallic) materials. The Italian participants were responsible for wing flaps. Both the Japanese and Italian groups received government grants or loans for up to 50 per cent of the development costs of their components. Since Boeing retained sole responsibility for the development of the cockpit and the avionics package, as well as wing design and fabrication and final assembly of the airframe, project management, marketing and product support remained the responsibility of Boeing. Since Boeing retained overall control of design, production and marketing, the 767 venture was not organized as a separate corporate entity.

Although the major design decisions on the 767 had been made by Boeing by the time the consortium was formed in 1978, considerable development and design work remained on many components for the aircraft. A number of these design and development tasks were assigned to Boeing's Japanese partner firms. Japanese engineering personnel were transferred to Boeing headquarters for up to a year which aided the transfer of component design skills and technologies to the Japanese firms.

The technological and financial benefits for the Japanese and Italian participants in the 767 project have been modest thus far, due to the relatively slow sales of the aircraft. Boeing, however, appears to have benefited from the joint venture in a number of ways. By selectively transferring component design and production technologies to Japanese firms, Boeing has reaped a return that would have been unattainable through licensing.[12] Boeing's access to the Japanese market, and possibly to rapidly growing Southeast Asian markets, may have been enhanced by its partnership with Japanese firms.[13] The partnership with Japanese and Italian firms has reduced the size, cost and risks of Boeing's financial commitment to the development of these aircraft. Boeing also has benefited by supporting entry or expanded participation by Japanese firms in the aircraft components' industry, thereby increasing competition among component suppliers and subcontractors.[14] Finally, the potentially valuable contributions of capital, production expertise, and market excess that the Japanese consortium could offer Airbus Industrie, a major competitor, have been preempted by the link between Boeing and the consortium.

The 7J7

In March 1984 Boeing announced a collaborative development project involving the Japan Aircraft Development Corporation (JADC, a consortium of the firms involved in the JCAC, is charged with managing new aircraft development projects) to design and produce a 150-seat aircraft, then expected to be introduced in 1990. The memorandum of understanding between Boeing and the JADC that was signed in March 1984 committed the Japanese group to a share of 25 per cent in the '7-7' project (later the 7J7, an aircraft that was to employ 'unducted fan' engines). As outlined in the memorandum of understanding, Japanese participation in the 7J7 project differed qualitatively from the 767 venture. Rather than participating as a risk-sharing subcontractor, with responsibilities limited to design and production of a modest number of components to meet Boeing specifications, the JADC was to participate in all phases of the project, ranging from fundamental design to marketing, finance of aircraft sales and product support. Boeing remained the senior partner in this joint venture, however, a status reinforced by the American firm's insistence on a higher return on its investment as an acknowledgement of its superior design project management, marketing and product support experience.[16]

The 7J7 venture appeared to be an extension of the alliance of Boeing and Japanese firms in commercial aircraft, albeit one in which Boeing remained the senior partner. A series of decisions by Boeing, however, reduced the importance of this venture and its potential benefits for the Japanese participants. The date of introduction of the new aircraft was postponed from 1990 to 1992 in 1985 and to 1993 in 1987, and the V2500 engine, produced in part by Japanese firms, was rejected by Boeing for the aircraft.

In November 1987 Boeing reduced the staff of the 7J7 project from 1,000 to 200 and subsequently unilaterally cancelled the project (*Aviation Week and Space Technology*, 1987d and 1987e).

In its announcement Boeing explained that the 7J7 project was being cancelled because of serious uncertainties concerning the market for this aircraft, uncertainties that were compounded by the technological risks of the 'propfan' technology that had been chosen as the engine for the 7J7. Boeing's decision was also influenced by its rapidly mounting backlog of orders for aircraft, the production demands of which were severely straining corporate resources. The bulging orderbook also reduced Boeing's incentives to create an all-new, jointly developed aircraft that might compete with existing products.

General Electric–SNECMA

The joint venture between General Electric and the Societe Nationale d'Etude et de Construction de Moteurs d'Aviation (SNECMA) is centred on the production of the CFM56, a high-bypass engine of 20,000–30,000 pounds' thrust. The collaboration of these two firms is formally managed by a separate entity (CFM International) in which each partner holds 50 per cent of the equity. Despite the equal division of equity ownership, the technological and managerial senior partner within CFM International is General Electric.

The CFM joint venture originated in the early 1970s, when engine producers on both sides of the Atlantic recognized the market possibilities for a high-bypass engine of 20,000–30,000 pounds' thrust, to be employed on medium- and short-range aircraft. Following talks with both General Electric and Pratt and Whitney, SNECMA chose General Electric as a partner in the development and production of the so-called 'ten-ton engine'. SNECMA's choice of General Electric built on a relationship that included SNECMA's major subcontracting role in the production of the CF6-50 and CF6-80 engines, employed on the Airbus A300 and A310.

Several aspects of this joint venture are noteworthy. Since the CFM56 incorporated an engine core that originally was developed for military purposes, the United States' Defense Department imposed restrictions on transfer of this technology from General Electric to SNECMA.[16] Although these restrictions complicated the development of the engine and contributed to higher costs, they did not jeopardize the development programme. The relative ease with which the central compressor could be manufactured separately and shipped to SNECMA from General Electric in a sealed black box reflected the fact that General Electric's design for the CFM56 exploited modular design principles in order to reduce maintenance costs. In addition, General Electric did most of the development and systems integration for the engine, reducing somewhat the requirements for information and data exchange between the two partners. None the less, some observers suggest that the CFM56 incurred performance penalties, due to restrictions on sharing of technology and design data between the parties responsible for the compressor and the rear sections of the engine.[17]

Negotiations over the restrictions on technology transfer, as well as the restrictions themselves, delayed the development of the CFM56 by about one year. The slow pace of development of the CFM56, however, reduced somewhat the complexity of project management. Had the CFM56 been a tightly time-constrained programme, project management might have been more difficult. Management of the CFM56 project was further simplified by the fact that General Electric was the acknowledged technological and managerial senior partner within the venture, receiving a fee from SNECMA for project management. Major design decisions typically were made by General Electric with input from SNECMA. General Electric also provides virtually all of the product support for the engine.

The CFM International has been a commercial success — SNECMA now is a leading French exporter of aerospace products, and the CFM56 engine is one of the best selling commercial aircraft engines and will be used on more than 50 per cent of the commercial transports ordered in 1986. General Electric also has benefited from SNECMA's contribution of 50 per cent of the development costs of the CFM56, which totalled more than £1 billion. The importance of SNECMA's financial contribution, however, goes beyond its absolute magnitude. In the view of senior managers at General Electric's Aircraft Engine Group, SNECMA's financial contribution prevented the termination by General Electric of the CFM56 programme in the mid-1970s. Moreover, the adoption of the CFM56-5 for the Airbus A320 undoubtedly was aided by the engine's substantial French content, providing a good example of enhanced market access through the strategic choice of joint venture partners.

Although the CFM venture has proven financially rewarding for SNECMA, the technological benefits for the French firm are less visible. SNECMA gives no signs of undertaking the development of a commercial engine in this or any higher-thrust class without General Electric's participation, either independently or in cooperation with other European producers. SNECMA's participation as a prime contractor in the engine business is unlikely, but the firm may well have become more competitive as a supplier of spare parts. Spare parts sales for the CFM56 are regulated by the GE–SNECMA agreement, but SNECMA could produce spare parts for other military or civilian engines.

Recently, General Electric and SNECMA have extended their alliance to include the development of an unducted-fan (UDF) engine. The financial burdens of the UDF project will exceed those of the CFM56, a possibility that makes joint development more attractive to General Electric. Thus far in the UDF programme, General Electric has assumed primary responsibility for development and testing, although SNECMA also has tested engine components. As of this writing, however, the outlook for the UDF engine is quite uncertain. Boeing's rejection of the engine for the 7J7 on the grounds of the unproven nature of the technology undoubtedly has not helped the engine's prospects, although McDonnell Douglas is pursuing development of a derivative of the MD-80 that will employ the UDF.

The International Aero Engines' V2500

The V2500 joint venture involves Pratt and Whitney, Rolls Royce, Fiat, MTU and Japan Aero Engines Corporation (JAEC, itself a consortium of Kawasaki Heavy Industries, Mitsubishi Heavy Industries, and Ishikawajima-Harima Heavy Industries), in one of the most complex joint ventures in the commercial aircraft industry. Announced in 1983, the joint venture had by 1989 developed a new 25,000-pound-thrust engine. International Aero Engines, an entity incorporated in Switzerland, has been formed to coordinate development, production, marketing and product support for the V2500. Although the formal structure of the V2500 venture is complex, the venture in fact appears to be an alliance of two multifirm groups, centred respectively around Rolls Royce (partners with Japan Aero Engines) and Pratt and Whitney (partners with MTU and Fiat). Prior experience in the joint development or production of aircraft engines is reflected in the division of production and design activities among the participants.

The decision by Rolls Royce and Pratt and Whitney to join forces in the development of a new engine followed by several years the demise of a joint venture between these firms. The JT10D project had as its goal the development of a high-bypass engine generating 28,000 pounds of thrust for the Boeing 757. The JT10D partnership lasted less than a year, breaking up 'amicably', according to the participants, in the spring of 1977 (*Aviation Week and Space Technology*, 1977a:17). Dissolution of the JT10D project occurred because of several factors. As the design of the aircraft for which it was intended (the Boeing 757) changed, the JT10D's design also was altered, and the engine increasingly was competing with the RB211-535, an engine developed independently by Rolls Royce. Transatlantic cooperation in the development of this engine also was complicated by restrictions on the transfer of 'dual-use' American engine technology imposed by the United States' Defense Department.

Before its discussions with Pratt and Whitney on the JT10D, Rolls Royce had joined Japan Aero Engines in the early 1970s in the development of the RJ500, a high-bypass engine producing 20,000 pounds of thrust. It became apparent that any engine for a 150-seat aircraft would have to generate more than 20,000 pounds' thrust and incorporate new technologies in materials and controls in order to increase fuel efficiency. Faced with these costly requirements, the RJ500 group in 1982 began exploring the possibilities for cooperation with either General Electric or Pratt and Whitney.

The other group within the V2500 venture consists of Pratt and Whitney and the two European firms with whom Pratt and Whitney worked closely on the PW2037, an engine developed for the Boeing 757 after the termination of the JT10D project. Although Pratt and Whitney recognized the potential market for an all-new engine in the 25,000-pound-thrust class, the firm's ambitious development agenda precluded the unaided launch of yet another multi-billion-dollar engine development programme. The American firm accordingly re-entered negotiations with Rolls Royce. In

1982 the Rolls Royce and Pratt and Whitney groups agreed to collaborate in the development of an all-new 25,000-pound-thrust engine.

Rolls Royce and JAEC originally were responsible for the forward section of the engine (the low- and high-pressure compressors), utilizing the advanced technology for fan-blade fabrication developed by Rolls Royce for its RB211 family of engines. The Pratt and Whitney group was responsible for the rear sections of the engine, employing technologies developed and applied in the PW2037. Within the group, Pratt and Whitney was responsible for the core section of the engine, while MTU and Fiat respectively developed and produced the low-pressure turbine and the gearbox. Assembly of the engine will take place in both the United States and Great Britain. Marketing is carried out by International Aero Engines, which also has responsibility for systems integration and project management.

IAE's autonomous control of project management and marketing is important, due in part to the numerous possibilities for conflicts of interest if either Rolls Royce or Pratt and Whitney were given primary responsibility for marketing the engine.[18] Such conflicts between jointly and independently developed products, after all, undermined the JT10D venture. Product support is delegated by IAE to the member firms best able to provide such support. These firms are likely to be Pratt and Whitney and Rolls Royce. The governments of the nations in which the foreign participants in the V2500 venture are based all have provided significant financial assistance.

The senior partners in the V2500 venture (Pratt and Whitney and Rolls Royce) devoted considerable effort to minimizing technology transfer in the development of this engine. Some of these efforts were motivated by American government scrutiny of Pratt and Whitney's role within the consortium and the desire of the Pentagon to prevent transfer of the American firm's high-pressure-engine core technology to foreign firms.[19] Much of the concern over technology transfer within the V2500 consortium, however, reflected the senior firms' commercial interests. In order to minimize technology transfer, the engine programme emphasized the separate development of engine components by member firms, with limited exchange of technical data among the partners.[20] Interfaces among these components were designed to facilitate the assembly and testing of the entire engine without extensive knowledge about the internal design specifications of the individual components.

Although this development strategy may have reduced technology transfer among the participants, it impeded the testing and integration of the components of the V2500. Development and testing of the V2500 were proceeding ahead of schedule until late 1986, but serious problems since then have necessitated a significant redesign of the engine's compressor by Rolls Royce. Rather than continuing as an equal partner with Rolls Royce, Pratt and Whitney has been forced to assume overall leadership of the engineering and systems integration for the project (Kandebo, 1987a). The strict divisions of responsibility between the senior partners thus appear to be blurring somewhat as a result of the requirements for systems integration and testing (see *Aviation Week and Space Technology*, 1987b:32–3; 1987c:31).

Like CFM International, the IAE consortium announced in late 1986 that a successor to its initial product, the so-called Super Fan engine, would be developed for the Airbus A340. In April 1987, however, IAE announced the indefinite postponement of the of the Super Fan project. Combined with the recent development and testing problems in the V2500 project, the Super Fan engine episode created additional doubts about the long-term viability of the IAE consortium and contributed to several order cancellations. Questions have thus been raised about the ability of the IAE to manage the activities of its independent partners in an extraordinarily complex development project.

Airbus Industrie

Airbus Industrie is one of the most durable joint ventures in the commercial aircraft industry. The longevity of the airbus Industrie consortium suggests that its structure and management have implications for the management of other joint ventures. These implications, however, should not be overdrawn since Airbus remains in many ways a consortium of governments or of firms largely controlled by the government participants. This discussion of the consortium's development and performance focuses on the tensions among the shifting goals of the national participants.

A central tension running through this history is the use by both the British and French governments of the Airbus venture as a means of sustaining their national aircraft industries. The history of the Airbus consortium is punctuated by clashes between the engine and airframe 'national champions' of France and Great Britain (SNECMA and Aerospatiale in France, Rolls Royce and British Aerospace in Great Britain). Conflicts have also erupted between the engine and airframe industries of each nation. Throughout the 1970s, for example, Rolls Royce was interested primarily in cooperation with American airframe firms, especially Boeing. British Aerospace, on the other hand, gradually came to support collaboration with Airbus. SNECMA's financial and technological prospects during the 1970s were tied to the CFM56 engine project with General Electric, while Aerospatiale was concerned primarily with Airbus.

In 1966 the West German, French and British governments began discussions of the design and production of a wide-body aircraft. The 1967 agreement among the three governments outlined a joint venture in the development of both an airframe and an engine. Great Britain acquired a 75 per cent share in the engine project, with West Germany and France each accounting for 12.5 per cent. The French won responsibility for design leadership and final assembly of the airframe. Consortium members also agreed to employ as many European components as possible in the airframe and engine.

Following this agreement, the consortium developed an airframe design that proved unacceptable to the national airlines of the member nations (capacity expanded from an original target of 250 passengers to more than 300) and was much more costly than originally planned. Rolls Royce lost interest in the Airbus project, however, due to its preoccupation with developing an engine for the ill-fated Lockheed L1011. The British government therefore began to reevaluate its participation; since the French had overall design responsibility for the airframe, the Airbus project held fewer attractions for the British airframe firm taking part in Airbus (British Aircraft Corporation, the predecessor to British Aerospace). Britain withdrew from the venture in 1969.

Following the withdrawal of Great Britain, the Airbus project was reorganized. West Germany and France initially attempted to continue developing the aircraft, now known as the A300B, on a bilateral basis. The Spanish and Dutch governments soon were brought in as partners. The loss of Great Britain proved to be a blessing in disguise. Before 1969, the consortium had been influenced (or immobilized) by the desire of both Great Britain and France to use the airbus project to support their domestic aerospace industries. The tensions created by the participation of the technologically equal British and French firms were replaced after British withdrawal by the binding agent of technological inequality between the remaining major participants. The consortium also dropped its earlier plans to develop both an engine and an airframe simultaneously and abandoned the goal of maximizing European content in the airframe. As a result of these changes and an extensive redesign, the early A300B aircraft had an American content of nearly 50 per cent, including the CF6 engines assembled by SNECMA.

After 1969, then, the goal of advancing European commercial aircraft and engine technology through the Airbus venture receded in importance. Airbus contrasts in this regard with many European collaborations in military aircraft and in other technologies, most of which have pursued extremely ambitious economic and technological goals. During this phase, Airbus Industrie also began to develop an independent administrative structure, albeit one that was dominated by French personnel and subject to the vetoes of participant governments.

During the third phase of the airbus project, spanning the mid-1970s, the commitment to the consortium of the French government wavered. The government goals of maintaining employment and technological capabilities within the French industry required the development of a new aircraft, since the design and production capacity of Aerospatiale were severely underutilized. The French government was also anxious to find an airframe on which to employ the CFM56 engine. Just as the British commitment to Airbus had been undercut by conflict between the interests of its airframe and engine 'national champions', France underwent a period of tortuous manoeuvring among U.S. airframe and engine firms, the Airbus partners and (occasionally) the British aircraft industry in evaluating numerous independent and cooperative projects. This phase culminated in the agreement in 1977 with McDonnell Douglas to develop the Mercure 200, a venture that soon collapsed.

Great Britain rejoined the Airbus consortium in 1979, inaugurating a period of dramatic growth and maturation. Two new aircraft, the A310 and A320, have been introduced during the 1980s, and the A300 product line has been rationalized. The product design decisions are extremely important, since they have established Airbus Industrie as a credible supplier of a 'family' of medium-range aircraft in a number of different sizes. The consortium has placed increasing pressure on American producers, accounting for a steadily growing share of new orders (from 11 per cent of worldwide orders in 1985 to 23 per cent in 1986),[21] and has achieved very substantial market shares in such high-growth areas as east and south Asia. Moreover, the impending introduction of the A330 and A340 should establish the consortium as a producer of long-range aircraft.

The mere survival of Airbus Industrie is a considerable achievement in the turbulent atmosphere of European cooperation in developing products in high-technology industries. In contrast to other cooperative ventures, Airbus has achieved trans-European cooperation and technological parity (at least) with American products. The success of the consortium owes much to the fact that the independent development of a national aircraft industry was beyond the financial capacity of any single European government. In this regard, commercial aircraft in the 1960s and 1970s foreshadowed the current and future technological and competitive conditions prevailing in such industries as computers, semiconductors and telecommunications equipment. Although trans-European cooperation in these other industries historically has been extremely difficult, it now appears increasingly likely.[22]

Despite its political and technological success, however, Airbus is not yet a commercial success. The success of the A320 follows the introduction of two aircraft, the A310 and A300B, which have not recouped their development costs. Financial returns, however, are only one of several criteria that should be employed to evaluate this investment. Much of the motivation for the Airbus venture stems from the desire of European governments to maintain, for reasons of national security and economic development, a national aircraft design and production capability. Airbus Industrie therefore cannot be judged solely on economic criteria.

Nevertheless, Airbus Industrie has not achieved all of the ambitious 'developmental' goals that were prominent in the early discussions of the consortium. Although the non-European content of Airbus aircraft now is declining, the early models of the A300 relied heavily on American-made components (in addition to the engines). The goal of commercial feasibility conflicted with the desire to strengthen an indigenous European components sector. The consortium's member firms increasingly specialize in the development and production of specific portions of the aircraft, a policy that has improved the cost performance and responsiveness of the consortium at the cost of diffusing a broader array of skills among all of the participants. Here again, one can see the immanent conflicts between the use of this consortium as a device for advancing indigenous technological capabilities and its commercial performance.

In a more positive vein, the contrast between the structure of Airbus

Industrie and the organization of a previous Anglo-French venture, the Concorde, is instructive. Despite its duration and complexity, the Concorde project never developed an autonomous management structure comparable to that of Airbus Industrie. Design and management disputes flourished and created delays, exacerbated by the need to seek intervention by senior management of the two 'cooperating' firms. Coordination of the activities of the erstwhile partners was such that for the first two years of the venture, the British participants designed a long-range, and the French a medium-range, aircraft.'

A closely related difference between Concorde and Airbus is the fact Concorde operated on a cost-sharing basis, which produced dramatic cost escalation over the life of the project, from the original estimate of £450 million in 1962 to more than £4 billion by 1978. By contrast, the organization of Airbus Industrie as an independent *groupement d'intérêt économique* means, among other things, that the relationship between Airbus and its partner firms resembles that of a prime contractor and suppliers in that fixed-cost contracts are employed for procurement of aircraft components and assemblies. As a result, airbus partner firms face strong incentives to minimize costs in contrast to the Concorde experience.

Conclusion

Governments and private firms in Western Europe, the United States and Japan all have pursued international collaboration in the commercial aircraft industry in recent years. The motives of each of these players are different and underline the heterogeneous nature of international collaboration. Even within a single industry, with a number of joint ventures focusing on a common set of activities (product development and manufacture), one observes considerable heterogeneity.

Collaboration clearly does not guarantee commercial success in this industry any more than it does in other global industries. Moreover, collaboration in product development appears to be one of the most difficult forms of international collaboration (See Mowery, 1989, for additional details). At the same time, however, the failure rate of joint ventures does not appear to exceed significantly that of independent product development programmes in an industry known for high risk (no more than five of twenty-four aircraft designs introduced since 1950 have been produced in large numbers).

The composition of the 'glue' binding together the partners in these collaborative ventures is complex. One of the most important bonding agents, observed in the Boeing 767 and General Electric–SNECMA ventures and in the participation of Japan Aero Engines, Fiat, and MTU in the V2500 project, is a technological disparity among the participant firms. The presence of such a disparity creates the basis for an exchange of technology, provided by the technologically advanced partner, for capital or market access, provided by the less-advanced firm.

The structure of joint ventures of this variety does not seem to be a serious issue when the more-advanced firm assumes responsibility for overall management and design. Ventures founded on the existence of such technological disparities have operated reasonably well as an equity partnership of financial equals (CFM International) or as a partnership between a prime contractor and a risk-sharing subcontractor (the 767 and JCAC, or Japan Aero Engines, Fiat and MTU within the V2500 project).

An important source of tension within ventures between technologically 'junior' and 'senior' partners, however, concerns the amount of technology transfer. Technology transfer within these joint ventures has thus far involved few if any of the key components of the senior firms' most advanced technologies. The internal barriers to technology transfer erected by the senior partners, however, appear to have hampered the performance of at least one venture, the V2500.

Restrictions on technology transfer imposed by the technologically advanced firms within collaborative ventures mean that the aspirations of technologically 'junior' firms for extensive learning and technology acquisition may be disappointed. This consideration is especially relevant to Japanese and NIC firms (as well as their governments) currently active in international ventures in this industry. Firms interested in establishing a specialized subcontracting capability or in stabilizing their workforce and capacity utilization through a subordinate role in a joint venture, a group that includes many Western European enterprises and governments ,however, are more likely to achieve their goals than are firms that use this role to obtain high-level capabilities in management, design and systems integration.

Ventures involving firms of comparable technological endowments require greater attention to organization and management. The cases discussed above suggest several sources of difficulty within such partnerships. The resolution of design disputes between the partner firms proved to be difficult and time-consuming in ventures without a strong management staff that was independent of the partner firms.[23] The structure of the V2500 venture, in which the high-level systems integration and overall design activities are the responsibility of an independent staff that works with the participant firms as subcontractors and suppliers seems to have advantages in this regard, although recent events suggest that even this structure can be difficult to manage.

Despite its other problems, an organizational structure like IAE, in which systems integration responsibilities are combined with those of marketing and the management of product support, re-establishes an essential link that was severed or weakened in the MDF100 and SF340 ventures. As the history of such projects as the Boeing 757 and 767 or the Airbus Industrie A310 and A320 demonstrate, close consultation between potential customers and both the marketing and design personnel of the airframe producer is critical to successful introduction of a new product. Joint venture organizations in which the links between marketing, product support and design are not preserved may make inappropriate design compromises and decisions.

An additional problem in joint ventures among technological equals is the emergence of competition between the product being developed within the joint venture and those produced independently by participant firms. This problem was particularly important in the unsuccessful JT10D venture between Pratt and Whitney and Rolls Royce and contributed to the demise of the MDF100 project. Since the degree to which aircraft and engines may substitute for one another varies greatly across customers and markets, uncertainty about such product encroachment is likely to be present in many such ventures.

Considerable concern has been raised in some accounts (for example, Reich, 1986) about the effects of international collaboration on the competitiveness of the American commercial aircraft industry. The evidence thus far, however, does not support a pessimistic assessment. Joint ventures are not likely to result in significant near-term foreign threats to the supremacy of established American 'prime contractor' firms in commercial aircraft. The costs and risks of independent entry into this industry are high, and maintenance of the research infrastructure necessary for an internationally competitive industry requires a level of public and private investment that exceeds the political tolerance of most foreign governments. Moreover, the flow of technology through joint ventures and multinational collaboration within this industry does not consist solely of technology 'exports' by American firms. In a number of cases, foreign-partner firms have made or are making significant technological contributions.

Any evaluation of these ventures also must consider the counterfactual case. Although offshore production of aircraft components and assemblies may reduce the American content of each aircraft or engine sold, if such teaming increases total sales the number of American jobs created or preserved through collaborative ventures may in fact exceed those associated with independent development and production. Pre-emption also plays an important role in the collaborative strategies of American and foreign firms. If the financial and other contributions of the Japanese airframe consortium can be denied to Airbus Industrie through an alliance with Boeing, market access and project finance for Boeing are enhanced and the American firm's commercial capabilities strengthened in the near term regardless of the amount of technology transfer taking place.

Recent international collaborative ventures nevertheless may be eroding the competitiveness of one group of American aerospace firms—supplier firms. Many of the collaborative ventures examined will strengthen the production and competitive capabilities of foreign suppliers of parts, assemblies and components—improvement in these capabilities is one of the goals of the American firms involved in some collaborative ventures. International collaboration among supplier firms also is likely to grow in the near future in order to gain market access and capital.[24] As in the automotive industry, increased international collaboration among first-tier firms is expanding collaborative ventures among suppliers.

Trade policy motivates much of the international collaboration within the commercial-aircraft industry. Foreign government financial subsidies or restrictions on market access are especially important influences on the commercial strategies of American producers.[25] Paradoxically, the pursuit by the industrialized nations of nationalistic policies of support for domestic industries has encouraged the development of consortia spanning national boundaries. Although the postwar growth of multinational firms and direct foreign investment raised the prospect in some assessments of 'global firms' to whom national boundaries would mean little or nothing, much of the current wave of international joint-venture activity reflects the opposite phenomenon. National governments are able to influence not only production but, increasingly, the product development and technology-transfer decisions of firms through the use of trade and other policies.

The perceived importance of the aircraft industry of the industrial and technological development of foreign economies, and the belief by the United States and foreign governments that a strong domestic aircraft industry is an important national security asset, nevertheless mean that government involvement and trade-distorting policies will remain permanent features of the international commercial-aircraft industry. International collaboration in this industry therefore is likely to flourish in the foreseeable future.

Notes

1. Earlier versions of this chapter were presented at meetings of the working group on 'Oligopolies and Hierarchies'. I am grateful to John Alic, Keith Hayward, Lynn Mytelka and Francois Chesnais for comments and suggestions. Preparation of this chapter was aided by support from the Haas School of Business and the Technology and Economic Growth programme of the Center for Economic Policy Research at Stanford University.
2. More detailed discussions of these and other collaborative ventures are contained in Mowery (1987, 1988).
3. In the design of the Boeing 727, Steiner (1982) noted that this process consumed two and one-half years and produced at least nine complete aircraft designs. More recently, the 'design definition' phase of the development of the Boeing 767 lasted for nearly six years.
4. 'Although the time between design and service release of civil and military aircraft increased over the years in the United States as it did in Europe, data for the late 1960s showed the United States well ahead of the United Kingdom and France. The average development time for civil aircraft was 52 months in the United Kingdom and 62 months in France, but it was 43 months in the United States.' [Hochmuth, 1974a, p. 149]
5. The National Research Council's US Civil Aviation Manufacturing Industry Panel projected that the American share of world air traffic would decline to roughly 36 per cent by 1990 from 57 per cent in 1971 (see National Research Council, US Civil Aviation Manufacturing Industry Panel, 1985).
6. Airbus Industrie, however, appears to be reducing the U.S. content in its new aircraft designs:

    To ensure that the European partners obtain a bigger share on the A320, the past reliance on U.S. manufacturers will be reduced. There are two other reasons for this trend: with the experience of the A300 and A310 behind it, Europe now feels more technically able to produce its own equipment. Second, the Europeans believe that they have lost aircraft sales due to the amount of U.S. equipment which the aircraft contained. They cite a potential contract for the A300s with Libya which was blocked because Libya is on the U.S. embargo list. [Reed, 1984:33].

Current estimates of the American content of the A320, for example, are as low as 20 per cent, and federal officials have projected that no more than 13–17 per cent of the A330 and A340 will be American components. See *Aviation Week and Space Technology*, 1986:36; 1987a:18.

7. The aircraft industry is a typical knowledge-intensive industry, characterized by high added value and far-reaching technological spin-off. It will play an important role in the national plan to remold Japan's industrial structure into an innovative knowledge-intensive type . . . At present the aircraft industry is smaller in scale in Japan than in advanced Western countries and relies excessively on demands from the defense industry. It should direct more attention to the manufacture of planes for civil transportation which has a big future . . . It seems realistic that the private sector should bear the ultimate risks involved in an aircraft development project, but for the time being the government will subsidize projects on the condition that a percentage of profits be contributed to the government, contingent on success . . . It is hoped that Japan will build up a system for basic research and development of aircraft engineering so that it may be fully ready for the expected technological innovation in the 1990s for the manufacture of the next generation aircraft. Development of aircraft engineering must be conducted on the initiative and assistance of the government as it involves highly sophisticated and complex technology'.

Ministry of International Trade and Industry, Industrial Structure Council, (1980) *The Vision of MITI Policies in the 1980s* (Tokyo, Industrial Bank of Japan), pp. 291–2.

8. This general basis for the choice by MITI of particular industries for focused assistance has been noted by Hadley in a survey of Japanese industrial policy: 'Japanese target industries have been selected not only for their own importance, but for their ramifying effect on other industries'. (Hadley, 1983b).

9. 'This trend toward subcontracting for services and renting or borrowing talent also is part of the [Boeing Company's] desire to avoid the huge buildup of manpower that marked the late 1960s and the subsequent wholesale layoffs that rocked the entire state of Washington . . . An interesting trend is revealed by a chart comparing Boeing sales in constant dollars with total manpower. (From 1957 through the late 1960s the curves traveled closely together. Since then, a wide gap has opened, indicating the company is achieving more total sales with considerably fewer employees. [O'Lone, 1978:48–9].

10. 'According to Boeing, Japan was considered for the "risk-sharing subcontract" only after U.S. companies had been approached and showed no interest in the program. The U.S. companies were either unable or unwilling to risk the investment'. (1982), (US General Accounting Office. 16, note).

11. The terms of the Boeing contract with the JCAC were describing as 'severe' by officials at MITI and the participating firms, requiring considerable efficiency and productivity improvements. Moreover, 'a Mitsubishi Heavy Industries executive said openly early in the program that the 767 is "not an effective —

program because the investment is too large and the profit is small'". (*Aviation Week and Space Technology* 1978:31).

12. The Japanese partners in the 767 project are making an extra payment of £143 million to Boeing as a royalty for the American firm's production and design experience, as well as its global sales and product support network. See *Aviation Week and Space Technology*, 1977c:201.
13. Aeritalia's participation in the 767 project has not enhanced Boeing's access to the European market, due to the superior political saliency and strength of the Airbus Industrie, whose A310 competes directly with the 767.'
14. A similar argument may be found in Moxon *et al.*, 1985: 53–4.
15. The JADC also insisted that Boeing provide at least 51 per cent of the equity in the 7J7 project, so as to ensure the American firm's participation as project manager.
16. These restrictions included the shipment of the compressor by General Electric in a sealed 'black box' module for installation by SNECMA on its CFM56 assembly line, a delay of eighteen months before the compressor could be shipped to France for testing and the payment to the United States government of a royalty on each engine.
17. One account of the negotiations between the United States government and Pratt and Whitney over technology transfer within the JT10D venture with Rolls Royce cited David Pickerell, a Pratt and Whitney executive: 'If the restriction [on technology transfer] is not lifted and the European partners are forced to operate under the same conditions as SNECMA on the CFM56 — SNECMA is not permitted access to GE core engine technology on the program — 'you can be certain the JT10D will not be as good an engine as it could be,' Pickerell said (*Aviation Week and Space Technology*, 1976: 109.
18. According to one account, 'IAE already is facing potential conflicts of interest among its members, Keen [J.M.S. Keen, executive vice president of International Aero Engines] said. There could be a "clear conflict of interest for a manufacturer", he said, if an airline were trying to decide between a Boeing 757 equipped with Rolls Royce RB.2111-535 engines and a 150-passenger aircraft equipped with the IAE V2500, for example. "That is one reason we believe we have to have our own marketing organization", Keen said' (Feazel, 1984: 108). Despite these efforts to insulate the V2500 from conflicts of interest, recent accounts suggest that middle-level executives at both Pratt and Whitney and Rolls Royce continue to view IAE as a competitor with existing and prospective products (Kandebo, 1987).
19. The review and approval of this venture (in September 1983) by the United States Department of Justice also is interesting in light of recent arguments (Nelson, 1984; Jorde and Teece, 1989) that American antitrust restrictions provide incentives for American firms to team with foreign enterprises. It is difficult to think of another American industry with a comparably concentrated market structure (three firms account for virtually 100 per cent of sales of large transport engines in the noncommunist world market) in which a joint product development venture between two of the three major competitors would be approved. Moreover, one of the two groups that have joined forces in the V2500 project (Rolls Royce and the JAEC) had a product, the RJ500 engine, that might have supported separate entry into this segment of the engine market. The approval of the IAE proposal by the Department of Justice lends some support to the view that joint ventures between American and foreign firms receive less

thorough scrutiny than those involving only American firms. Nevertheless, this case is an isolated one (See Mowery, 1988).

20. 'Technology transfer questions were raised by both Pratt and Whitney and Rolls Royce early in the consortium negotiations', according to Samuel L. Higginbottom, chairman and president of Rolls Royce. Both companies feel there will be a minimum of exchange of proprietary data in the final assembly process. "We will have to know interfaces, and there obviously will be some exchange of data involved in that", Higginbottom said. "But we will not have to get into the details of technology . . ." It took a lot of work to match the technology split to the work-sharing formula, one official said. But now that it is completed, final assembly essentially will involve bolting together the separate modules.' [Fink, 1983, p. 29].
21. See Golich, 1989.
22. See the discussion of the European ESPRIT Programme in Chapter 9 of this volume.
23. This problem was particularly characteristic of the MDF100 and Saab-Scania/Fairchild joint ventures, both of which eventually collapsed. See Mowery, (1987, 1988) for additional discussion.
24. Donne (1987) discusses a recent joint venture between the Bendix aircraft brake division of Allied-Signal Aerospace of the United States and Dunlop Aerospace of Great Britain that was formed to supply wheels and carbon brakes to the Airbus A330 and A340 aircraft now being developed.
25. Conflicts between the United States' government and European governments over public subsidies for Airbus Industrie have subsided somewhat, reflecting modest reforms in the financing and structure of the consortium and, far more important, the fact that the global large-transport market now is very much a seller's market. With both American and Western European firms facing large order backlogs, there is far less transatlantic conflict over marginal orders, as Hayward (1989) has noted.

References

Aerospace Industries Association, Foreign Competition Project Group, Commercial Transport Aircraft Committee (1976), *The Challenge of Foreign Competition*, Washington, DC, Aerospace Research Center.

Aviation Week and Space Technology (1976), 'Rolls Confident of Major JT10D Task', 6 September, p. 109.

—— (1977a), 'Rolls Royce Leaves JTl0D Turbofan Developments Programe', May 16, p. 17.

—— (1977b), 'Eastern Lease, New Sales Bolster Airbus Prospects', 6 June, pp. 234–41.

—— (1977c), 'Japanese Doubts Rising Over F-15, P-3C', 6 June, p. 201.

—— (1978), 'New Efforts Task Japanese Firms', 2 October, pp. 31–3.

—— (1982a), 'McDonnell Douglas/Fokker Cancel 150-Seat Aircraft', 15 February, p. 34.

—— (1982b), 'Dutch, Swedes Use Innovative Financing'. 6 September, pp. 171–3.

—— (1985), 'Fairchild Withdrawing from 340 Aircraft Project', 21 October, p. 23.

—— (1986), 'U.S.–European Trade Talks Focus on Subsidy Issues', 31 March, p. 36.

—— (1987a), 'U.S., Europeans Clash Over Airbus Subsidies', 9 February, pp. 18–20.

—— (1987b), 'Pratt and Whitney Expands Role in V2500 Compressor Work', 16 March, pp. 32–3.

—— (1987c), 'IAE Delays V2500 Certification to Develop New Components', 25 May, p. 31.

—— (1987d), 'Airline Observer', 23 November, p. 43.

—— (1987e), 'News Digest', 14 December, p. 30.

Brown, D.A. (1986), 'Short Brothers, Saab-Scania Join Boeing 7J7 Program', *Aviation Week and Space Technology*, 31 March, pp. 32–33.

Donne, M. (1987), 'Dunlop Joins U.S. Group in Airbus Contract Bid', *Financial Times*, 17 September, p. 6.

Feazel, M. (1984), 'Large Engine Design Costs Dictate Consortium Efforts', *Aviation Week and Space Technology*, 18 June, pp. 108–9.

Fink, D.E. (1983), 'Pratt, Rolls Launch New Turbofan', *Aviation Week and Space Technology*, 7 November, pp. 28–9.

Golich, V. (1989), 'Market-Induced State Cooperation: State Autonomy and the Internationalization of the Aerospace Industry', presented at the meetings of the International Studies Association, London, 28–31 March 28–31.

Hadley, E.M., (1983), The Secret of Japan's Success Challenge *Challenge* **26**.

Harris, J. (1986), 'Spies Who Sparked the Industrial Revolution', *New Scientist*, 22 May, pp. 42–7.

Hayward, K. (1986), *International Collaboration in Civil Aerospace*, London, Frances Pinter.

—— (1989), 'Competition and Collaboration in the Development and Manufacture of Large Commercial Aircraft', presented at the meetings of the International Studies Association, London, 28–31 March.

Henderson, D. (1977), 'Two British Errors: Their Probable Size and some Possible Lessons', *Oxford Economic Papers*, **29**, 159–205.

Hochmuth, M.S. (1974a), 'Aerospace' in R.S. Vernon, (ed.), *Big Business and the State*. Cambridge, Mass., Harvard University Press.

—— (1974b), *Organizing the Transnational: The Experience with Transnational Enterprise in Advanced Technology*, Cambridge, Mass., Harvard University Press.

Japan, Ministry of International Trade and Industry, Industrial Structure Council, *The Vision of MITI policies in the 1980's* Tokyo: Industrial Bank of Japan, 1980.

Jordan, W.A. (1970), *Airline Regulation in America*, Baltimore, Johns Hopkins University Press.

Jorde, T. and Teece, D.J., (1989), 'Innovation, Cooperation and Antitrust Balancing Competition and Cooperation', *High Technology Law Journal*, **4**, pp. 1–113.

Kandebo, S.W. (1987a), 'International Aero Engines Seeks Solutions to V2500 Development Problems', *Aviation Week and Space Technology*, 13 April, pp. 88–9.

—— (1987b), 'Engine Makers Examine IAE to Avoid Pitfalls in Collaborative Efforts', *Aviation Week and Space Technology*, 15 June, pp. 245–6.

Killing, J.P. (1983), *Strategies for Joint Venture Success*, New York: Praeger.

Lorell, M.A. (1970), *Multinational Development of Large Aircraft: The European Experience*, Santa Monica, Rand Corporation.

Mowery, D.C. (1985), 'Federal Funding of R&D in Transportation: The Case of Aviation', presented at the National Academy of Sciences Symposium on the Impact of Federal R&D Funding, Washington, DC, 21–2 November.

—— (1987), *Alliance Politics and Economics: Multinational Joint Ventures in Commercial Aircraft*, Cambridge: Ballinger.

——(1988), *International Collaborative Ventures in U.S. Manufacturing*, Cambridge, Ballinger.

—— (1989), International Joint Ventures and the Commercialization of Innovations', presented at the Conference on Commercializing Innovations, Stanford University, 11–12 September.

—— and Rosenberg N, (1982), 'The Commercial Aircraft Industry' in R. R. Nelson (ed.), *Government and Technical Progress: A Cross-Industry Analysis*, New York: Pergamon Press.

—— (1985), 'Competition and Cooperation: The U.S. and Japanese Commercial Aircraft Industries', *California Management Review*, **27**, pp. 70–92.

Moxon, R.W., Roehl T.W., Truitt J.R. and Geringer J.M., (1985), *Emerging Sources of Foreign Competition in the Commercial Aircraft Manufacturing Industry*, Washington, DC, US Department of Transportation.

National Research Council, Committee on NASA Scientific and Technological Program Reviews (1982). *Aeronautics Research and Technology: A Review of Proposed Reductions in the FY 1983 NASA Program*, Washington, DC, National Academy Press.

—— (1983a), Manufacturing Studies Board, Committee on the Machine Tool Industry. *The Machine Tool Industry and the Defense Industrial Base*, Washington, DC, National Academy Press.

—— (1985), US Civil Aviation Manufacturing Industry Panel, *The Competitive Status of the U.S. Civil Aircraft Manufacturing Industry*, Washington, DC, National Academy Press.

Nelson, R.R., (1984), *High-Technology Policies: A Five-Nation Comparison*, Washington, DC, American Enterprise Institute.

O'Lone, R.G. (1978), 'Boeing Facing New Set of Challenges', *Aviation Week and Space Technology*, 12 November, pp. 43–55.

Reed, A. (1983), 'Fokker Moving Ahead with New P&W-Powered F27', *Air Transport World*, August, pp. 19–25.

Reich, R., (1986), 'A Faustian Bargain with the Japanese', *New York Times*, 16 April, section 3, p. 2.

—— (1984), 'Airbus Talks About A320, Future Projects', *Air Transport World*, May pp. 33–7.

Ropelewski, R. (1976), 'Mercure 200 Pact Sparks Uproar', *Aviation Week and Space Technology*, 23 August, pp. 12–13.

Samuels, R.J., and Whipple B.C., (1989), 'Defense Production and Industrial Development: The Case of Japanese Aircraft in C. Johnson, L. Tyson, and J. Zysman (eds), *Politics and Productivity: How Governments Create Advantage in World Markets*, Cambridge: Ballinger.

Steiner, J.E. (1982.), 'How Decisions Are Made', AIAA Wright Brothers' Lectureship in Aeronautics, Seattle.

US Department of Commerce, International Trade : Administration (1987), *U.S. Industrial Outlook: 1987*, Washington, DC, US Government Printing Office.

US General Accounting Office (1982), *US Military Co-production Agreements Assist Japan in Developing its Civil Aircraft Industry*, Washington, DC, US Government Printing Office.

5 Towards a new Europeanism: French firms in strategic partnerships

Michel Delapierre and Jean-Benoit Zimmerman

Many factors have altered the environment within which European firms must now compete. Previous chapters in this volume have stressed changes in the knowledge intensity of production and in the pattern of internationalization. Here the focus is on two aspects of each of these processes that have a particular bearing on the strategies of European firms in general and on French firms in particular: the development of combinative strategies and the interpenetration of transnationalized industries and national productive systems.

Sections one and two of this chapter analyse these processes and the strategic options to which they are giving rise. Section three examines the alliance pattern of French firms from this perspective.

Combinations at the Heart of New Competitive Strategies

Combinative practices now pervade all levels of industrial activity, from research and development (R & D) to manufacturing and marketing. With the progressive merging of previously distinct scientific sectors such as chemistry, physics or biology, a multidisciplinary approach is rapidly evolving at the R & D level and giving rise to the emergence of new technologies through the combination of existing ones. This fusion of technologies is well illustrated by the multiplication of new industrial fields such as optoelectronics, mecatronics, biotronics or chemitronics and of new patterns of corporate organization that involve the merging of industrial functions through the use of computer-aided design and manufacturing systems.

Combinations can also be found at the product level. An increasing number of goods are made through the assembly of components produced by a variety of distinct industries. Microprocessors, for example, can now be found in cars, household equipment and machine tools as well as in computers. To manufacture these goods also requires the combination of specific technologies and manufacturing capacities. Innovation,moreover, increasingly takes place at the component level, thus allowing for the rapid multiplication of new combinations.[1] At yet another level, products themselves are being combined into complex systems by designing and integrating specialized equipment including software. Computing systems are an example of this.

Combinative strategies have thus become a way of providing solutions in the form of both technologies and products. In turn, they stimulate innovation that further widens the range of potential applications, increases variety and facilitates the development of customized products. This enables the firm to position itself on a higher value added segment of the market.

The process of combining and recombining technologies and products, however, leads to a continuous shifting of knowledge and industry boundaries. Strategies aimed at increasing the speed of response to a dynamic environment are contributing in turn to its turbulence. Faced with uncertainty and change in their most stable markets, firms are taking a variety of strategic initiatives. Some corporations are attempting to build new forms of industrial capacity by relying on a combinative strategy to supplement the exploitation of a core of accumulated knowledge.

In order to incorporate combinative skills and capabilities, other companies are adopting new forms of organization that rely on modular structures. By splitting their operations into semi-autonomous units, R & D, manufacturing and commercial functions can be integrated, communication lines shortened and innovation speeded up. At the same time, modular structures can work as a tool of diversification. Thus the Compagnie General d'Electricité (CGE) is attempting to reinforce the industrial coherence of each of its core activities: services, power — centred on its subsidiary Alsthom—and telecommunications, based on Alcatel and its newly acquired share in ITT.

Modular strategies are also being used in the management of combinations. A large number of firms in assembly activities, in the automobile industry or in information processing, for example, are trimming back the number of their subcontractors but involving them more in design activities that enhance innovation at the component stage. Networking of this sort is becoming the industrial form that gives effect to combinative practices. In such networks corporations work increasingly in parallel rather than in sequence.

Still another type of combinative strategy is technology bunching — the combination of knowledge and skills and their systematic exploitation over a wide range of applications. Through technology bunching strategies, the activities of the firm are no longer restricted to or defined by a given set of goods or end-markets. Companies that adopt this strategy provide performance or 'solutions' instead of a range of goods. They do not, for example, sell bottles or cans, but packaging technologies.[2]

Modular organization strategies allow for the bunching of technologies and the ensuing combination of components into final applications. Thus the firm can reach the market with new solutions much more rapidly. This articulation of several combinative layers produces a multiplier effect that broadens the range of possible applications. Given the variety of possible applications, it also enables R & D expenses to be spread over several markets, thus reducing size constraints, allowing for further market segmentation and facilitating the emergence of new products.[3]

The adoption of combinative strategies favours the creation of strategic partnerships that cut across industries and bring together partners who can exploit their complementary skills, manufacturing and marketing abilities. As combinative strategies widen the range of possible product outcomes, strategic partnerships that entail joint production of knowledge or components, moreover, do not necessarily preclude competition in final goods. They may, however, lead to new industrial structures especially where segmentation and the diverse and changing core of suppliers blur industrial boundaries.[4] Under these conditions, new oligopolies are likely to form among groups of large companies through the sharing of knowledge, the exercise of control over the process of knowledge development and the exploitation of applications across a wide range of different applications (Delapierre and Mytelka, 1988). Such networks, however, do not displace more traditional internalization or integration strategies but rather constitute a complementary dimension within a firm's global strategy. It is not surprising, therefore, to find that in a survey of inter-firm relationships in the high-technology industries, covering the period June 1987–September 1988, 54 per cent of the agreements were contractual alliances or joint ventures but fully 46 per cent were mergers or acquisitions (Ferrands, 1988).

Global Industries and the European 'National' Space

Given this context, even the largest French firms can no longer limit their strategic options to protect their positions of strength on well-defined and fixed markets. The emergence of new markets or market segments, the rapid saturation of existing markets and swift changes in manufacturing processes and in buyers' requirements are redefining and reshaping industrial activities. To survive in this new milieu, French firms will need to define their position relative to their competitors, from within and from outside Europe and to adjust to the main technological changes underway.

A similar problem faces the French state within the context of European policymaking. In the past, states were responsible for achieving national goals which included actively contributing to the development of coherent national productive systems. But Europe is not a single nation and its economic coherence must be built differently. It cannot merely become the sum of national coherences as we will argue below.

From both the strategic planning and the policy perspective, the creation of a European Single Market in 1992 complicates this picture still further. On the one hand, it could provide European companies with the skill, manufacturing and market base from which to mount effective operations world-wide. Conversely, it could lead to the massive penetration of Europe by non-European firms and products.

To cope with the challenges presented by this changing industrial context, French firms will have to choose a new strategy. Three options appear to be the most serious candidates: going world-wide, which emphasizes the international context at the expense of the domestic base; fortress Europe, which is less responsive to the world-wide structure of industries and springboard Europe, which attempts to conciliate both needs. In what follows we discuss some of the weaknesses and strengths of each of these.

Going world-wide

In highly transnationalized industries characterized by world-wide oligopolies dominated by large multinationals, standardized products and important economies of scale, national firms are forced to internationalize rapidly and to implement their strategies on a global basis. For these firms, Europe is merely a local market. The EC market for data-processing equipment, though a big one, absorbs only 25 per cent of the total sales of French manufacturers. The United states market is potentially their largest and establishing a strategic position within it is of utmost importance.

For firms that are 'going world-wide', strategic partnerships focus upon market-orientated operations through distribution agreements and equity participations, mainly with American companies, in order to build market share. In the more transnationalized industries size constraints of markets and manufacturing often lead to acquisitions rather than partnerships.

Bull, the French data-processing national champion, for example, took over its American partner and previous owner, Honeywell Information Systems in 1988.[5] Given its internal growth rate, Bull could not have achieved a global dimension on its own (Chabert, 1989). To reinforce its position in microcomputers, Bull also acquired Zenith Data Systems, an American microcomputer manufacturer ranked fifth world-wide, in October 1989. Similarly, Thomson swapped its medical electronics business for General Electric's RCA consumer electronics subsidiary, thus acquiring 23 per cent of the American market (Electronic Business, 1988). By moving the headquarters of its consumer electronics division to the United States, Thomson further deepened its integration in the American market. During the same period, Thomson also re-orientated its core activities, easing out of the public switching business and domestic computers and linking its semiconductor division in a joint venture to SGS ATES, Italy.

The principal danger in pursuing world-wide strategies, however, is that firms attempt to jump directly from the national level to the world level, without first having built a national power base from which to compete globally. Thus many French firms have chosen to form alliances with dominant American and Japanese companies, rather than with their closer European competitors. In so doing, however, they have traded domestic market share for products and technologies they do not master.

In other cases, firms trying to penetrate the American market have been unable to withstand a vigorous counter-attack by their American competitors because of their weaker domestic base. They adopt product, manufacturing and commercialization standards established elsewhere and more suitable for these environments. They are thus likely to be at a disadvantage in playing a competitive game whose rules they do not control. The result is a cycle of continuing dependence on their suppliers as they attempt to catch up in industries characterized by permanent innovation.

In still other instances, firms trying to penetrate the American market have been unable to withstand a vigorous counter-attack by their American competitors because of their weaker domestic base. When Thomson, for example, bought Mostek, an American electronic components manufacturer, in 1985, it was unable to gain entry into new cooperative ventures being set up between North American producers, notably the SEMATECH consortium for semiconductor technology.[6] The lack of technical backing by its parent company, moreover, led ultimately to the decline of Mostek in the American market.

Fortress Europe

Over the past two decades a number of large French industrial groups have grown accustomed to working primarily for the domestic market. This was especially true in the defence industry and in telecommunications prior to deregulation. For these 'national champions', the Single European Market represents an extension of this national logic to the regional market carrying with it the expectation that they will remain protected through public procurement policies. For these firms, strategic partnerships are aimed largely at defending the existing market base in a context of globalizing industries. This has led French companies to conclude agreements that involve a rationalization of production through joint ventures, asset switching and market sharing.

In telecommunications, the French government induced Thomson to enter the industry in 1975, through the acquisition of LMT and Ericsson France, affiliates of ITT (American) and Ericsson (Swedish). The objective was to create domestic competition for CGE, the main French telecom equipment manufacturer, while keeping the outcome of this competition under national control. By 1984, with growing size constraints in a globalizing industry, the French state allowed CGE to acquire Thomson's telecommunications activities and subsequently to take over ITT's European telecom affiliates.[7] CGE thus became a European-based champion.

National champion policies and strategies, however, are rapidly becoming obsolete for a number of reasons. First, technology-bunching strategies, based on a combination of knowledge, components and products, with a wide array of applications, gave rise to perpetually changing industrial boundaries. Companies, focusing the major part of their activities on a single market, risk suddenly being faced with an unexpected foreign competitor, marketing the same goods or a new type of product or manufacturing process. Second, the logic of combinative practices rests on horizontal trans-industry circulation of knowledge rather than vertical control of technology. National champion strategies based on unique contenders limits the scope for innovative combinations and its self-multiplying potential. Third, there is a new recognition in government circles that former national champions can no longer be sustained solely through national procurement and concentration policies. The French government has thus shifted resources away from industrial policies and towards technology policies which, by promoting inter-firm technology cooperation agreements, seek to stimulate the accumulation and dissemination of knowledge throughout the entire national industrial fabric.[8] Whereas earlier, only a handful of large firms in the data-processing industry received nearly two-thirds of all public R & D funds, the 1989 'filière électronique' budget will devote FF150 million to collective research and more significantly FF200 million to the diffusion of technologies (Teillac, 1989). Collaboration through strategic partnerships has thus replaced cartel-like collusion as a preferred strategy of the French government.

Many of the same problems would simply be reproduced at the European level if a 'fortress' Europe policy, based on choosing single 'European champions' for a given market were adopted. Collective pressure for a return to protectionism by these slow moving giants, retrenched within a fortress Europe, would then diminish the stimulus for innovation. Fortunately this scenario is improbable given the political difficulties of selecting a European contender from among the national candidates. But the lack of an industrial policy of the old type does not imply that other policies should not be attempted since, in the absence of new industrial policies, it is likely that the opening of national borders in 1992 would give rise to cut-throat competition between local champions in all industries. While this could lead to a general shake out that eliminates the weakest, it would leave the victors too exhausted to face their non-European competitors.

Springboard Europe

Some French firms seem to have recognised that a compromise had to be found between the opposing strategies of going world-wide and fortress Europe. In contrast to a 'fortress' Europe strategy through which a number of 'European champions', protected by trade and European procurement policies are created, a 'springboard' Europe strategy constitutes a more flexible approach based on a mixed forms of international regulation of the sort described by Charles-Albert Michalet in Chapter two. In addition by contributing to the organization of an industrial system based on networking, it would enable firms simultaneously to benefit from economies of scale, reach necessary thresholds and engage in combinative practices. A strong position in Europe built on and adapted to its productive structure and market specificities could thus act as a springboard for the penetration of world markets, turning European firms into leaders of the pack rather than followers of the leader.

Airbus Industrie provides a good example of such a strategy. Based on the development of a type of aircraft more suited to the specificities of short-haul flights within Europe, the A300 product line did not duplicate, but rather provided an alternative to Boeing, caught out of its fields of strength. As sales in Asia and North America developed, the European market could be seen to have been a springboard and not a retrenchment.[9]

The new Europeanism, implied in a springboard Europe strategy, involves a systematic combination of the different specializations of European industrial groups, cutting across national and industrial boundaries. Because it is mainly built on combinations, it calls for partnerships in preference to mergers and acquisitions. The systematic combination of distinct specialized skills which results from such partnerships enables participating firms to remain competitive by creating the flexibility needed to react to a changing environment and by enhancing the capacity to manage the process of change itself. In addition, European research programmes such as ESPRIT, RACE or BRITE, and national technology policies in France itself, are aimed at developing the self-supporting capacity within Europe to design product, process and competition norms based on the specificities of the EEC economic and social system. Europe would thus become a norm-giver rather than a norm-taker.

A policy of using the European space as a springboard for global competition is also important because the commercial viability of many new products depends upon the existence of multiple producers. The personal computer market, launched by Apple in the late 1970s, for example, did not find its professional customer base and its growth potential until IBM and other major main-frame computer manufacturers entered the market in 1982. Today electronic consumer goods manufacturers are attempting to strike agreements on video CD systems, with at least some of their partners, thus avoiding a replay of the intense struggle which characterized the video tape recording market. Standards are also a prerequisite for the development of markets for systems products, where components and specialized equipment from different and independent manufacturers are combined. Here the main form of partnership between European manufacturers would be those that involve the joint design of common technical solutions, leading to differenciated but compatible products.

The new Europeanism has not entirely replaced the old Europeanism, which remains deeply entrenched as an industrial strategy, rooted in nationalistic trends and policies favouring domestic manufacturers. However, at the same time, European firms are entering into alliances with leading firms from the United States and Japan. These two trends are typical of French firms as we will see in the next section.

Strategic Partnering by French Firms

The LAREA/CEREM data base includes agreements reported in the public press, involving European firms, concluded in four technological or industrial areas — biotechnologies, civilian aviation and aerospace and information processing from 1980 to 1988 and materials[10] from the years 1982 to 1985.[11] From this data base, 652 agreements involving French companies have been extracted. Fifty-one per cent of these are in the information-processing field. This comes as no surprise considering the broad scope of the industry. Biotechnology and aeronautics constitute 19 per cent each,

Table 5.1: Agreements by French firms by nationality of partners and function (in %)

	Knowledge	Production	Commercial	Global	Total
Aerospace/aircraft					
France	28	20	39	52	32
EEC*	37	41	30	35	32
USA	23	25	22	9	23
Japan	0	0	0	0	0
Others	12	14	9	4	11
Total	50	42	19	19	100
Biotechnology					
France	40	38	36	33	35
EEC*	16	12	11	16	16
USA	24	38	32	30	30
Japan	4	8	11	2	7
Others	16	4	7	16	11
Total	36	21	22	34	100
Information technology					
France	25	15	20	54	35
EEC*	24	15	13	10	20
USA	32	46	49	31	39
Japan	6	13	8	1	6
Others	10	8	11	2	5
Total	19	12	37	46	100
Materials (1982–5)					
France	31	20	14	14	21
EEC*	8	17	21	21	18
USA	51	29	35	26	32
Japan	8	20	14	8	11
Others	2	14	11	21	18
Total	17	22	20	62	100
Total					
France	30	22	25	44	33
EEC*	25	25	15	15	18
USA	28	34	42	29	34
Japan	4	8	8	2	6
Others	11	9	10	9	9
Total	27	20	29	37	100

*excluding French firms

Source: LAREA/CEREM database

while materials, due to the shorter time coverage, lags at 10 per cent (see Table 5.1).

Not all of these agreements can properly be termed strategic partnerships.

Table 5.2: Strategic orientation of French partnerships

Partner nationality	Knowledge	Production	Commerce	Global
French	F	F	F	F
Other EEC	S	S/F	S/F	S/F
Extra-EEC	W	W	S/W	S/W

Keys: F = Fortress
S = Springboard
W = Going world-wide

The LAREA/CEREM data base, therefore, distinguishes between knowledge production which constitutes 27 per cent of our sample; manufacturing (production) which accounts for 20 per cent; commerce, amounting to 29 per cent of the agreements and global partnerships, where the agreement covers the entire range of industrial functions from R & D to sales. The latter generally lead to either the setting up of a separate business entity as a joint venture between the partners, or the exchange of shares in a minority equity participation. These total 37 per cent of the agreements involving French firms. When the exchange of shares or the taking of an equity position in a company concerns the entire range of activity of either firm, the strategic autonomy of the participants may be quite limited. It is thus no longer appropriate to call this type of an agreement a partnership.

Since the 1980s French firms have been increasingly involved in collaborative agreements (see Table 5.1). This pattern coincides with global trends observed in other studies (Chesnais,1988; Mytelka,1987). By examining the pattern of French partnering activity, it is possible to distinguish country-specific and industry-specific characteristics of these agreements and to relate them to the three broader strategies discussed above. To begin this process it is necessary to describe the kinds of agreements that would correspond most closely to each of these strategies. Table 5.2 summarizes these distinctions.

Fortress Europe strategies would most likely be built upon global, commercial and production agreements that in the first instance link French firms to each other and then to European partners. This is a defensive strategy built more on the rationalization of existing bases of production than on the design of new products and technologies. Where knowledge-production agreements were concluded, one would expect them to be limited to intra-French partnerships.

'Going world-wide' implies a search for non-European partners. These would mainly be American for operations aimed at the penetration of large markets and American or Japanese where French companies are trying to capture market shares in Europe with imported technologies and products.

Table 5.3: Modal tendencies in the strategic orientations of French firms by partner nationality and function (in %)

Partner nationality	Knowledge	Production	Commercial	Global	Total
French	30			44	33
Other EEC	25				
Extra-EEC	28	34	42		34

While a large proportion of such partnerships will concern global and commercial functions, a true world-wide strategy would also lead to some collaboration in knowledge production with a view to designing world products.

Springboard strategies, as a combination of elements from each of the previous two, are much more difficult to single out. However, their main characteristic is likely to be partnerships with European firms and and a focus on knowledge production, standardization activities and joint production. Alliances such as these could then be expected to evolve into or be supplemented by commercial and global agreements in order to structure the complementarity of the European offer. In addition, the true springboard effect would be seen through the development of partnerships with non-European companies downstream on the commercial side, thus showing a move towards the penetration of world markets.

It should be kept in mind that firms do not exclusively pursue one type of strategy. Rather, they adopt a mix of these various forms. As a result, only broad tendencies can be drawn in the analysis that follows.

Table 5.3 gives the distribution of agreements of French firms by nationality of partners and functions. Drawing on data for total agreements from Table 5.1, it selects for each function the partner with which French firms have the highest proportion of agreements. Thus, for agreements involving the commercialization of products, French firms tend mainly to form alliances with American companies. Where over one third of the agreements are with a particular partner, as for example, 44 per cent of all global agreements by French firms are with French partners, only that cell is filled.

From the predominance of French and non-EEC partners, particularly in global and commercial agreements, it is evident that French firms tend mainly to pursue either a fortress or global strategy. The high proportion of French–French agreements, moreover, suggests that the fortress tendency continues to be more restricted to the French market than extended to Europe as a whole.

The strong orientation of French firms toward market protection or penetration is further shown by their high propensity for outright acquisition of assets abroad. In 1988, French groups were second only to British

Table 5.4: Patterns of strategic partnership by French firms: by industry

	Knowledge	Production	Commercial	Global	Total
France	BIO	BIO	BIO AERO	BIO AERO INFO	BIO AERO
EEC	AERO	AERO			AERO
USA	INFO MAT	BIO INFO MAT	INFO MAT	MAT	INFO MAT

companies in foreign acquisitions world-wide, with an overall total of 143 deals valued at £11.2 billion (Waller, 1987).

Some hints of the emergence of a new Europeanism, however may be identified at the knowledge-production level where partnerships with EEC companies (25 per cent) are a close third behind partnerships with other French (30 per cent) or non-EEC (28 per cent) companies. These figures exclude the far more numerous knowledge-production and sharing agreements concluded by French firms with their European partners through EEC programmes such as ESPRIT. Taking these into consideration, the new Europeanism would appear to be a more prominent feature of the behaviour of French firms. It must nevertheless be noted that it is the deliberate policy of the European Commission, rather than the independent initiative of the firms that plays a pivotal role in the development of this springboard strategy.

Table 5.4 looks within the 'country-specific' pattern at the distribution of agreements by industry. Some important distinctions in strategic orientation exist across these four industries. Biotechnology, for example, is mainly characterised by fortress strategies with some hints of a 'going world-wide' tendency. Information technology and the materials are mainly following the global route, while only aeronautics and aerospace firms, taken collectively, are implementing a springboard strategy. A closer look at each of these industrial sectors enables us to understand the basis for these differences.

Biotechnologies

Companies with operations in biotechnology are either large groups such as Lafarge-Copee, ELF or Rhône-Poulenc seeking to enter new areas of growth and diversify, or new firms such as Transgene, which are working exclusively in biotechnology, but need financing and access to markets. In both cases, the first priority seems to have been the establishment of a strong national base, as approximately one out of two agreements in the period 1980–5 involved a French partner (35 per cent of the agreements in Table 5.1). In contrast, European firms were seen to constitute a strong threat and only 16 per cent of the alliances were concluded with them. Consistent with the predominance of a national champion syndrome is an emphasis on global agreements with American and Japanese world leaders to reinforce the national position. In biotechnology, therefore, the two strategies, 'going world-wide' and fortress Europe, are being implemented either simultaneously or sequentially. This can been seen in the cases of Rhône Poulenc and ELF, two of the main French industrial actors in this field.

In both companies, R & D strategies predominated until 1983 and these were mainly with French firms. From 1983 to 1986, Rhône Poulenc, unlike ELF, kept its strong emphasis on the production of knowledge, but with a deliberate search for American partners. More recently it has taken a more European perspective, but has done so by moving away from alliances and towards the acquisition of European and American companies. This European orientation and the acquisition policies that gave it effect were reinforced in 1990 when the French government ceded its minority shareholding in Roussel-Uclaf to them. Rhône Poulenc thus became a partner of the German chemical and pharmaceutical company, Hoechst. From 1984 to 1986, ELF pursued a 'going world-wide' strategy by focusing its cooperative ventures in biotechnology on the market side — acquiring businesses, creating joint ventures and signing commercialization agreements with either French or American corporations. Since 1987, ELF has focused on Europe, like Rhône Poulenc, mainly through acquisitions. This, however, is in line with their 'going world-wide' orientation, since the pattern of their acquisitions (LAREA/CEREM data base) shows that they see Europe more as a market itself than as an industrial base from which to penetrate the world market.

Information technologies

Information technology constitute a relatively more mature sector, despite the continuous introduction of new products. The major industrial groups are 'national champions' with strong government backing. They are deeply entrenched in the national market, with a large volume of sales. Strategic partnerships are formed to further global integration and joint sales. However, two different trends appear to be emerging. On the one hand, French companies are more actively seeking transatlantic alliances with American corporations to gain market access. This takes three forms: manufacturing licences (46 per cent of their alliances with American companies as opposed to 15 per cent with European partners), commercialization agreements (49 per cent with American firms as opposed to 13 per cent with European companies) and global agreements (31 per cent with American partners as compared to 10 per cent European). On the other hand, when it comes to R & D functions, French firms are also seeking alliances with their European counterparts, and the share of knowledge-related agreements has grown to 26 per cent in the period from 1986 to 1988, suggesting that this Euro-centred trend is on the rise. However, 50 per cent of the new knowledge agreements are between French firms and this despite the success of EEC multinational research programmes in promoting intra-EEC cooperative agreements. One can, therefore, question the extent to which such programmes are laying the basis for a more integrated European industry if they do not stimulate the formation of new, intra-European partnerships apart from those directly sponsored by the EEC.

Definitive conclusions about the strategic orientations of French information processing firms are difficult to draw using an analysis based solely on the number of agreements rather than the volume of resources involved. If, however, we take into consideration some of the very large projects that were recently launched through the EUREKA programme, then the growth of a 'springboard' orientation seems to emerge in a more prominant place in so far as the information technology sector is concerned.

The EUREKA programme, a complement to ESPRIT, is more directly concerned with market applications. It constitutes a response to the challenges European firms face in the international component industry. European manufacturers control less than 10 per cent of the world-wide production of semiconductors. Several EUREKA projects have been designed to increase that share. The first EUREKA programme in 1985, involving seven participants, helped establish a company, European Silicon Structure (ES2), for the manufacture of prototypes or small batches — less than 50,000 units — of full custom circuits.

In 1988, a new venture, the Joint European Submicron Silicon Initiative — JESSI — was launched by Siemens, Philips and SGS-Thomson, with the support of EUREKA. This project also involves thirty-two other partners from business and research organizations in the design and manufacture of high-level integrated semiconductor components (*Financial Times*, 1989); FF27 billion is to be invested by 1996.

Difficult negotiations, lasting about a year, between the largest European electronics groups preceded the launching of JESSI. Siemens and Philips, both previously involved in the megaproject—conceived to design and manufacture of 1 and 4 Mb memories—were reluctant to include a third partner and competitor, SGS-Thomson. However, as a result of strong state intervention, particularly by the French government, and the prospect of substantial financing through EUREKA, SGS-Thomson was admitted as a full founding partner. JESSI is to be based on a combination of each of the partner's specific strengths: static memories (SRAMs) in the case of Philips; dynamic memories (DRAMs) for Siemens and erasable programmable memories (EPROMs) for SGS-Thomson. The main members of JESSI and of the American company SEMATECH — all multinational firms with affiliates in both Europe and North America — at first undertook talks on the possibility of cooperation between the two projects. SEMATECH,[11] however, refused to reciprocate by opening its membership to JESSI participants and talks were then broken off.

Many of the strategic partnerships in the information technology sector are centred on standardization.[13] The very nature of information-processing products — complex systems, computing, data storage, data capture, data retrieval and data transfer units — is such that even the largest integrated groups can no longer cover the entire range of applications. Thus, some level of complementarity, hence compatibility, is needed for manufacturers in order that the combination of their products can be turned into virtually customized systems. The principal partners such as Bull, Siemens and ICL continue to remain competitors with respect to end market applications, but their agreements on common interconnection standards ensure larger potential markets for all of them. Strategic partnerships are thus a positive-sum game.

Materials

Materials constitute a more complex case. The sector is shaped by old traditional activities, characterized by huge volume markets of bulk commodities and by the introduction of very sophisticated new products or new materials such as ceramics or composites. The established European producers, whether in the traditional materials industry or in the chemical industry, have achieved a strong international position. However, both are facing technology-induced changes in their most stable markets. The development and emergence of new materials constitute powerful forces, destabilizing product based oligopolies.

Two major partnership strategies have thus been pursued. In the more mature and oligopolistic sectors, restructuring deals — hence a fortress Europe perspective — are dominant. Global agreements, quite often involving the exchange of activities through equity swaps, constitute 62 per cent of the reported agreements. These tend to build a strong European base rather than a domestic one, as 21 per cent of the global agreements are intra-EEC while only 14 per cent are exclusively domestic ones. Furthermore, they are intended to develop stronger positions in the American market. Many European alliances lead to the sharing of large manufacturing facilities for basic products in bulk, while each partner concentrates its investments in activities designed to develop its own specialty products. Chemical companies are thus reorganizing their industrial activities, shifting from volume to specialty production, closely attuned to the growing trends in R & D and customization.

In the newest sectors, competition rather than collaboration appears to be the norm. Only 8 per cent of the knowledge-production agreements involve European partners, whereas 51 per cent are transatlantic alliances. Rhône Poulenc's activities are typical of this dual strategy. Over the eighties it has withdrawn from heavy chemicals to concentrate on specialty chemicals. In organic chemistry, for example, equity swaps have permitted the group to rationalize its production within Europe. In ceramics the strategy goes nearly in the opposite direction. Agreements for knowledge production between American and French partners are being concluded in order to build the technological capacity for further diversifications (LAREA/CEREM 1988: 61–86).

Aeronautics and Aerospace

Civilian aviation and aerospace companies seldom have recourse to partnerships that involve the entire range of their activities and lead to a process of rationalization with foreign firms. The industry's base is national. The principal manufacturers are national firms, not heavily engaged in foreign direct investment. Governments, moreover, are eager to preserve their strategic independence and generally discourage takeovers of national aircraft firms by foreign groups. However, as large aircraft programmes require technological and financial resources which exceed the capacity of any single national European manufacturer, this sector is the locus of many cooperative ventures among European firms. Airbus industries discussed by Mowery in Chapter 4, is one example. Because of the growing merger of R & D and manufacturing activities, moreover, the number of knowledge- and production-related agreements has also risen. Purely commercial agreements, only 19 per cent of the total, are less significant in this type of industrial activity where no single group is currently able to design and manufacture large aircraft on its own. Furthermore, the unit value of less expensive items, such as helicopters, is sufficiently large to warrant a direct sales force.

Conclusion: Towards a New Europeanism

From the previous analysis, it is evident that there is an old Europeanism, based on market considerations and emphasizing size. Its centre-piece is the national champion. In contrast, the new Europeanism is based on a combination of diverse skills from different European industrial groups. It relies more heavily on horizontal strategic partnerships than on vertical integration.

In evaluating the implications of this strategy, the long-term stability of such relationships constitutes an important issue and a source of concern. According to a study of 880 joint ventures and cooperative agreements, only 60 per cent of them lasted for more than four years and only 14 per cent of them lasted longer than ten years (*Global Finance*, 1988). Although there is relatively little information on the consequences of severed partnerships, there is some indication that they may have ended in mergers or the absorption of one partner by another. They may also have led to the complete cessation of cooperative activities. This, however, should not necessarily be judged a failure. As we have stressed above, flexibility is the central and distinguishing characteristic of strategic partnerships. This implies that just as strategic partnerships can be formed with great speed, so can they be terminated quickly in response to changing technical opportunities and competitive conditions. In other words, strategic partnerships, given their distinctive nature, must be evaluated by criteria other than those used to assess direct foreign investment.

Europe's diversity constitutes its greatest handicap as well as its greatest source of potential strength. The building of a European scientific and technological capacity through the adoption of harmonized technological options would provide a framework for the introduction of new technologies, new products and new ways to compete in world markets. It would thus give Europe the ability to participate in shaping the evolution of technological trajectories.

The development of standardization in Europe, moreover, would allow for a more efficient process of specialization where economies of scope can be appropriated not only by large integrated concerns but by small companies operating through flexible networks. A division of labour based on the scale of the EEC market thus offers an alternative to a strict specialization among firms and nations and permits a new type of differentiation based on complementarities.

To a large extent, inter-firm agreements, mergers and equity participation are themselves guided by the rationale of industries at a world-wide level. To focus exclusively on a strategy based on this logic, however, results in the enhancement of outward orientated forces and rapid integration into structures presently organized by dominant groups from the United States and Japan. This type of strategy entails the generation of long-term dependence on foreign firms. In order to avoid these consequences, state intervention and the political willingness to construct a new Europe is essential. The challenge which Europe is currently facing centres on its ability to initate strategies and policies that can simultaneously ensure the development of global capacities which can identify and implement proper operating standards as well as support flexibility of action, grounded in the diversity of its components.

Notes

1. Japanese car makers have been able to reduce the launching time of a new generation of automobiles from seven to four years by utilizing only 40 per cent of newly designed components as compared with their American competitors whose newly designed components comprise 80 per cent.
2. A detailed presentation of technology bunching can be found in GEST:1986.
3. It should be pointed out, however, that while some French companies are adopting technology bunching strategies, others are pursuing strategies of retrenchment within tight industrial boundaries. Pechiney, for example, is building a strong knowledge base in non-ferrous metals, ceramics and composites, and doing so through a close relationship with its customers. Thomson and CGE, in contrast, are mainly seeking to establish dominant market positions, with the former eyeing consumer electronics and defence goods and the latter telecommunications, transportation and power equipment. Both do so, however, at the expense of their industrial flexibility.
4. The blurring of industrial boundaries is further reinforced by a strategy of selling performances or solutions.
5. See also Chapter 8 in this volume.
6. Interview with senior management at Thomson, Paris, 1987.

7. See Chapter 8 in this volume.
8. See Delapierre, Lemettre, Mytelka, Vavakova and Zimmermann, 1988.
9. For further details on the Airbus case, see Chapter 4.
10. Materials is a description used to cover a number of traditional industrial sectors such as: glass, ceramics, cement, bulk chemicals. Some of these products have become involved in producing 'new' materials such as composites.
11. An analysis of the data from 1980 to 1985 was presented in LAREA/CEREM 1988. Work is presently in progress to update the data base to 1988 and to cover two additional sectors: automobiles and ground transportation services. The data base excludes agreements concluded within the context of European programmes such as ESPRIT, RACE or BRITE. ESPRIT is analysed in Chapter 9. For a description of the data base see Chapter 1.
12. For a discussion of SEMATECH see Chapter 7.
13. Competition is still a distinct feature among standards-setting groups. A group of microcomputer suppliers have joined a consortium of nine international manufacturers to design and implement a standardized bus in order to improve on the interconnections within microcomputer systems and challenge the new, proprietary, *de facto* standard introduced by IBM with its P/2 range. Called EISA, Extended Industry Standard Architecture, it is based on IBM's PCs and is intended to allow compatible manufacturers to hold on to their market shares as well as prevent IBM from remaining the norm setter (*01 Informatique*, 1989). The initiatives taken by European standards associations have been supported by the EC in an attempt to shape a truly European information industry, one which can compete globally. In an effort to shift from *ex-post* to *ex-ante* standardization, the European Commission has organized a committee of high-ranking civil servants from national standards bodies. It has supported the final recommendations of the 1983 round-table conference involving twelve leading European information technology companies which culminated in the setting up of SPAG (Standard Promotion and Application Group), established to work on the implementation of open-systems interconnection protocols (Adoux, 1986) Shortly thereafter, a similar initiative, COS, was introduced in the United States and Japan. SPAG has since accepted membership applications from non-European manufacturers such as IBM, Hewlett-Packard and DEC and is cooperating with COS to harmonize their protocols-testing tools. Additional information on standards-setting through the ESPRIT programme is contained in Chapter 9.

References

Adoux, M. (1986), 'La politique communautaire de normalisation dans le domaine des technologies de l'information et des télécommunications', *La Rouge et la Jaune*, No. 4.

Caincara, G.C., Colombo, M.S. and Mariotti, S. (1987) 'Cooperative Agreements in the Information and Telecommunications Industrial System', Milan Polytechnic, Department of Electronics, October, (mimeo).

Chabert, P. (1989), 'Bull affirme sa strategie mondiale', *L'Usine Nouvelle*, no. 2205, 2 February.

Chesnais, F. (1988), 'Les accords de cooperation technique entre firmes independantes', *STI Revue*, No. 4.

Delapierre, M. and Mytelka, L.K., (1988), 'Decomposition, recomposition des oligopolies', Cahiers de l'ISMEA, *Economie et Société*, 11–12, pp. 57–83.
Electronic Business (1988), 15 March.
Ferrands, C. (1988), 'High Technology Alliances for 1992', *The Economist* Intelligence Unit, *European Trends*, No. 4.
Financial Times (1989a), 22 February.
— (1989b), 22 March.
— 'U.S. and Europe May Open up Chip Research Efforts', 13 June.
— (1989d), 'Sematech in EC Chip Talks', 21 June.
GEST (1986), *Grappes technologiques: les nouvelles strategies d'entreprise*, Paris, McGraw Hill.
Global Finance (1988), December.
LAREA/CEREM (1986), 'Les politiques d'industrialisation du tiers monde, face aux complexes industriels transnationalisées, Nanterre, (mimeo).
— (1988), 'Les Strategies d'accord des groupes de la CEE. Integration ou éclatement de l'espace industriel éuropéen', Action de Recherche Thematique en Economie Internationale, Programme Europe Industrielle et Technologique; Commissariat General au Plan, Paris, October (mimeo).
Michalet, C.A., Delapierre, M., Madeuf, B. and Ominami, C. (1983) *Nationalisations et internationalisations: strategies des multinationales françaises dans la crise*, Paris, La Découverte, 1983.
— (1985), *Le Capitalisme mondiale*, 2nd ed. Paris, PUF.
Mytelka, L.K. (1987), 'The Political Economy of Strategic Partnering', *Investment Canada*, March.
Teillac, J. (1989), 'L'Economie française souffre-t-elle d'une insuffisance de la recherche?' *Avis et Rapports du Conseil Economique et Social*, no. 13, 2 June.
Waller, D. (1987), 'Britain Leads in Overseas Takeovers', *Financial Times*, March.

6 Institutions and innovation: research collaboration as technology strategy in Japan

Jonah D. Levy and Richard J.Samuels

The Japanese have the poorest spirit for cooperation. [Nippon Oil President Naito referring to failed oil cartels in the 1920s.]

Joint action for the common good apparently had little appeal to the Japanese mind. [United States Strategic Bombing Survey referring to the failure of Japanese aircraft manufacturers to collaborate during World War II.]

Collaboration is Everything. [Organizing slogan for the Japanese Research Programme in very large scale integrated circuits]

Introduction - the landscape

Inter-firm research collaboration in Japan is widespread, structurally diverse, and increasing rapidly in both absolute terms and as a proportion of total R & D.[1] A 1986 survey by the Japan Key Technology Centre revealed that nearly two-thirds of the 261 firms surveyed have engaged in inter-firm research projects.[2] The Economic Research Institute of the Machinery Promotion Industry Association reported a rapid increase in the filing of joint patent applications (JPA's) by Japanese firms. In the case of materials research alone, more than twice as many JPA's were filed in 1985 as in 1980. The same study found that as many as one-quarter of all patent applications in selected sectors, such as plant engineering, are filed jointly. In steel, heavy equipment and automobiles, JPA's accounted for more than 10 per cent of all patents filed in 1980–2.[3] That percentage has risen subsequently, as Japanese firms, no longer able simply to take superior foreign technology off the shelf, increasingly band together to push back technological frontiers.

Collaborative research has become the defining feature of Japanese research practice and the *sine qua non* for competitiveness in many technology-intensive sectors. Indeed, cooperation is more common in technologically innovative sectors than in other areas. Within the machinery industry, for example, 80 per cent of all joint patent applications are generated by high-tech electronic equipment manufacturers. (Tomiura, 1985, 23) As we shall document, the most striking features of interfirm research cooperation in Japan are the diversity of its participants, the nature of the research conducted, and the institutional forms through which collaboration is organized.

Debate has raged over the kind of research (basic versus applied) that is most amenable to interfirm collaboration. The argument on behalf of basic research is twofold. (Kurokawa, 1987) First, basic research is essentially a 'public good' — firms will not invest in it singly, since the results are almost impossible to withhold from non-investors. The second argument is that firms are unlikely to cooperate in applied research, since they fear the loss of valuable proprietary information. Because basic research is further removed from the competitive dictates of the marketplace, it is better suited to cooperative undertakings.

The argument on behalf of cooperation in applied research is that this is the only kind of research which interests firms. Companies are in the business of making money, not winning Nobel Prizes; they are unlikely to devote scarce resources and valued research personnel to undertakings that are far removed from commercial applications.[4] Some theorists try to straddle the two claims: research should be conducted at an 'intermediate' level, not so close to the market that it incites misgivings over compromising proprietary knowledge, not so far that firms are uninterested. (Johnson, 1982)

The evidence from the Japanese case is mixed. A government survey found that 14 per cent of inter-firm collaboration was directed at basic research, whereas one-third involved applied research and more than half was devoted to product development. (Rokuhara, 1985: 40). While the share of joint basic research may seem low, consider that there has been little basic research of any kind in Japan (whether cooperative or by a single firm) until quite recently. What is more, the incidence of cooperation in basic research appears to be increasing, especially within government-sponsored programmes.

A certain amount of the debate about Japanese practice arises, no doubt, from the fact that scholars are not always discussing the same phenomenon. The forms of cooperative research are multiple. They run the gamut from simple contracts between two private firms to elaborate government-backed consortia. Applied research is typical of purely private agreements, whereas government-backed initiatives tend to be more orientated toward basic research. Even this generalization must be qualified, however. Government interest in basic research is a relatively recent development. When Japanese industry lagged behind world technological leaders, policy sought primarily to promote the transfer and application of existing technology, rather than the generation of new technology. These priorities have shifted as Japanese industry has reached the technological forefront.

Distinctions between basic and applied research and between private and publicly sponsored cooperation are not the only dimensions along which joint research varies. Each cooperative undertaking raises a host of questions: what the research agenda will be; which participants will perform which tasks; whether the research will be conducted cooperatively in a common facility, or whether each firm will undertake its own research, with a sharing of results. Government support further complicates the matter. Public and private actors must negotiate how much money the firms will contribute and how much will be covered by public coffers, as well as who will have rights to resulting patents. As will be seen, there is no single response to these and many other questions; arrangements vary from case to case.

Like the forms of cooperative research, the nature of the participants cannot be subsumed under any simple generalizations. Most cooperative efforts involve straightforward agreements between two private firms, but some bring together literally dozens of firms under the aegis of public authorities.[5] Nor is the public authority always the same. MITI, the Ministry of Posts and Telecommunications (MPT), the Science and Technology Agency (STA), and the Ministry of Education, Science and Culture (Mombusho) all direct research consortia, as do a number of public and para-public agencies, most notably the Nippon Telegraph and Telephone Corporation (NTT) and various 'public policy companies' (*kokusaku gaisha*) or 'external agencies' (*gaikaku dantai*). In some cases, a single ministry or agency supervises a particular joint research project, but increasingly, the responsibility is shared between two or more public authorities.

Many apparently common-sense assumptions about the kinds of firms that would most likely be interested in cooperative R & D are belied by Japanese practice. For example, it is often argued that small firms are most in need of collaborative ventures since they lack the resources to make substantial investments on their own. Indeed, the goal of helping small firms was the primary motivation for the creation of government-sponsored research consortia, the celebrated 'Engineering Research Associations' (ERA's), in the early 1960s. However, over time, the ERAs have come to be dominated by industrial giants, such as Hitachi, Mitsubishi, and NEC. Nationally, large firms engage in joint research more frequently on average than small firms, perhaps because their superior resources place them in a better position to commercialize the results of joint efforts. On the other hand, if large firms participate more frequently in joint research, the rate of increase of this practice is greater among small firms. Between 1980 and 1982, the number of inter-firm contracts for joint R & D increased by 60 per cent among firms with a capitalisation of smaller than 10 billion yen, twice the increase for firms larger than 10 billion yen. (Rokuhara, 1985, 37)

Another plausible but inaccurate assumption is that inter-firm alliances should be found primarily among members of the same *keiretsu* (the large, integrated finance-centred groups such as Mitsui and Mitsubishi, which originated in the pre-war Japanese *zaibatsu*). Members of a *keiretsu* are bound together by mutual equity holdings and ties to a common financial institution, and they often give preference to each other with regard to investment or purchase decisions.[6] They would, therefore, seem to constitute natural research partners. Survey data, however, tell a different tale. Most inter-firm research is undertaken by unrelated firms, especially in the most innovative sectors. Of nearly 200,000 cases of joint patent applications by twenty-nine different firms, most were among otherwise unrelated partners[7]. To take but one example, six of Nissan's twenty-one joint patent applications between 1980–85 were filed with Toshiba, the electronics giant nominally affiliated with Toyota in the Mitsui Group. By contrast, Toyota and Toshiba did not collaborate on a single patent in that period (Teraguchi, 1985). In the late 1980s, one-half to four-fifths of all research consortia involving non-competing firms took place among unaffiliated firms.[8] Indeed, a MITI study showed a corollary development: firms within the same group have begun to compete with each other for the technological high ground in emerging areas such as bioengineering, new materials, and electronics (Tsusansho, 1987)

One common-sense assumption about participants in joint R & D does hold true: the vast majority of joint research is conducted among non-competing firms, rather than direct rivals. Fully four-fifths of interfirm research collaboration in Japan is 'vertical', involving firms operating at different phases of the production process. Common examples are 'maker–user' combinations such as steel firms and automakers or ceramics and semiconductor manufacturers. None the less, a significant minority of cases, one-fifth of all joint research in Japan, are conducted by competitors. It is these 'horizontal' combinations that are the subject of our analysis.

Why focus on what is clearly a minority phenomenon? First, because cooperation among competitors poses a puzzle for conventional economic theory. That a firm should be willing to cooperate with a company producing for a completely different market is not so surprising; that it would share valuable technology with a direct rival, and that it would do repeatedly and successfully, requires explanation. Second, horizontal collaboration is of substantive, as well as theoretical, significance. Although horizontal alliances account for only one-fifth of Japanese research collaboration, their numbers have increased and their forms have diversified. As we shall see, there has been a startling acceleration in the creation of new institutions to generate knowledge in Japan, and these new institutions uniformly involve competing firms. Every legislative initiative regarding technology policy in the 1980's was directed at least in part at stimulating inter-firm research collaboration. It is not uncommon for Japanese firms to participate in as many as several dozen such consortia, dispatching their researchers as well as mailing their checks to support the effort. The purpose of this chapter, then is to understand how inter-firm cooperation in R & D has become such a prominent feature of the Japanese landscape.

Understanding research collaboration in Japan: Institutional stability and political struggle

The widespread and growing incidence of collaboration in R & D among Japanese firms raises a number of fundamental questions. Why are collaborative practices so much more extensive in Japan than anywhere else? How is cooperation among competitors established and how is it maintained?

What are the economic and technological implications of this practice? Our understanding of Japanese practice emphasizes a political and institutional context that is broadly favourable to collaboration, but in which the specific modes of cooperation are subject to constant tension and renegotiation. It comprises four basic elements: (1) the centrality of technology to Japanese development strategies; (2) state activism to foster collaborative research; (3) a stable institutional context on both the public and private sides; 4) extensive conflict and bargaining among public and private actors.

The centrality of technology

Seventy-five years ago, the Austrian economist Joseph Schumpeter (1983) argued that innovation is the central component of economic competitiveness. Schumpeter scoffed at neoclassical economic theory's emphasis on price competition and incremental improvements, asserting that these factors paled in comparison to the competitive advantages conferred by innovation. This was the reasoning behind Schumpeter's argument on behalf of monopolies: monopolists may increase prices in the short term, but in the long term Schumpeter believed that their vast resources would make it possible to fund far greater research efforts than under conditions of perfect competition. Thus, the static inefficiencies due to higher prices would be more than offset by the gains in dynamic efficiency resulting from accelerated innovation.

Schumpeter's obsession with the technological dimension of competition resonates throughout Japanese economic practice. Price has always taken a backseat to technology acquisition in the motivations of Japanese industrialists and policymakers. Consider the aircraft industry. It costs Japan twice as much to produce the F-15 under licence from the United States or to co-produce the next generation FSX fighter than it would to simply buy the plane from an American manufacturer (Samuels and Whipple, 1989). However, the long-term gains in technological know-how are thought to justify the up-front expenditures. Japanese citizens, whether as consumers or taxpayers, are routinely called upon to pay higher prices for inferior goods, while domestic producers work to close the technological gap with foreign rivals.[9] The Schumpeterian outlook of Japanese producers is further reflected by the fact that purchases of technology (patents, licences, royalties etc.) are one of the few areas in which the country continues to run a sizable (though now shrinking) trade deficit.

State activism and economic nationalism

While the obsession of Japanese economic actors with the technological dimension of competition echo Schumpeter's analysis, the same cannot be said of the modalities they deploy. Schumpeter saw little role for public authorities, and indeed, blamed them for seeking to preserve the status quo by enshrining restrictive practices that constrain would-be entrepreneurs. This is in striking contrast to Japanese practice, in which a range of government policies are designed to promote indigenous technological development. These policies have evolved considerably over the last century and include: subsidies and protection for targeted industries; generous government procurement contracts, which are essentially closed to foreign companies; insistence on technology transfer to domestic firms by foreign companies seeking to sell or produce in Japan; and, of course, support for joint research consortia.

The changing role of the state in a late-developing economy was anticipated by the nineteenth-century German mercantilist Friedrich List. List argued, against Ricardo, that comparative advantage is not bequeathed by God and nature, but can be created:

> . . . in any nation already advanced in agriculture and civilisation, by means of moderate protection, its infant manufactures, however defective and dear their productions at first may be, can by practice, experience, and international competition readily attain ability to equal in every respect the older productions of their foreign competitors. [List, 1922, 32]

List's brief for protectionism informs our understanding of Japanese practice in which the costs of protection are considered different in kind from the benefits. Protection costs the nation 'values', that is, wealth in the short term. In return, however, through the development of a competitive domestic industry, the nation increases its 'productive powers', that is, its potential to create wealth. In List's mind, as in the minds of Japanese economic planners, there is no question but that the latter is far more valuable than the former: '. . . the forces of production are the tree on which wealth grows, and ... the tree which bears the fruit is of greater value than the fruit itself.'[11] For List, as for Japanese economic elites, state jurisdiction in markets enables successful arboriculture.

But states must be flexible. List anticipates how the economic development that derives from these practices begets institutional change. He notes that when firms reach world-class levels of productivity and quality, they no longer need protection from foreign competition. What is more, they are confronted by foreign industrial powers who insist that the late developer stop free-riding and open its markets. In this way, economic development makes some institutional arrangements less practicable or salient.

Cooperation, both in research and product markets, under a national banner (*hi no maru*) has long been encouraged by the Japanese state. But, as if following List's script, support for inter-firm research collaboration in Japan has taken a variety of different forms over the years. Beginning in the 1930's, half-public, half-private 'national policy companies' (*kokusaku gaisha*) were created to promote collective research and development. In the early postwar years, public policy companies were largely supplanted by 'success conditional loans' (*hojokin*), which were, in fact, little different from direct subsidies.

Since the 1960s, MITI's celebrated 'Engineering Research Associations' (ERAs) have become the most important institution supporting joint research. Like many Japanese institutions, the ERA was borrowed from

Table 6.1: Participation by large firms in engineering research associations in 1987 (Number of projects)

Nippon Steel	6	Toray	6
NKK	9	Teijin	5
Asahi Kasei	9	Kobe Steel	15
Sumitomo Metals	4	Kurare	5
NEC	11	Fujitsu	6
Hitachi	18	Toshiba	16
Mitsubishi Electric			14
Kawasaki Heavy Industries			15
Ishikawajima Harima Heavy Industries			15
Mitsubishi Heavy Industries			16

Source: Kodama, 1987

abroad. Dr Masao Sugimoto,[12] Director of MITI's Mechanical Engineering Laboratory (Kikai Shikenjo) in the late 1950s, was impressed by a British system of cooperative research associations that had been created after World War I out of concern that Britain was losing its technological leadership. Of particular interest to Sugimoto (and to the Japan Auto Parts Industry Association that lobbied for new public research initiatives) was the support provided by the British government through ERA's to small- and medium-sized firms. The first research associations were *ad hoc*, subsidized by Sugimoto's lab and supervised by the Japan Auto Parts Industry Association.

In 1961, the ERA system was legally established under the Research Association for the Promotion of Mining and Industrial Technology Act (*Kogyo Gijutsu Kenkyu Kumiai Ho*). Small- and medium-sized firms remained the primary target and the purpose was applied rather than basic research. Between 1961–5, twelve ERAs were established and their sectoral composition began to broaden. With Japanese industry reaching world-class levels of technology in the mid-1960s, it was uncertain whether ERA's would be needed any longer and none were created between 1965–70. This hiatus, however, turned out to be but a pause; it was followed by an ERA 'boom'. Fifty-nine research associations, representing fields as diverse as polymers, aircraft jet engines, microelectronics, fine ceramics, and biotechnology, were established between 1971 and 1983 (twenty-five in the period 1981–83 alone).

At the end of 1985, fifty-two of the seventy-nine ERAs established under the 1961 law were still operating, but both the nature of their participants and their *raison d'être* had been transformed. Although small-and medium-sized firms were still active in ERAs (136 firms belong to only one association), seven firms were involved in ten or more, and thirty firms account for nearly one-third of the memberships. Much of the stimulus for these ERAs, moreover, seemed to come from Japan's largest firms (see Table 6.1).

As Sigurdson points out, the aims of ERAs have also changed '. . . from generating specific technical results to that of broadly influencing certain industries or a whole industrial sector' (Sigurdson, 1986, 10). This shift was abetted by MITI policy encouraging the use of ERAs for broadly-based 'national projects' in such areas as microelectronics (the super high-performance computer and VLSI projects), materials science, and biotechnology.[13] ERAs have become a high priority, with government support doubling between 1977 and 1982 alone. Although accounting for less than two percent of total Japanese R & D spending, ERAs receive nearly 50 per cent of government R & D subsidies and act as a critical stimulus for significant private research spending (Wakasugi, 1986, 157). In the late 1980s even foreign firms were invited to participate in Japanese research consortia.[14]

The tax system in Japan provides further incentives for joint research. The most explicit tax benefit allows firms engaging in collaborative research to depreciate capital equipment by a full 100 per cent in the first year of the project, using a process euphemistically known as 'compressed records' (*asshuku kicho*). Each research consortium may own its own equipment nominally valued at one yen, and fixed property taxes for joint research ventures are reduced to 75 per cent after three years.[15]

The 1980s have witnessed a veritable explosion of new forms of government-backed joint research. Among these arrangements are: informal collaborative institutions known as 'forums' or 'centres', which often precede the formation of an ERA;[16] research cartels within the jurisdiction of the Structurally Depressed Industry Law; programmes to enhance the access of private consortia to government labs and researchers; and, the Japan Key Technology Centre, to be discussed below. In addition, new life has been breathed into some of the old institutional arrangements. For example, several of the most important current consortia are organized as public policy companies.

In short, collaborative research has become the modal pattern of state support for research in Japan. Roughly 80 per cent of all government research loans are extended to joint projects. (Suzuki, 1986) The institutional forms may vary, but the Listian logic remains the same: the government subsidizes private firms to work together to devise solutions to their common technical problems. As Japan moved from technological backwater to world leader in many industries, research consortia, the institutions of collaborative research, were not eliminated but reconfigured and readapted to meet the country's new needs. This stability of function, if not of form, is related to another feature of Japanese research collaboration — the stability of the partners.

Stable Public and Private Interests

We believe that the stability of the players, both public and private, is a central factor in the ability of Japanese firms to achieve cooperation. Game theory models the problem of cooperation among rivals as a so-called 'prisoners' dilemma'. In the prisoners' dilemma, two players are better off if they both cooperate with each other than if they both 'defect' (cheat). However, each player taken individually receives a higher payoff from defecting than from cooperating, regardless of what the other player does. Consequently, self-interested actors will always defect and, as a result, both players will fare worse than they would have if they had cooperated.

Robert Axelrod (1984) proposes a simple, yet persuasive 'solution' to the prisoners' dilemma. He argues that cooperation can become rational in a context of iterated interaction. This is because players might be willing to forego the opportunity to achieve a higher payoff in the short term through cheating if they know that defection will hurt them in the long run by reducing chances for future cooperation. A series of plays allows for contingent behaviour, that is, each player's cooperation can be made contingent on the prior good behaviour of its partners. As a result, according to Axelrod, unless future payoffs are discounted heavily, a strategy of contingent cooperation (tit for tat) will fare better than any other strategy. (In other words, rational utility maximizers will find it in their interests to cooperate voluntarily.

The oligopolistic structure of Japanese industry closely approximates the conditions for voluntary cooperation identified by Axelrod. The bulk of joint research is conducted among large, diversified industrial firms and groups centred around giant financial institutions. These firms participate in approximately 90 per cent of MITI's ERAs and lead virtually every one. In extreme cases, such as the computer and aircraft industries, the same four or five firms have been involved in virtually every single research consortium during the past twenty-five years!

Logically, the stability of industry participants should make it possible to establish self-policing cooperation, since consortia members would be able to punish non-cooperative behaviour by excluding the offending firm from future collaborative enterprises.[17] Interviews with managers in participating firms indicate that fear of exclusion from future projects often compels firms to join consortia when they would rather conduct research on their own and to behave cooperatively, rather than hoard information or free-ride.

None the less, two important qualifications to Axelrod's claims must be made. First, even with a stable set of players, firms do cheat. The instances of non-cooperative behaviour — lead firms in an industry refusing to join a consortium, information hoarding, lackadaisical research efforts — are too numerous to describe here. The second and more important qualification is that, in the absence of a state authority which rewards cooperation and occasionally punishes defection, research consortia are almost never established among competing firms. This suggests that Axelrod underestimates the difficulties inherent to self-policing cooperation.[18] In short, the oligopolistic structure of Japanese industry facilitates cooperation in the context of active state support, but it is insufficient to generate inter-firm collaboration by itself.

Axelrod's insights can be applied fruitfully to public actors as well as private actors. Monolithic visions of MITI-dominated industrial policy fail to recognize that MITI rarely has sole jurisdiction over a particular policy area. MITI's authority to promote joint research is challenged by a number of ministries. As will be seen, in the increasingly intertwined telecommunications and computer industries, the Ministry of Posts and Telecommunications (MPT) is a constant rival. So, too, is the Nippon Telegraph and Telephone Company (NTT), the recently privatized national telecommunications monopoly. The Ministry of Education, Science, and Culture (Mombusho) supervises basic scientific research within universities, and consequently, has come into conflict with MITI as it has sought to promote industry–university ties. Finally, the Science and Technology Agency (STA), which was established in the 1950s to coordinate government research and to assume jurisdiction in areas not controlled by other ministries, inevitably crosses paths with either MITI or Mombusho whenever it tries to intervene. Superimposed on these jurisdictional disputes is the unwavering hostility of the powerful Ministry of Finance (MOF) to any new public expenditures.

While the institutional picture in Japan is far more complex than simple statist interpretations suggest, one also finds an important element of stability. Japan is not a pluralist paradise. On the contrary, one of the most striking features of Japanese research consortia is the relative stability of the participants, both public and private. On the public side, this means that, for any given industry, MITI competes for jurisdiction with one or perhaps two other ministries. As a result, much as Axelrod would predict, some kind of *modus vivendi* tends to be reached. For example, although MITI and STA often encroach on each other's turf, by and large both agencies have accepted a division of labour by which MITI is responsible for applied research and STA for basic research.

A similar process has occurred on the private side. The stability of players has led to the establishment of a basic division of labour acceptable to all. Japanese firms, ever distrustful of their competitors, have by no means cast away all their fears and embraced full-scale cooperation. Rather, they have developed a set of practices which allow them to pool resources while keeping their partners at arm's length. Typically, researchers from different companies do not work together on the same technical problem. Instead, each participant company assumes responsibility for a specific task. Research is performed independently in each firm's own labs, with the patents then shared. This practice, referred to as 'distributed cooperation' by the Japanese, suggests an exchange of roughly comparable, independently-produced technologies rather than genuine collaboration.[19] Since technologies are generated independently, it is very difficult for a participant to do nothing while hiding behind the efforts of its partners. Thus, 'distributed cooperation' helps assuage participants' fears of being victimized by free-riders.

Political Bargaining

The features described in the preceding sections — a shared view among public and private decisionmakers that technology, not price, is the central component of competitiveness; public support for joint research; stable players on both the public and private sides — offer fertile ground for interfirm research consortia in Japan. However, neither the success nor the broad features of these cooperative arrangements are predetermined. Rather, deals are put together (or not put together) on the basis of complex negotiations among public and private actors.

Each research consortium is preceded by a prolonged process of conflict and negotiation. Typically, MITI formalizes the process — at its own initiative or at the behest of private industry —[20] by proposing a joint research venture in a particular area. Almost immediately, a host of criticisms is lodged. Some firms decry the project as technologically unfeasible and too far removed from the market. Excluded firms demand entry. MOF declares that it cannot be financed, given current budget constraints. Rival ministries complain that MITI is encroaching on their terrain and often counter with a proposal of their own.

The main lines of cleavage are threefold: between ministries, between government and industry and among firms. In the first category, one finds battles over who will direct the venture (MITI versus MPT versus NTT versus STA) and over how much will be spent by the government (MITI versus MOF). In the second category are conflicts over the nature of the research to be conducted (basic versus applied), over control of resulting patents and over relative financial contributions of government and industry. In the third case, firms have to sort out the division of labour, in the process reminding each other of past bargains and behaviour. The outcomes of these struggles are neither consistent nor predetermined. Sometimes, compromises are reached; often, they are not, as the many instances of duplicate ministry-sponsored projects indicate. As the cases of telecommunication and computers in the next section will illustrate, the organizing principles, jurisdictional boundaries, and modes of financing are very flexible and vary tremendously across cases.

A tale of two industries

This section examines collaboration in R & D in the telecommunications and computer industries in order to highlight certain salient features of Japanese practice. The telecommunications case focuses on the politics of cooperative R & D, on the often elaborate process of bargaining which precedes and sustains cooperation. It is an extreme example, almost a caricature of the kinds of complex bureaucratic negotiations that create institutions for collaborative research. In our study of the computer industry, we shift our attention from the political underpinnings of research collaboration to its economic consequences. The computer case demonstrates the essential role that cooperation has played in permitting Japanese firms to survive in an industry in which rapid technological change is the *sine qua non* of competitiveness.

Telecommunications: the politics of cooperative R & D

At first glance, the Key Technologies Research Promotion Centre seems like a prototypical initiative of the 'strong', developmentalist Japanese state. Established in 1985, on the initiative of MITI, the Centre provides several forms of support for joint research in basic high-tech areas (telecommunications, computers, aeronautics, etc.). It represents the most recent and most ambitious government programme for collaborative research to date. A logical conclusion would be that the powerful Japanese state, having recognized the need for Japanese industry to move from a strategy of emulating and diffusing existing foreign technology to one of developing new technologies independently and in advance of foreign competitors, has designed, in a coherent, rational manner, an institution to support this strategic shift. Closer inspection, however, challenges this neat, statist image. While the Key Tech Centre was devised in part in response to Japan's changed economic circumstances, it was shaped as much by a political logic as by an economic logic.

The Key Tech Centre grew out of the so-called 'Telecom War' of the early 1980's, a turf battle between MITI and MPT, in which NTT was also deeply involved.[21] Several converging developments led to this bureaucratic war and to the creation of the Key Tech Centre as a means of re-establishing the peace. The first development concerned international trade frictions. The special relationship between NTT and its associated firms was assailed by American trade negotiators in the 1980s.[22] They resented efforts to shelter NTT's $3 billion procurement programme from Japan's promises to liberalize trade, and believed (incorrectly as it turned out) that an agreement for open NTT bidding and procurement would reduce the bilateral trade deficit through an increase in American sales of high-technology telecommunications equipment.

The second development had to do with fiscal austerity. Senior LDP leaders, MOF officials, and business leaders had long been engaged in negotiations to reduce government spending and to relieve the public treasury of financial responsibility for some of its most inefficient operations such as the national railways. It occurred to private-sector leaders that the NTT monopoly might be challenged as well. Fiscal austerity also affected research budgets. The government's share of R & D spending was already lower in Japan than in any other industrial democracy when, in 1984, the Finance Ministry instituted its 'zero minus ceiling' budget system. MOF announced that it would disallow any budget requests larger than the previous year's allocations.

Fiscal austerity could not have come at a worse time for MITI, which was trying vigorously to redefine its industrial policy mission and to enhance its role in industrial research. In addition to increased research funding for the AIST, MITI sought approval to establish a new Basic Technology Promotion Center for telecommunications, materials technology and biotechnology in the fiscal 1985 budget. MITI's objectives clashed not only with LDP and MOF budget-cutters, but also with the ambitions of MPT, which was lobbying vigorously to maintain and to enhance its own administrative jurisdictions. Indeed, MPT's problems were far more menacing than MITI's. Even though MPT had not fully controlled NTT for most of the postwar period, the NTT privatization would further dissipate MPT powers. To make matters worse, MPT was threatened with loss of control of the lucrative Postal Savings Programme, 'the world's largest financial institution.' (Johnson, 1989). The private banks and MOF were each eager to wrest control of these funds from MPT. Taken together, these developments could snuff out MPT's aspirations to re-establish its prewar status as a 'policy agency' equal to MITI or MOF.

Changes in the nature of the telecommunications industry further complicated the picture. The emergence of a hybrid 'information industry' out of the computer industry (MITI's bailiwick) and a newly competitive communications industry (regulation of communications circuits is indisputably MPT's job) gave both MITI and MPT legitimate claims for policy jurisdiction in the new high-growth telecommunications business. The result was a duplication of efforts, as each ministry sought to assume exclusive jurisdiction in this budding industry. MITI and MPT each supervised separate and uncoordinated research in its national laboratories; each stimulated and supported inter-firm research collaboration in telecommunications designed to establish it as the national telecommunications policy champion. In 1983, each ministry initiated a separate regional information network system: MPT's 'Teletopia' and MITI's 'New Media Community.' In the summer of 1984, each submitted separate draft bills outlining and telecommunications' research and regulatory programme that would secure its own policy jurisdiction.[23] But it was clear that neither MOF nor the private firms would put up with the duplication and competition for long.

The privatization of NTT provided opportunities for reconciliation of MITI and MPT aspirations, a reconciliation achieved only after extensive bureaucratic infighting and mediation by the LDP. Once it became clear that NTT shares would be sold, MPT (fearing the loss of its research infrastructure) proposed that a special Telecommunications Research Promotion Centre (Denki Tsushin Shinkö Kikō) be established with funds from the sale of shares (*genbutsu shusshi*). MOF preferred to use the funds to offset the fiscal deficit, a move that would have separated MPT from the NTT funds. Senior LDP politicians intervened between MOF and MPT and induced MITI to redirect its own proposal for a new research centre.

Their reconciliation required three separate compromises. The easiest was the name. MPT deferred to MITI here, and the MITI proposal for a Key Technology Promotion Centre was accepted. MPT preferred that the new centre focus only on telecommunications technology, while MITI sought a broader mandate. MITI again prevailed. But MITI's effort to have unilateral control of the centre was rebuffed by the LDP, MOF, and business leaders. The new centre would be controlled jointly. In the final compromise, MITI had its financial windfall and MPT had its policy windfall. As Johnson aptly puts it: 'The center is a typical Japanese hybrid: the product of bureaucratic competition, funded from public but not tax monies, and incorporating private sector supervision and participation.'[24]

The Key Technology Promotion Centre was established by the Key Technology Research Facilitation Law of June 1985. The centre is the latest institutional manifestation of Japanese cooperative research promotion. It is engaged in three categories of activities providing: (1) equity for research and development companies comprised of private firms engaged in joint research (up to 70 per cent of total capitalization); (2) loans to private joint-venture research firms (interest repayment is 'success conditional'); and (3) basic infrastructure to collect and diffuse scientific and technical information, to promote international research cooperation and to facilitate other forms of joint research, including access for private researchers to national research facilities. One-third of government dividends from NTT shareholdings are earmarked for the Centre. In addition, it receives funds directly from the Japan Development Bank, other government financial institutions and private firms.

The list of 'Key Tech' projects (Table 6.2) reflects clearly the political compromise that created the centre. There are two kinds of projects: the MPT-supported 'teletopias' which provide regional information systems to local governments, and the MITI supported 'R & D projects,' which look very much like its ERAs, but which give the state an equity stake. This suggests that MITI may have been induced to compromise its own 'new media community' regional policy programme, while MPT lost its bid to expand its research base. In 1989, six of the centre's eight new capital investments were in media technologies, as were nearly half of its twenty-two new loan projects. Every one of these thirty new projects is led by a major technology-based multinational corporation such as Hitachi, NEC and Fujitsu.

Table 6.2: Key technology center investment projects initiated in 1989

Number:	1
Field:	Electronics
Theme:	R & D of Superconducting Quantum Interference Device SQUID Systems
Organization:	SQUID System Laboratory
Period:	March 1990 – March 1996 (6 years, 1 month)
Planned budget: (Center investment in parentheses)	5700 million yen (3990 million yen)
1989 Center investment:	30 million yen
Primary participants:	Hitachi Ltd Yokogawa Electric Sumitomo Electric Shimatsu Manufacturing Daikin Industries and 3 other organizations

Number:	2
Field:	Network
Theme:	Basic research to enhance the reliability and operation of large-scale communications systems
Organization:	Advanced Communication System Laboratory
Period:	March 1990 – March 1996 (6 years, 1 month)
Planned budget: (Center investment in parentheses)	3158 million yen (2211 million yen)
1989 Center investment:	18 million yen
Primary participants:	Hitachi Ltd Tohoku Electric Power NTT Oki Electric Sumitomo Electric and 6 other organizations

Number:	3
Field:	Radiocommunication
Theme:	Experimental research of a public-personal mobile communication system
Organization:	Mobile Communication System Laboratory
Period:	March 1990 – March 1995 (5 years, 1 month)
Planned budget: (Center investment in parentheses)	2885.8 million yen (2020 million yen)
1989 Center investment:	26.6 million yen
Primary participants:	NEC Oki Electric Toshiba Fujitsu Matsushita Mitsubishi Electric

Number:	4
Field:	New Media Community
Theme:	R & D of an information system to promote the tourist industry (Kisennuma City)
Organization:	Kissennuma Regional Information Center
Period:	March 1990 – March 1993 (3 years, 1 month)
Planned budget: (Center investment in parentheses)	180 million yen (90 million yen)
1989 Center investment:	2 million yen
Primary participants:	Kisennuma City Miyagi Prefecture Kisennuma Chamber of Commerce

Number:	5
Field:	New Media Community
Theme:	R & D of an information system to promote local industries
Organization:	Wakayama;Kainan Regional Industrial Information Center
Period:	March 1990 – February 1995 (5 years)
Planned budget: (Center investment in parentheses)	540 million yen (270 million yen)
1989 Center investment:	15 million yen
Primary participants:	Kainan City Kainan Household Product Industry Association Wakayama Prefecture Wakayama Prefecture Lacquer Ware Commerce Association Nokgmi Town Misato Town and 16 other organizations

Number:	6
Field:	New Media Community
Theme:	R & D of a research and reference support system – R & D of an information system to promote dispersed industries
Organization:	Okayama Wide Area Industrial Information System
Period:	March 1990 to December 1993 (3 years, 10 months)
Planned budget: (Center investment in parentheses)	300 million yen (150 million yen)
1989 Center investment:	3 million yen
Primary participants:	Okayama Prefecture Okayama City Kurashiki City NEC Chugoku Bank and 27 other organizations

Number:	7
Field:	Teletopia
Theme:	Experimental research of a comprehensive snow information system through computer mapping
Organization:	Joetsu Information Center
Period:	February 1990 – May 1993 (3 years, 4 months)
Planned budget: (Center investment in parentheses)	538 million yen (269 million yen)
1989 Center investment:	5.4 million yen
Primary participants:	Joetsu City Nigata Prefecture

NTT
Daiyon Bank Hokuetsu Bank
and 13 other organizations

Total for 7 projects

Total planned budget:	13302.7 million yen
Total KTC investment:	9000 million yen
1989 KTC investment:	100 million yen

The Key Tech Centre, then, is not simply the product of the recognition by enlightened Japanese bureaucrats that industry should be encouraged to collaborate in basic research. Rather, its creation and mode of operation reflect a series of compromises — between MITI and MPT, between both of these ministries and MOF and between government and industry. The case of the Key Tech Centre underlines the centrality of political bargaining and specific institutional arrangements in any collaborative enterprise. As we shall see, even in the case of the computer industry, which is often held out as a model of successful collaboration, conflict is everpresent and compromise a necessity.

Global Competition and Domestic Alliances: The Computer Industry[25]

The computer industry represents a high hurdle, a kind of 'critical case' by which to measure the value of collaborative research (Wakasugi, 1987 and 1988). This is true for several reasons. First, competition in computer manufacturing is waged primarily through innovation, by developing new products which render existing offerings obsolete, rather than by simply lowering the price of a standard item. Products have an extremely short life-span (Wakasugi, 1987, 11–12). Adding to the challenge, Japanese manufacturers have long lagged far behind the state of the art. Thus they not only had to match the competition's rapid innovative pace; they had to exceed it in order to become viable. Finally, the global leader of the industry, IBM, has not stood by while foreign and domestic rivals worked to catch up. Far from acting the sitting duck, IBM has played the role of hunter, repeatedly introducing new generations of products which rendered existing Japanese offerings — and often prototypes of machines not yet in production — obsolete.

Given the intensity of the technological challenge and the potential commercial rewards, it is not surprising that the computer industry has seen more ERAs (fourteen) than any other industry. From day one, MITI's ERAs have been formulated to help Japan's computer makers respond to IBM's incursions. MITI has provided substantial incentives for collaborative research, covering anywhere from one-half to 100 per cent of costs. From a static perspective, it would have been more efficient for Japan to buy its computers abroad. For many of the past thirty years, IBM's offerings have been cheaper, more reliable and more powerful. However, taking a dynamic view of efficiency, public officials regularly sacrificed immediate consumption opportunities to future productive potential and channelled vast resources to the industry.

The configuration of actors on both the public and private sides has provided the ideal circumstances for the development of cooperative practices as described by Axelrod. In the private sphere, six firms dominate the Japanese computer industry: Fujitsu, Hitachi, NEC, Toshiba, Mitsubishi Electric and Oki Electric. These same firms have participated in virtually every MITI-sponsored venture since the mid-1960s. What is more, they have been the *only* participants in these ventures. Prior to the 1980s, efforts by electronics giants such as Sharp and Sanyo to gain admittance were rebuffed by MITI. Firms know that it is in their interest to cooperate with their partners because bad behaviour can be reciprocated in future projects. In addition, as Fujitsu's Tajiri Yasushi notes, there is always the threat of government reprisals: 'If we ever said, "forget about Fujitsu [for a given project] and do it with someone else," we would never be invited to join a government project again.'[26] Tajiri's fears seem well founded. Matsushita, once a member of the computer oligarchy, left the industry in 1964, believing that 'seven firms was too many'; it was unable to re-enter MITI-sponsored computer consortia for two decades.[27]

The government side also finds a stable set of players. Since 1968, virtually every MITI ERA has been matched (and sometimes preceded) by NTT. The relationship between the two agencies has been both cooperative and competitive. They share a common goal — to channel resources to a strategic industry — and a common set of enemies — the tight-fisted MOF and American lobbyists demanding a more open Japanese computer market. NTT has proven to be a valuable ally against both of these enemies. Awash in cash and with a giant procurement budget, it is able to channel vast resources off-budget to the four telecommunications makers who also happen to operate in the computer industry (Fujitsu, Hitachi, NEC, and Oki). At the same time, because these resources are channelled through inflated prices paid for telecommunications equipment, the subsidies are less visible.

This cooperation between MITI and NTT has also been facilitated by an unstated agreement on the division of labour. (Doane, 1984; 142–6). MITI and NTT tend to sponsor complementary, rather than duplicative, research. Typically, NTT's ventures are more applied than MITI's. Whereas ERAs have focused on developing prototypes, to be translated into commercial products through each firm's independent research efforts, NTT has sought working machines for its telecommunications network. NTT has also compelled its suppliers to develop sophisticated testing and quality assurance methods, features which are less relevant to prototypes.

ERA's have formed the central weapon in the battle between Japanese computer makers and IBM over the past twenty-five years. Consider the ways in which the Japanese responded to IBM in the 1960s and 1970s, with research consortia expressly designed to parry IBM's innovative thrusts. As Wakasugi puts it, 'Cooperative R & D projects were the place where domestic makers exchanged the information necessary to devise strategies to compete with IBM'. (1987: 32) In fact, from the first ERA in 1962 to the

Table 6.3: Japanese research consortia in computer technology

Year*	IBM Product	Collaborative Japanese response	Japanese product
1962		Computer Basic Technology Research Association (FONTAC)	
1964	360 series		
1965			FACOM 230–50
1966		Super High-Performance	NEAC 2200, TOSBAC 5000
1967		Computer Project	HITAC 8000, FACOM 230–60
1968			
1970	370 series		
1971	370VS series		
1972		New Series Project	
1973	370/VS enhanced		
1974			M series, ACOS series
1975			COSMO series
1976		ERA in VLSI	
1977	303X series		
1978			M-200, ACOS-900
1979			M130F–160F, M140H–160H ACOS 250

*The dates of model introductions are somewhat deceptive because there can be as much as two or three years between new product announcements and the beginning of volume production

Source: Wakasugi, 1988: 24; Anchordoguy, 1989

celebrated VLSI project of the late 1970's, every research consortium was targeted at some segment of IBM's technological advantage:

From the early 1960's to the late 1970's, each ERA enabled Japanese producers to eat away at IBM's technological advantage. At the beginning of the FONTAC project, the Japanese had nothing to compete with what for IBM was an aging model (the 1401 series). Three years later, FONTAC had helped the Japanese match the 1401 series, but IBM had already moved to a new generation of products. The Super High-Performance Computer ERA lifted Japanese industry into the same product generation as IBM, although just barely. IBM introduced the 370 series shortly after Japanese competitors for the 360 hit the market. By the end of the New Series Project, however, IBM's lead had been narrowed to two, maybe three years, and protectionism was becoming less necessary for Japanese sales.

With the VLSI ERA, which operated from 1976 to 1979, Japan forged ahead in semiconductors. As in the New Series Project, MITI again covered approximately half the costs. For the first time since the FONTAC project, however, all six domestic manufacturers did not participate. Oki Electric was dropped because it had failed to commercialize the results from its New Series partnerships with Mitsubishi, a condition for the receipt of government subsidies. In addition, the company was struggling and did not appear to be in a position to contribute to the VLSI project.

Another novel feature of the VLSI ERA was its division of labour. In all previous projects 'distributed collaboration' had been the rule: each firm conducted research independently, with its own personnel in its own laboratories, and results were then exchanged at group meetings. The VLSI consortium brought all participants together in a common facility. But for the most part, old practices were reproduced in the new setting. Five independent work teams were composed, each dominated by the representatives of one firm. Still, the teams were not entirely homogeneous, which necessitated an unprecedented degree of cooperation and informal exchange between researchers from different firms.

By all accounts, the VLSI ERA was a striking success. in less than four years, the consortium generated some 1,000 patents, sixteen per cent of which were held jointly. The perfecting of techniques for tracing designs on silicon wafers and for controlling quality not only enabled Japanese manufacturers to become world leaders in VLSI, but made it possible for them to capture increasing shares of the global market for memory chips and to introduce a range of powerful fourth generation computers that could compete with IBM's 303X and 4300 series (Anchordoguy, 1989, 180A).

With Japanese hardware manufacturers having finally closed the technological gap with IBM and having reached a level of profitability permitting them to make substantial R & D investments on their own, one might think that ERA would have receded into the background. Instead, the ERA of the 1980s were redesigned to push back technological frontiers rather than simply to match results achieved elsewhere (Wakasugi, 1987: 23). Three major MITI initiatives were launched in the 1980s: the Optoelectronics Applied Systems ERA lasted from 1981 to 1986; the Scientific Computer Research Association, which is seeking to develop the components necessary to build a supercomputer (notably densely integrated, high-speed logic and memory chips); and the well-publicized Fifth-Generation Computer Project, which is seeking to develop a radically new kind of computer, one that is capable of 'thinking' on its own, of inferring new knowledge from its data base and writing its own software (Anchordoguy, 1989).

The ERAs of the 1980s share the objective of advancing the level of technology of Japanese computer makers, but several changes have been made. Whereas earlier ERAs sought to build working prototypes, which could be commercialized easily, the ventures of the 1980s are orientated toward basic research with at best distant links to the market. In the Fifth-Generation Project, for example, there is no expectation that the goal of creating a thinking computer will be realized by the time the project is scheduled to end in 1992.

Because there is less proprietary technology at stake, participants appear to be comfortable with more involved forms of cooperation. The practice of 'distributed collaboration', which had been the rule prior to the VLSI project, has been greatly diluted during the 1980s. Whereas in the past, firms conducted research separately in their own labs, all three ERAs mentioned above have been housed in common facilities. What is more, the work teams for each task are no longer drawn solely from one firm but are increasingly heterogeneous.

Although the computer industry is often cited as a model of successful Japanese research collaboration, conflict has been rife at several levels: between rival firms; between rival ministries; between government and industry. The relationship between two 'partners' in the New Series project, Fujitsu and Hitachi, was replete with dirty tricks.[28] Fujitsu and Hitachi were responsible for building four 'M series' mainframe computers. By agreement, Hitachi was to manufacture the intermediate-size machines, the M-170 and M-180, and Fujitsu the largest and smallest machines, the M-190 and M-160. However, Fujitsu immediately launched a competitor to Hitachi's M-180, whereupon Hitachi cloned Fujitsu's M-160, and so on, with the result that both firms wound up selling all four models. In a recent interview, a Fujitsu executive declared: 'while above the desk we were shaking hands, below it we were kicking . . . with one hand we were shaking hands and with the other hand hitting each other.'[29]

The relationship between MITI and NTT has also seen tense moments. MITI's celebrated VLSI (Very Large-Scale Integrated Circuit) project, for example, was targeted not only at IBM, but at NTT, the latter having established a VLSI consortium a year earlier. MITI tried to absorb NTT's VLSI consortium into its own, but NTT refused to go along (Anchordoguy, 1989, 170–6). Another source of conflict between MITI and NTT is the fact that NTT's 'family' of telecommunications suppliers is not identical to MITI's clientele. Thus, when Oki Electric was barred from MITI's VLSI ERA, it was none the less able to gain access to VLSI technology through its work with NTT (Anchordoguy, 1989: 290).

The sharpest battle line within the research consortia has been between MITI and private industry. One point of conflict has been the structure of the industry. As in many other industries, MITI has sought to consolidate computer manufacturing into a few 'national champions'. In the early 1970s, with the industry in crisis due to the introduction of IBM's advanced 370 series and with market liberalization on the horizon, MITI proposed some $500 million in aid on condition that the six manufacturers merge their operations into two or three groups. The computer makers balked, and MOF slashed MITI's budget, so the mergers never occurred.[30]

While failing in its efforts to induce a *de jure* consolidation of production, MITI has used the ERAs to create a *de facto* consolidation. The assignment of tasks and public resources within each consortium have consistently favoured the three largest producers, Fujitsu, NEC and Hitachi, at the expense of three much smaller producers, Toshiba, Mitsubishi and Oki Electric. In the Super High-Performance Computer ERA, the big three were assigned the work on the mainframes and integrated circuits — the heart of the system — whereas the little three were consigned to printers and cables. Concurrent with this project, MITI organized a software ERA, which excluded the little three. In the New Series ERA, established shortly after MITI's failed consolidation effort, Fujitsu and Hitachi were given responsibility for developing the largest and most sophisticated models and received 45 per cent of the public funds. At the other end of the spectrum, Mitsubishi and Oki were put in charge of the smallest and least sophisticated machines and received only 15 per cent of the available subsidies.

The second major source of disagreement between MITI and industry has been over the agenda and financing of the ERAs. Typically, MITI favours basic research, since this is the area in which private industry is most likely to be deficient. Private firms, while agreeing in principle with MITI's analysis, invariably seek to modify MITI's projects so as to receive subsidies for immediately commercializable research. As for the funding of the projects, MITI seeks to have industry shoulder at least half the financial burden, so that it can make its limited budget go further. Participant firms, by contrast, lobby for 100 per cent public subsidies.

The Fifth-Generation Computer ERA illustrates these conflicts over the financing and agenda of joint research (Anchordoguy, 1989, 188–92). MITI originally budgeted Y100 billion ($455 million) for the venture, half to be provided by public funds and half by the participants. However, private industry balked at committing funds to what it viewed as vague and unrealistic goals. MOF, for its part, refused to make up the difference. In the end, MITI scaled back the programme, preserving the basic research component, while eliminating funding for commercial applications. The government is contributing Y50 billion as promised and industry participates with planners and researchers, but not with cash.

The computer industry offers powerful testimony to the salience of inter-firm research collaboration. In a business in which introductions of revolutionary new products occur on a regular basis and from which electronics giants, such as GE, RCA, and Matsushita have been forced to exit, the participants in MITI's ERAs have not only maintained a presence, but actually gained market share against IBM (Wakasugi, 1987, 1988). Indeed, by 1983, Japanese computer exports totalled four times imports (Anchordoguy, 1989, 130A). The dualism of the Japanese industry also reflects the impact of MITI's ERA's. For all of their financial and industrial muscle, giant conglomerates Toshiba and Mitsubishi have been unable to overcome the handicap posed by their second-level position within the ERAs. They scramble for crumbs in a domestic computer market dominated by IBM, (Fujitsu, NEC, and Hitachi (Wakasugi, 1988: 29). What is more, their inferiority is technological as well as commercial: they are confined to the low technology end of the market — microcomputers, personal computers, peripheral equipment — and do not manufacture the largest and most sophisticated machines.

While the impact of ERAs has been undeniable, it has not been the only factor in the rise of the Japanese computer industry. Government subsidies, protectionism and the Japan Electronic Computer Corporation (a public policy company, which helped rig prices and promote the use of Japanese machines) have each been critical additional tools. Even in the realm of technology, Japan's progress cannot be attributed solely to joint research. Much of the technology necessary to build IBM-compatible machines was licensed at low cost from American firms, rather than generated domestically.

The case of the Japanese software industry also seems to urge caution in attributing Japanese economic or even technological success solely to ERAs. There have been as many ERAs in software (seven) as in hardware, and yet the industry is widely viewed as backward. Virtually all operating systems and programs must be purchased from abroad.

The practices associated with inter-firm research consortia contravene many of the most widely held interpretations of Japanese political and economic life. Cultural models of a nation of consensual, harmonious, cooperative citizens do not account completely for the recurrent conflict and concern for the preservation of proprietary information which pervade Japanese research consortia. The late development model, with its vision of collaborative practices as a response to the challenges posed by economic backwardness, better explains catch-up than innovation. Statist visions of an all-wise and all-powerful MITI devising research consortia as the one-best solution to Japan's economic needs are confounded by the fact that MITI has faced considerable resistance from both private and rival public actors and has often been forced to abandon or at least scale back its projects.

We believe that inter-firm research collaboration is perched precariously upon an institutional structure and a political will to find cooperative solutions in the face of real divergences of interest among players, both public and private. In our concluding section, we consider the implications of this set of arrangements for Japanese competitiveness and for efforts to emulate Japanese methods abroad.

Conclusion — Japan's national system of innovation

Cooperative R & D is but one method among many for promoting technological development. Research consortia have become the method of choice for public officials in Japan in large part because many of the alternatives have been foreclosed for political and historical reasons. Spin-offs from military procurement, as practiced in the United States and France, were limited by the postwar ban on military exports and by heretofore low defence expenditures. Direct foreign investment, the strategy employed by Sweden, ran up against a deeply held xenophobia, born of centuries of isolation. MITI attempted at various times to implement a French-style 'national champions' strategy', merging Japanese firms into one or two giants, but was invariably checked by private industry, often in alliance with MITI's political rivals.

We believe that research consortia are becoming modal, particularly in basic research, because they correspond to the incentives created by the Japanese institutional context. These include, on the positive side, developmental state officials and stable institutional actors; on the negative side, limits on military expenditures, a distrust of things foreign (foreign firms have not been part of the Axelrodian iterative game) and limits on MITI's power that include bureaucratic and industrial rivals. Christopher Freeman captures this interplay between historical and institutional structures and 'national systems of innovation':

> When Britain opened up a major 'technological gap' in the first industrial revolution, this was related not simply to an increase in invention and scientific activities . . . but to novel ways of organizing production, investment, and marketing, and novel ways of combining invention with entrepreneurship. When Germany and the United States overtook Britain . . . their success was also related to major institutional changes in the national system of innovation ... (The same is true of Japan today.) [Freeman, 1987: 31]

Japan's 'national system of innovation' seems to offer a number of advantages over classic, firm-based innovation. As resources are pooled and risks are shared, participants in research consortia may be willing to undertake more ambitious technology strategies than if they were working alone. Rapid diffusion of technologies and the avoidance of unnecessary duplication mean that resources may be employed more efficiently. Finally, collaboration permits Japanese industry to enjoy the advantages of size and scale without vitiating competitive pressures. Indeed, it could be argued that, by creating a 'level technological playing field' throughout the nation's industry, research consortia actually increase competition.

Although we believe that this Japanese system of innovation with its distinctive institutions and practices has proven itself superior to standard practice in the West in important cases, our analysis should not be interpreted as suggesting that research consortia offer *the* way for the United States and Europe to match Japan's technological dynamism. Many factors have contributed to Japan's technological performance: a well-educated labour force, with a per capita engineering population twice that of the United States; one of the highest investment rates in the world; a history of 'reverse engineering', of absorbing and improving upon foreign technologies; managerial practices which encourage worker initiative and suggestions. Research consortia are an important features of Japan's 'national system of innovation', but they are not the only feature.

The other grounds for caution before rushing to emulate the Japanese system is that, as we have sought to demonstrate, this system is very much rooted in Japan's historical and institutional context. Japan's historical and institutional legacy have ruled out certain technology strategies (spin-offs from military procurement, direct foreign investment etc.), which might prove viable in other countries. Conversely, efforts to replicate research consortia are likely to prove difficult in countries lacking such features as public authorities willing to underwrite private research efforts or stable institutional actors whose regularized interactions create incentives for developing high-trust relations and who are willing to accommodate a significant (if negotiated) role for the state. Economic practices cannot be imported as simply as automobiles or computers. Any effort to transplant research consortia to radically different national circumstances are conditioned — and possibly precluded — by the historical and institutional characteristics of the recipient nation. None the less, we believe that Western understanding of the purposes, processes and meaning of collaboration must be adjusted in light of Japan's experiment with this innovative national system of collaborative research.

Notes

1. For a description of the full range of collaborative practices in Japan, see Samuels (1987), from which this account is drawn.
2. *Key Tec News* (October, 1986).
3. See Kikai Shinko Kyokai Keizai Kenkyujo (1984) and Tsusansho (1987).
4. Evidence in support of this view is provided in Doane (1984).
5. Wakasugi (1986) p. 152 reports that 86 per cent of all inter-firm research involves a single partner.
6. See Gerlach (1989) for analysis of *keiretsu* linkages.
7. Kikai Shinko Kyokai Keizai Kenkyujo (1984) p. 21. Indeed, the preface to this report notes that it was undertaken in response to the boom in joint patent applications, particularly between 'unaffiliated' firms (*kotonaru shihon keiretsu*) including competitors.
8. For a list of such group-based collaborative research projects, see Keizai Chosa Kyokai (1986).
9. Elsewhere Samuels (1989) explores how Japanese consumers pay too much for commodities as well.
10. Research consortia represent a particularly unSchumpeterian practice because collaboration vitiates what Schumpeter viewed as the essential motivation for innovation: the possibility of achieving a decisive edge over the competition and reaping monopoly rents.
11. List (1922), p. 37. This metaphor presages the Japanese use of trees to characterize the 'roots to fruits' logic of technology development for national security. See Samuels and Whipple (1989).
12. Sugimoto had worked for Hitachi before World War II. He returned to Hitachi in 1964 after a distinguished career at MITI and after serving as the Director of the Science and Technology agency. Sigurdson (1986) contains a more complete account of the history of engineering research associations in Japan. See Kogyo (1985) for details on the legal, financial, and administrative regulations guiding the operation of Japanese ERAs.
13. See Yamamura (1984) for details on basic research and Sigurdson (1986), Doane (1984), and Sakakibara (1983) for details on joint development of products for the market.
14. Their response has been unenthusiastic. Best known is the 1987 MITI pro-

gramme in High Temperature Superconductivity; although designed expressly as an international consortium, it attracted only limited foreign participation.

15. These tax benefits are outlined in Kogyo Gijutsu Volume 27, Number 4 (1986). See also Wakasugi (1986), p. 159.
16. See Tsusansho, ed. (1987), p. 31 for a list that includes: Powdered Materials Centre; Fine Ceramics Forum; New Materials Centre; BioIndustry Forum; New Glass Forum; New Diamond Forum; Artificial Intelligence Centre; New Chemical Development Association.
17. Wakasugi (1987: 51) calls membership in Japanese research consortia 'effectively perpetual' and adds that participants:

    > . . . have an intimate knowledge of each other's research and development strategies, technological levels, and even know the faces of each other's R & D personnel. These companies expect to take part in future cooperative R & D projects, and it is not in their long term interest to try to get a free ride on one project and thereby jeopardize their chances of participating in the future.

18. For an excellent critique of Axelrod, see Gowa (1986).
19. Doane (1984) calls it 'separate but together.' The phrase 'distributed cooperation' (*kyodo no naka no bunsan*) was used by the executive director of the Japan Key Technology Centre. (interview, January 1989). It is not insignificant that of the 1,000 patents that resulted from the VLSI research consortium, only 16 per cent were filed jointly. See Fong (1987), p. 30.
20. In the beginning, the process by which inter-firm research collaboration becomes an object of public policy is very informal. Pepper *et al.* (1985, p. 220) sketch the process leading to the creation of the Biotechnology Research Association emphasizing its origins in an industry 'roundtable' (*kondankai*). Doane (1984) argues that with the exception of NTT's procurement-based collaborative development programmes, most joint research in Japan is 'industry initiated.' (p. 159). Yamamura (1986) stresses MITI's 'open leadership' of joint research projects. We believe that debates about whether this process is industry or government initiated obscure a more complex reality.
21. The term 'Telecom Wars' and much of this account is from Johnson (1989). Readers interested in a throughly compelling and deftly nuanced account of relations between MPT and MITI are urged to read his essay. Note that NTT was supervised directly by MPT until it was reorganized as a joint stock company in 1986.
22. NTT conducts basic research in three laboratories that together comprise its electrical communications Laboratory (ECL), one of the most prestigious research institutes in Japan. Like the Bell Labs of AT & T, three times its size, the ECL is engaged in a wide variety of telecommunications research. NTT has no production facilities, but provides a final market for the products conceived in its labs. Products for NTT are developed by a stable 'family' of contract suppliers. Whereas MITI subsidizes research before it is undertaken, NTT pays its contractors only after their goals are reached. These firms — NEC, Fujitsu, OKI Electric, and Hitachi — therefore find additional incentives for collaborative research and development.
23. The MPT program was embodied in its draft bill: 'Denki Tsushin no Kiban Seibi Hoan'. MITI's was in its 'Joho Sangyo Kyugo Kiban Hoan.' See *Shukan Toyo Keizai*, 15 September, 1984; *Asahi Shimbun*, 31 July, 1984; *Shukan Toyo Keizai*, 11 August, 1984; Tsusho . . . (1985).
24. Johnson (1989); see also *Shukan Toyo Keizai*, 19 January, 1985.

25. This account draws from the works of Doane (1984), Wakasugi (1986, 1987, 1988), and especially Anchordoguy (1989).
26. Cited in Anchordoguy (1989), p. 186.
27. Anchordoguy (1989), p. 59. Having been kept out of the early information technologies consortia, Matsushita is now very active in the newer ones in materials, magnetics and related areas.
28. These are described in Doane (1984), pp. 162–3 and Anchordoguy (1989), pp. 132–40.
29. Cited in Anchordoguy (1989), p. 133.
30. Elsewhere, Samuels (1987b) has developed a general model of this process.

REFERENCES

Anchordoguy, Marie, 1989, *Computers, Inc.: Japan's Challenge to IBM*, Cambridge, MA: Harvard University Press.

Axelrod, Robert, 1984, *The Evolution of Cooperation*, New York: Basic Books.

Doane, Donna Lisa, (1984), *Two Essays on Technological Innovation: Innovation and Economic Stagnation, and Interfirm Cooperation for Innovation in Japan.* unpublished Ph.D. dissertation, Department of Economics, Yale University, New Haven.

Dore, Ronald, (1973), *British Factory — Japanese Factory: The Origins of National Diversity of Industrial Relations*, Berkeley: University of California Press.

Freeman, Christopher, (1987), *Technology Policy and Economic performance: Lessons from Japan*, London and New York, Pinter.

Fong, Glen R., May (1987), 'State Capacity, Industrial Structure, and Industrial Policy: American and Japanese Experience in Micro Electronics,' unpublished, (mimeo).

Gerlach, Michael, 1989, 'Keiretsu Organization in the Japanese Economy: Analysis and Trade Implications,' in C. Johnson *et al.*, eds. *Politics and Productivity: How Japan's Development Strategy Works*, Cambridge, Mass, Ballinger.

Gershenkron, Alexander, (1963), *Economic Backwardness in Historical Perspective*, Cambridge, Mass, Harvard University Press.

Gowa, Joanne, (1986), 'Anarchy, Egoism, and Third Images: The Evolution of Cooperation and Industrial Relations'. International Organization,Winter, **4**, No. 1.

Johnson, Chalmers, (1982), *MITI and the Japanese Miracle: The Growth of Industrial Policy, 1925–1975*, Stanford: Stanford University Press.

Johnson,Chalmers, (1989), 'MITI, MPT, and the Telecom Wars: How Japan Makes Policy for High Technology', in C. Johnson, *Politics and Productivity: How Japan's Development Strategy Works*, Cambridge, Mass, Ballinger Publishing Co.

Keizai Chosa Kyokai (ed.) (1986), *Keiretsu no Kenkyo Nenpo*, (The Group Research Annual), Tokyo, Keizai Chosa Kyokai.

Kikai Shinko Kyokai Keizai Kenkyujo, (ed.) (1984), *Tokkyo Shutsugan Shutai Oyobi Shutsugan Keino Kara Mita Kikai Kogyo ni Okeru Gijutsu Kaihatsu Katsudo no Bunseki*, (Analysis of R & D Activities of the Machinery Industries from the Perspective of Patent Applications), Tokyo.

Kodama, Fumio, (1987), 'Kyodo Kenkyu ni Kansuru Kenkyu' (Research Concerning Collaborative Research), Tokyo, unpublished mimeo.

Kogyo, Gijutsuin, (ed.) (1985), *Kokogyo Gijutsu Kenkyu Kumiai Seido ni Tsuite* (concerning the Industrial Research Association System), Tokyo, Ministry of International Trade and Industry.

Kurokawa, Susumu, (1987), 'An Economic Analysis of Collaborative R & D.', unpublished seminar paper, Sloan School of Management.

List, Friedrich, (1922), *The National System of Political Economy*, London: Longmans, Green and Co.

Nakane, Chie, (1970), *Japanese Society*, Berkeley, University of California Press.

OECD, (1965), *The Structure of Industrial Research Associations*, Paris, Organization of Economic Cooperation and Development.

Okimoto, Daniel I., (1989), *Between MITI and the Market*, Stanford, Stanford University Press.

Pepper, T. Lomas Merit, E. Janow and Jimmy W. Wheeler et al., (1985), *The Competition: Dealing with Japan*, New York, Praeger.

Rokuhara, Akira, (ed.) (1985), *Kenkyu Kaihatsu to Dokusen Kinshi Seisaku* (R & D and Anti-Monopoly Policy), Tokyo, Gyosei.

Sakakibara, Kiyonori, (1983), 'From Imitation to Innovation: The Very Large Scale Integrated (VLSI) Semiconductor Project in Japan', Cambridge, Mass. Massachusetts Institute of Technology, Sloan School of Management Working Paper No. 1490–83.

Sakakura, S., 1984, 'Problem of Present Evaluation of Public Investment and Purpose of New Evaluation of R & D Investment as Reflationary Policy', in H. Eto and K. Matsui, (eds), *R & D Management Systems in Japanese Industry*, Amsterdam: North Holland.

Samuels, Richard J., (1987a), *The Business of the Japanese State: Energy Markets in Comparative and Historical Perspective*, Ithaca, NY: Cornell University Press.

— 1987b, 'Research Collaboration in Japan', Working Paper, Massachusetts Institute of Technology, Japan Science and Technology Program.

— (1989), 'Consuming for Production: National Security, The Domestic Economy, and Nuclear Fuel Procurement in Japan', *International Organization.*

— and Whipple, Benjamin, 1989, 'Defense Production for Industrial Development', in C. Johnson, (ed.), *Politics and Productivity: How Japan's Development Strategy Works*, Cambridge, MA: Ballinger.

Saxonhouse, Gary. (1985), 'Japanese Cooperative R & D Ventures: A Market Evaluation', unpublished seminar discussion paper No. 156, Department of Economics, University of Michigan, August.

Schumpeter, Joseph A. (1983), *The Theory of Economic Development: An Inquiry into Profits, Capital, Credit, Interest, and the Business Cycles*, New Brunswick, NJ Transaction Books. First published in 1911.

Sigurdson, Jon., (1986), *Industry and State Partnership in Japan: The Very Large Scale Integrated Circuits (VLSI) Project*, Lund, Sweden, Research Policy Institute, University of Lund.

Suzuki, Masabumi, (1986), 'Comparative Study of the American and Japanese Policies Concerning Cooperative R & D',Working Paper 86–00, Japan Science and Technology Program, Cambridge, Massachusetts Institute of Technology.

Teraguchi, Keiko, (1985), 'Tokkyo Shutsugan kara mita Jidosha Sangyo no Kyodo Kaihatsu Jokyo', (The Situation Concerning Joint Development in the Automobile Industry Viewed from Patent Applications), *Jidosha Kenkyu*, **7**, No. 4, pp. 8–13.

Tomiura, Azusa, 1985, 'How Nippon Steel Conducts Joint Research', *Research Management*, January–February, pp. 22–6.

Tsusansho, (ed.), 1987, 'Kigyo no Kenkyu Kaihatsu Katsudo no Arata na Tenkai, 'New Developments in the R & D Activities of Firms, unpublished mimeo, 12 March.

Tsusho Sangyosho Sangyo Seisakukyokyu, (1985), *Sangyo Gijutsu Kaihatsu Seisaku to Kiban Gijutsu Kenkyu Enkotsuka Ho*, (Law for the Facilitation of the Basic Technology Research and Policy for Industrial Technology Development), Tokyo, Toyo Hoki.

Vogel, Ezra F. (1987), 'Japan: Adaptive Communitarianism', in George C. Lodge and Ezra F. Vogel, (eds.) *Ideology and National Competitiveness: An Analysis of Nine Countries*, Boston, Harvard Business School Press.

Wakasugi, Ryohei, (1986), *Gijutsu Kakushin to Kenkyu Kaihatsu no Keizai Bunseki* (Economic Analysis of Innovation and R & D), Tokyo, Toyo Keizai Shimposha.

Wakasugi, Ryohei, (1987), 'Cooperative Research and Development in the Computer Industry: An Analysis of Actual Data', unpublished paper.

Wakasugi, Ryohei, (1988), 'A Consideration of Cooperative Organization: Joint R & D of Japanese Firms', Staff Paper Series, Faculty of Economics, Shinshu University, March.

Yamamura, Kozo, (1984), 'Joint Research and Anti-trust: Japanese vs American Strategies', unpublished paper prepared for delivery to the Conference on Japanese Industrial Policy in Comparative Perspective, New York, 17–19 March.

7 From weakness or strength: U.S. firms and U.S. policies in a global economy

John A. Alic

He a wind coptin, dass de trouble. He a sailin mon, and he used to de old-time way. All his life he been zigogin and zaggin, he don't know how to go straight.

Peter Mathiessen, *Far Tortuga*

The United States has adapted rather haltingly to the new international economy — an economy that has emerged in large part through actions taken, over a forty year period, by the United States government and by American corporations. Some American firms have adapted quickly and well, moving toward globally integrated operations and new forms of cooperation with suppliers and customers, as well as with putative rivals. Others have had difficulty: simultaneous competition and cooperation within networks of firms requires a balancing act that not all have been able to manage.

Companies that have learned to turn strategic alliances to their advantage, which may or may not imply mutual advantage, enter partnerships from a position of strength — strength based on experience. Even if they are the weaker partner in terms of technology, the ability to manage strategic partnerships themselves, with an awareness of what they are doing, will serve them well in the future. Other companies, including American firms whose corporate memories and institutional skills have been torn apart by mergers, leveraged buyouts and takeovers, may find themselves at a disadvantage in strategic partnerships.

This chapter pursues these themes by examining the responses to international competition of firms in two American sectors, automobiles and semiconductors.[1] Representing the old and the new, autos and semiconductors can stand for much of American manufacturing. Strategic partnerships have played steadily more important roles in both over the past decade, though in different ways.

American automakers are already embedded in extensive networks of linkages with foreign firms, often cemented with equity holdings. Semiconductor manufacturer's are seeking to manage networks that include both domestic and foreign competitors. Partnerships in the automobile industry like those in the aircraft industry[2] focus on joint product development and joint manufacture. They are central to corporate strategy. Many of the agreements among American semiconductor firms, however, stop with R & D. They do not have as much significance for strategy, though they may in the future and already do in Japanese and European firms.[3] Both American automakers and semiconductor firms, like steelmakers and consumer electronics firms before them, are being crowded into smaller and smaller market segments. As the 1990s begin, they must shed the remnants of the past if they are to devise new strategies and compete more effectively.

The United States Government, with its *laissez-faire* rhetoric and preference for macroeconomic tools, has done little to encourage or discourage strategic alliances. Indeed, federal agencies rarely devote much effort to understanding business activities or to competitiveness. Measures such as financial support for the microelectronics R & D consortium SEMATECH continue the nation's *ad hoc* tradition.

Technology levelling and the new competitive dynamics

American competitiveness in both smokestack and high-technology industries has been declining for years.[4] In the earlier postwar period, the United States had potent sources of advantage, particularly in high technology: entrepreneurship and venture capital; a decentralized technology and science infrastructure with many centres of excellence; flexible labour markets with high mobility among engineers, scientists and managers. In a comparative sense, all these strengths have waned.

There is no mystery in this. Before World War II, American technology was seldom better than foreign technology; sometimes it was inferior. European industries held the lead in fields ranging from chemicals to automatic lathes to prestressed concrete. Japan had a well-developed industrial base by the onset of the 1930s. After the war, the Marshall Plan and other forms of American aid helped war-ravaged economies recover. Their scientific and technical establishments revived and they regained their accustomed places at or near the forefront of technology.

Following the establishment of the General Agreement on Tariffs and Trade (GATT) in 1947, American leadership, through seven rounds of multilateral trade negotiations, left tariffs at low levels. Although non-tariff barriers have multiplied, the international economy is more open today than at any time in the past. Even as the Europeans worried over technology gaps and inward American investment, their industries were catching up. While American technology accompanied American investment in Europe, the Japanese government restricted both imports and direct investment. With no alternatives for exploiting their advantages in the rapidly growing Japanese market, American companies licensed technology to the many Japanese firms that were scouring the world for know-how. Japan improved its production capabilities fast enough to become the world's low-cost supplier of goods ranging from ships to television sets by the 1960s, while also making rapid strides in product engineering. With remarkable speed, Japanese companies moved from commodity goods and simple consumer products to high-value-added manufactures.

In the world that has emerged since 1970, knowledge diffuses swiftly.

Firms in developing countries have greater ability to adapt and exploit technologies originating in the West or in Japan. They have been helped by Third World governments grown more sophisticated in bargaining with multinational corporations. With the newly industrializing countries (NICs) improving their skill bases, and continuing to benefit from relatively low labour costs (for technicians, engineers and managers, as well as blue-collar labour), competitive pressures on the triad of Japan, Western Europe, and the United States can only increase.

Shifts in the international economy, marked as they are by rapid growth in NICs like South Korea and Taiwan, now proceed largely beyond the influence of the United States' government. They bring political issues that must be dealt with: pressures for trade restrictions, for R & D support and for financial assistance; adjustment policies that can help people and communities accommodate to change. The United States is still searching for workable approaches to competition in a relatively open international economy, one that its policies helped create.

Alfred Chandler (1962) teaches us how slowly corporations respond to changing circumstance. When suddenly confronted, in the latter part of the 1970s, with Japanese firms selling high-quality integrated circuits (ICs) at low prices, American semiconductor firms had many strengths upon which they might have drawn. Their technological skills were as yet unmatched. They understood the market better than their new rivals. But they lacked financial resources and, more important, the strategic vision to see that the playing field had shifted beneath their feet. Where technological competition had earlier centred on product technologies, it increasingly became a matter of manufacturing capabilities. SEMATECH, which will put most of its resources into processing technology, represents a partial response — one that comes a decade after the nature of the competitive threat from Japan became plain. It took that long for the leaders of this industry in the United States to understand that accusing their rivals of unfair trade practices would accomplish little.

Strategies aimed at meeting the new competition more directly might, following Chandler's reasoning, have forced major structural changes in the American semiconductor industry. Mergers and consolidation would have helped the merchant firms — those selling on the open market (for example Intel, Texas Instruments) rather than producing for internal consumption (IBM, AT&T) — amass the financing needed to counter the Japanese. New strategies and new structures were not forthcoming in an industry dominated by much the same group of men that had gained their initial management experience at Fairchild Semiconductor and its descendents — a set of individuals who put a very high value on independence and who saw the threat from Japan largely as a matter of unfair competition rather than an export strategy centered on low-cost, high-quality manufacturing of relatively standardized IC designs (the usual Japanese entry technique).

Since its birth, the microelectronics industry has undergone rapid structural change. Comfortable competitive patterns never developed. Imported cars, in contrast, disrupted a long-established and comfortable pattern of competition among domestic automobile producers. Unlike the semiconductor firms, American automakers did have the financial resources to respond to new competition, despite a number of years of low profits or heavy losses in the late 1970s and early 1980s. But they lacked insight into what would be needed to counter Japanese product strategies, which initially focused on small cars. When, in the second half of the 1980s Japan's Big Three (Toyota, Nissan, and Honda) began moving strongly upmarket with higher-priced vehicles and new luxury nameplates, the American firms had little in their product pipelines to counter these new models.

Strategic partnerships — in essence, efforts to bring together a more potent array of complementary assets than firms can assemble on their own — represent one response to the imperatives of competing in a world with more, and more able rivals.[5] The major American automakers have more experience with alliances than their counterparts in microelectronics (See 7.1). All three have substantial equity holdings in second-tier Japanese producers (GM-Isuzu, Ford-Mazda, Chrysler-Mitsubishi), and joint production ventures within the United States. But they have fallen behind in both product and process technologies. Microelectronics firms are still groping for strategies that will enable them to survive in competition with financially powerful rivals benefiting from large captive markets. In both cases there is a learning process involved in using alliances strategically.

Automobiles: Toward a world industry

In 1971, imports accounted for 15 per cent of American automobile sales — a figure that no longer seems high, but certainly did then. By the end of that decade, Chrysler was barely saved from bankruptcy. In the mid-1980s, Japan surpassed the United States in total automobile production. By the early 1990s, Japanese automakers will have the capacity to produce at least two and a half million motor vehicles in the United States (cars plus light trucks) — more than they exported there a decade earlier.

The industry is changing literally day by day around the American automakers, as Japanese firms (and parts suppliers) increase their investments and broaden their product lines. The simple fact is that, during the 1980s, automobile production in the United States has shifted radically, from dominance by three American firms to dominance by a group of six firms, three American and three Japanese. The American automobile industry enters the 1990s, in some respects stronger than in 1980 (when Chrysler was still threatened with bankruptcy), but weak in terms of both product technology and manufacturing capabilities.

The Japanese Entry Strategy.

Hidden behind the more visible outcomes of their strategies, and largely responsible for their initial success, Japan's automakers have substantial

Table 7.1: Comparing the US automobile and microelectronics industries

	Automobiles	Microelectronics
Stage of industrial development	Mature: market growth slow; continuing over-capacity likely.	Maturing: market growth rapid but investment requirements high because of increasing R & D costs and capital intensity.
Stage of technological development	Mature: incremental engineering improvement important (for example multivalve cylinder heads, electronic traction control).	Maturing: rapid but predictable technical progress, driven by lithography for increases in circuit density; silicon likely to remain dominant, with only slight possibility of radical technical shift during the next several decades.
Strengths of US firms	Financial power; extensive marketing and distribution networks; ample multi-national operating experience.	Product design technology particularly for micro-processors and specialized chips; understanding customer needs and the market for advanced chip designs.
Weaknesses of US firms	Both product and process technology.	Process technology; financing.
Characteristic forms of strategic partnerships	Joint ventures with firms for design and production, with Korean firms for production.	Shared R & D; joint develop-ment of complementary products.
Characteristic form of shared or jointly developed knowledge	Product engineering particularly for small cars; process know-how, especially shopfloor organization and management.	Upstream R & D; conceptual design of products; process tool development.

advantages in costs and productivity (much greater for some firms than others). These stem from highly developed manufacturing systems that rely not so much on automation as on effective integration of process and product design, work organization, and shopfloor management.[6] They have managed to retain much if not all of this margin in their American plants.

American automakers have been trying to emulate Japanese practices, but productivity is a moving target, and although American firms have improved, the Japanese remain well ahead. Moreover, Japan's automobile manufacturers have moved in twenty years from product technologies that compared poorly with the best American and European design practice to a position of product leadership. On a cost-per-value basis, and in many cases in an absolute sense, this lead exists in almost all the market segments in which Japanese firms compete. Their success must be seen as even more remarkable given the inherent difficulties of entering a mature foreign market.

Japan's automakers suffered from many problems they failed to anticipate in their efforts to penetrate the United States during the 1970s. Powertrains wore out quickly in long-distance driving. Companies like Honda found themselves trying to sell cars with fenders that rusted through after one or two northern winters. Federally mandated recalls were frequent. Japanese automobile manufacturers overcame these problems. They redesigned their products to suit American needs and tastes, establishing deserved reputations for quality and reliability and, in contrast to European manufacturers, built strong dealer organizations that helped them understand American consumers.

Japan's automakers learned many lessons from their American rivals and learned them well. The credit goes to the industry, which benefited from government policies, but not nearly so directly as Japanese semiconductor manufacturers. In the past several years, with their upmarket moves and new brand names, Japan's automakers have taken another leaf from Alfred Sloan. In turning their cars into high-fashion products, they have introduced new models much more quickly than American or European firms — a necessary capability for implementing such an approach. Design/development/tooling cycles for Japanese automakers have shrunk to little more than half those in the United States; Honda's model cycle is down to forty months, while American firms take 5 or 6 years.[7]

Collaborative Arrangements

More than in any other sector, inter-firm collaboration has accompanied restructuring in automobile production. Joint ventures and other agreements, many of them aimed at sharing the costs and risks of product development, have nearly doubled since 1980 — from perhaps seventy worldwide to more than 125.[8] Of course, this was an international industry long before World War II. In Europe, General Motors and Ford have been major forces for decades. European companies have been pursuing joint development efforts among themselves, while Britain has welcomed Japanese firms.

In arrangements linking American and Japanese manufacturers, American companies typically get product technology for small cars, and in some cases process know-how as well (this is the case with the GM–Toyota joint venture, NUMMI). Ford and General Motors have also entered joint ventures with Korean firms, where the primary attraction lies in low labour costs. Although GM has recently placed the Geo nameplate on products from Isuzu, Suzuki, NUMMI, and a GM-Suzuki joint venture in Canada, the 'world-car' — widely anticipated early in the 1980s — has not materialized. Still, the global industry has been in a remarkable state of flux throughout the 1980s with vertical integration giving way to a complex and constantly shifting web of inter-firm linkages on a world scale. As the major automakers have pursued their product, manufacturing and marketing strategies, alliances have evolved further in this industry than perhaps any other.

Microelectronics: Managing conflict

Relatively speaking, the merchant semiconductor industry is still young. Since the 1950s, when ICs were developed, technological advance in both semiconductors and the products that incorporate them — notably computers — has spurred extraordinary market growth. Through the 1970s, the centre of engineering creativity and entrepreneurial vigour lay in the American-based suppliers, many of them located in the Silicon Valley region of California.

Product and Process Technologies

The competitive strategies of American merchant firms have been conditioned by technological skills and by their ability to finance expansion. Growing as rapidly as the world market — much less carving out larger shares — put great strain on the resources of relatively small firms, particularly as capital intensity rose.[9] By the middle 1970s, the options for American-based merchant firms were narrowing. Only the largest could hope to supply a broad line of products. Others were forced to specialize — in memory chips, microprocessors, semicustom ICs.

So long as American-owned firms competed primarily among themselves, the game remained one of product design and product strategy — a matter of developing circuits with features (ranging from pin configurations to microprocessor instruction sets) that would find favour with customers who were mostly other American firms. When the Japanese entered, in the mid-1970s, IC technology was stabilizing — especially for dynamic random access memory chips (DRAMs). Not only did everyone know that 256K chips would follow 64K DRAMS, with 1-megabit circuits next on the horizon, but DRAM design is straightforward compared with logic or microprocessors.

With fewer opportunities for differentiation, manufacturing technology became more important. On this ground, Japanese firms like NEC and Fujitsu, which also produced computers and telecommunications equipment, could compete quite effectively. Not only could they cross-subsidize, but, because they consumed many of their chips internally and the costs of finding and replacing defective ICs escalate rapidly once incorporated into end products, they had strong incentives for controlling their manufacturing processes and improving quality and reliability.

Japanese suppliers could also take advantage of the financing options accruing to large, diversified corporations in Japan. When semiconductor sales slumped, they continued to invest in new production capacity, emerging in a position to take advantage of capacity shortfalls in the United States once sales resumed their upward trajectory — a pattern repeated several times. As Japanese suppliers came to dominate the DRAM market in the 1980s, most of the American merchant firms dropped out, although able to maintain a slowly shrinking edge in lower volume, design-intensive chips such as microprocessors.

International agreements

Marketplace realities have often forced nominal rivals in the semiconductor industry to collaborate. Most ICs are incorporated in end products by manufacturers that seek multiple sources of supply to protect themselves. Thus an innovating semiconductor firm may have little choice but to license a chip design to competitors; to sell to foreign customers may mean licensing foreign firms. Companies have also begun to cooperate in developing families of chips. With the pace of technical development rapid and markets volatile, arrangements involving licensing, cross-licensing, second-sourcing and joint product development function as risk-sharing mechanisms. As Japan's capabilities in microelectronics improved, these relatively straightforward technical exchanges expanded beyond the circle of American firms to include Japanese companies.[10]

In contrast to automobile production, where export quotas helped push Japanese firms into joint ventures, access to the American market has played no more than a minor role in fostering agreements between American and foreign semiconductor firms. Although trade friction has been high, the American market remains open. Distribution, moreover, is straightforward. Collaborative agreements typically involve exchange of technology, or joint development, with a tightly focused technical agenda that brings firm-specific strengths to bear on problems of common interest. Thus Motorola, long a leader in microprocessors, and Toshiba, which has the largest share of the world DRAM market, negotiated an agreement in 1987 to establish a joint manufacturing venture, with Toshiba sharing some of its DRAM know-how in exchange for microprocessor technology.

While the Motorola–Toshiba agreement has so far held together, competitive forces have, in this industry, frequently overwhelmed the incentives for collaboration. Although formalized alternate sourcing agreements have largely but not entirely replaced the copying that was once so frequent, second-sourcing agreements sometimes still end in flurries of legal briefs. Over a period of a few weeks recently, MIPS Computer Systems was concluding an agreement to license its high-performance microprocessors to NEC and Siemens just as an arrangement between Motorola and Hitachi was coming apart. At the same time, the courts were handing down a decision in Intel's long-running lawsuit against NEC over copying of an earlier generation of microprocessors.[11]

Domestic collaboration: SEMATECH

Rising costs for R & D and production facilities lie behind many of the technology-sharing arrangements in microelectronics. R & D expenses were a major reason for the formation of Microelectronics & Computer Technology Corporation (MCC), organized as a profit-seeking joint venture with a relatively broad portfolio of projects. In part because of this breadth, few if any MCC members view their participation as central to business strategy. This is not the case with SEMATECH, a not-for-profit R & D consortium with half its $200 million annual budget coming from the federal government. SEMATECH represents a collective response by fourteen American Firms to the United States' lag in processing technology. The consortium's R & D will centre on lithography and other process tools for denser ICs.[12] Because the merchant firms know they cannot compete effectively without better manufacturing know-how, SEMATECH, with its focused R & D agenda, has greater strategic significance than typical consortia formed to engage in joint R & D.

SEMATECH had a rocky start, and will face continued scrutiny. Some of its members are simultaneously collaborating with Japanese firms – in addition to the Motorola–Toshiba link noted above, Texas Instruments has a major agreement to cooperate in DRAMS with Hitachi — so that internal tensions will probably be difficult to manage. Perhaps most important, SEMATECH will have to guard against excessively optimistic expectations in Washington. Parity simply in lithography — or even a lead over the Japanese — would not be enough to rebuild American manufacturing capabilities in microelectronics, much less American competitiveness in this industry. It is through their mastery of the systems aspects of production that Japanese semiconductor firms gained their advantage, just as in automobiles. Mastering the individual steps in IC fabrication (lithography being one of many) does not lead automatically to efficiency in high-volume production. SEMATECH has asked for five years of Federal support, pledging to wean itself from public funds by 1993. The question for American policymakers will be: what to do to support this industry over the longer term should SEMATECH succeed on its own terms? What to do if it does not?

From weakness or from strength?

Despite the rather gloomy picture painted above for the automobile and semiconductor industries, the United States as a whole retains major sources of competitive strength (See Table 7.2). Many of these stem from a vast and diverse economy — one that is therefore extraordinarily robust. Individual sectors, even the largest, can slump, with ripple effects smaller than in countries more heavily dependent on a few industries.

Table 7.2 U.S. Strengths and Weaknesses in International Competition

Technology base No other nation can match American capabilities across the board in technology and science, although Japan and several other rivals have been increasing their commercial R & D investments more rapidly, while American firms have often been slow in taking advantage of existing knowledge.

Industrial infrastructure Although competitive decline in semiconductor manufacturing equipment has hurt the American microelectronics industry, American companies in general can call on a vast array of vendors, suppliers and service firms. Few other countries have a comparable range of capabilities so easily available.

Entrepreneurial traditions As in the earlier years of microelectronics, entrepreneurial startups have given the United States a substantial lead in such industries as computer software and biotechnology. On the other hand, these same traditions contribute to the turmoil of mergers and buyouts.

Financial Markets Deep, flexible and deregulated capital markets also cut two ways: American corporations have more avenues for securing financing than those in other parts of the world, but American financial markets create strong pressures for short-term profits.

Labour Force American firms continue to draw competitive strength from a mobile work force, and from inward migration, although the poor quality of much secondary and high school education has begun to harm American competitiveness. Engineers — schooled according to an applied science model — have been insensitive, not only to the role of manufacturing, but to the significance of design and marketing.

Climate for Business and Industry Political stability in the United States underlies business and consumer confidence, encouraging risktaking. None the less, business confidence may have ebbed somewhat, a casualty of federal budget deficits, trade imbalances, rapid exchange rate swings and the evident inability of government to deal with these.

Policymaking system The Federal system has permitted states to experiment with support for industrial development. Washington, meanwhile, has pulled back from many forms of economic regulation, spurring competition in some sectors.

The United States has seemingly been able to shrug off even the massive adjustment pressures created by penetration of its automobile industry. By the same token, however, the United States is vulnerable at many points — to imports of ferrochrome and NIC steel, Italian pasta and Argentine beef, oil and copper. Narrower economies can focus their resources in ways quite impossible for the United States.

The size and wealth of the United States' economy, with its multitude of sophisticated customers for almost any imaginable product, creates an unequalled laboratory for innovation — one reason so many foreign firms have sought alliances with American partners. But as Table 7.2 also suggests, sources of weakness often mirror sources of strength: high priorities for science coupled with low priorities for commercial technology development, and for manufacturing; flexible, deregulated capital markets leading to an emphasis on short-term financial paybacks.

For many years, American companies failed to recognize that their accustomed advantages in technology and management expertise were slipping away. They blamed their loss of markets on low wages abroad, unfair trade practices and, in the first half of the 1980s, an overvalued dollar. None of these factors has been irrelevant, but none has been, by itself, decisive. Similarly, the favourite whipping boy of the late 1980s — high costs of capital, caused by the huge federal budget deficit and a low national savings rate — provides only a partial explanation.[13] Signals of competitive decline in industries like textiles, steel and consumer electronics can be easily found in the 1950s and 1960s, when American macroeconomic policies were far different than in recent years.

Even if the United States had managed to avoid the huge budget deficits of the 1980s, and the foreign borrowing these entailed, American firms would have found the world of the 1990s an uncomfortable place. Many will be forced abroad in search of technology, just as foreign firms came to them in earlier decades. Today, American companies — whether multinationals or those with exclusively domestic horizons — can hope at most to be first among equals. More and more will enter strategic alliances, not from positions of strength, but from positions at best of parity.

Government policies

The United States government has adjusted even more haltingly than business to the new realities of international competition. Policymakers were slow to recognize the depth and extent of the difficulties in American industry, in part because it is so much easier to focus on broad economic indicators than on the specifics of individual sectors. But it is companies that compete, not national economies; competitiveness can only be understood on a sector-by-sector basis, which requires delving at least to some extent into the activities of individual firms — which the United States' government normally avoids, except for regulatory reasons.[14]

Focusing on exchange rates or on broad indicators like productivity or gross domestic product makes it hard to discern underlying problems, especially in an economy as large and diverse as that of the United States. It, moreover, makes it easy to believe that macroeconomic policy will be sufficient remedy for all ills. Such a focus is fundamentally deceptive. The failure of American policymakers to confront competitive decline earlier and more directly stems in large part from this misplaced macroeconomic emphasis.

For many years, then, despite the visibility of symptoms in particular sectors — steel before autos, consumer electronics before semiconductors — the bigger picture tended to drop from sight. When imports of steel and autos mounted during the 1970s, and massive layoffs by steelmakers and automobile firms generated intense political pressures, Washington debated sector-specific remedies — voluntary restraint agreements (VRAs) limiting imports of steel, regulatory relief for the automobile industry. Sectoral responses were viewed as emergency measures, justified until the economy righted itself. Some officials continued to hold that structural adjustment should ideally (that is in a world without politics) be allowed to proceed without government interference of any kind.

During the 1980s, as the slippage in American competitiveness became obvious even to sceptics, the policy debate took its usual course: the search for simple solutions to complex problems. In looking for 'the problem' to be fixed, the United States has suffered from a particular form of schizophrenia. Sectoral difficulties generated *ad hoc* responses in the usual American fashion — trade adjustment assistance for labour, loan guarantees for capital, import restrictions for both.

But American trade policy has been of little help in the adjustment process. As Detroit laid off unionized employees, Japanese automakers, with their shipments to the United States limited beginning in 1981 by VRAs, invested in onshore plants. Incoming Japanese firms, mostly locating in rural areas with predominately white populations, screened large numbers of candidates before hiring a relatively young work force likely to remain non-union. They were able to postpone the pension bills American automakers were already paying, while adjustment costs fell heavily on displaced autoworkers who had the misfortune to lose well-paying jobs in plants that shut down permanently.

At the same time, it was said, if only government could get its macroeconomic policy right, the trouble would disappear — in heavy industry and light, steel as well as microelectronics. Even as they were forced to implement sectoral measures in response to political forces, decisionmakers persisted in asserting that the problems could be wished away through fiscal and monetary policy. If those arguing against government involvement in the economy could not halt reactive measures like VRAs or trade adjustment assistance, at least they could try to hold the line against proactive policies by proclaiming that government could not pick winners and losers (despite the fact that almost any government action does just that). The debate was sterile, and lapsed for a time (to resume at the end of the 1980s) as the United States moved on to a more exciting experiment: supply-side economics, an overvalued dollar, massive budget and trade deficits and huge inflows of capital.

Some of the sectoral pressures abated as economic expansion masked the start of a slide in living standards and inflation rates declined thanks to the Federal Reserve. Unemployment gradually fell from the near-10 per cent levels of 1982–83. But the high dollar contributed to trade imbalances even in high-technology sectors earlier regarded as bastions of American competitiveness. By the middle of the decade, the United States woke up to realize that competitive slippage would not be confined to smokestack industries. More than anything else, the sudden decline in microelectronics drove home the point. No industry was immune. American competitiveness was threatened, not only in sunset industries, but in high-growth, high-tech, sunrise sectors.

Industrial policy

During the first half of the 1980s, Democrats in Congress introduced many bills intended to deal, in one way or another, with competitive difficulties. Draft legislation coalesced around three principal thrusts:

— some form of economic cooperation council for helping build consensus among government, (business, and labour, and aiding in policy co-ordination;
— Federal financing for industries — whether declining and otherwise troubled, like steel, or technologically dynamic, like semiconductors — through a development bank;
— encouragement for R & D and innovation — a shift in the nation's science and technology policy to raise priorities for commercial (that is, non-military) technology development.

Many of the ideas had been under discussion for half a dozen years already. The ongoing debate set the stage for initiatives like SEMATECH and many of the provisions of the Omnibus Trade and Competitiveness Act of 1988 (which, among other things, established a Competitiveness Policy Council).

The Reagan White House, meanwhile, began its own study of the problems, appointing a Commission on Industrial Competitiveness composed mostly of businessmen.[15] Few of its recommendations stirred much interest in the administration that had requested it. In the dominant view within the executive branch, American competitive strength had been built on free, hence efficient, markets. A more explicit American industrial policy would sap this strength. Instead of creating competitiveness councils, the United States should continue to deregulate, seek a 'level playing field' internationally and unleash its entrepreneurs to compete.

None the less, by the close of the decade, many of the steps under debate had, in one form or another, been taken. While the federal government has not seriously contemplated a development bank, Congress did approve $100 million in 1988 and 1989 for SEMATECH, directing the Department of Defense (DOD) to fund the consortium after a widely publicized report of the Defense Science Board urged such a programme on grounds that a declining microelectronics industry threatened national security.[16] If the expenditures were rationalized in this way, everyone knew that commercial competitiveness was the goal. The consortium will not undertake defence-specific R & D: DOD became the vehicle because it was alone among federal agencies in having the ability to monitor large-scale industrial R & D, and because it was easy to channel the money in this way.

SEMATECH represents a turning point in American technology policy: an explicit decision to subsidize commercial R & D with the goal of helping an industry threatened by foreign competition. Along with the confused debate over high-definition television (HDTV) during 1989, SEMATECH points to a new American direction, in which technology policy can be seen as a slimmed down version of what had earlier been termed industrial policy. When paired with attempts at managed trade such as the United States–Japan Semiconductor Arrangement, resemblance to the more comprehensive approach debated earlier in the decade may seem relatively close. Certainly some advocates of SEMATECH and of federal support of HDTV have seen such proposals as models for the future. But it is just as easy to see in these *ad hoc* decisions little beyond a precedent for others in the same mould.

Systemic Problems, Systemic Response?

Government policies affect competitivenss in many ways: through education and training, tariffs and other trade restraints, the climate for innovation and R & D funding. The United States has always had an industrial policy, and always will, if by this we mean the set of laws, regulations, and customary practices through which the federal government, by design and by accident, affects the actions and decisions of private industry. But if almost any action can have a ripple effect, exerting subtle or not so subtle influences on corporate decisions, how to weigh the impact on competitiveness alongside the other concerns of policymakers?

Difficult as this might be, the United States has not tried. Policymakers have talked about international competitiveness, but when they have acted, have not acted as if the impact on competitive ability matters very much. Disarray seems as common today — illustrated by the brouhaha in 1989 over the FSX agreement with Japan — as when advocates of industrial policy called, a dozen years ago, for coherence and continuity in dealing with the problems of declining industries. In effect, the policymaking system has not caught up with the events of the past two decades. Major tax bills with substantial implications for the competitive position of American industries passed Congress in 1981 and 1986 with little analysis of those implications. Neither bill allayed the concerns of analysts who see financing difficulties underlying the competive slide of American industry. In a very different example, the United States deregulated its telecommunications industry largely for domestic reasons and out of government's inability to cope with the impact of technological change in this sector,[17] while other countries made their choices for reasons of trade and competition. Beyond the R & D funding for SEMATECH and a few other consortia, and minor changes to antitrust law, policies affecting strategic partnerships have been notable for their absence.

Federal agencies do pay somewhat more attention to the impacts of day-to-day decisions on competitiveness than fifteen or twenty years ago, although it is fair to say that international competitiveness still plays a minor role in American policymaking compared with countries that have learned to export as effectively as Japan, West Germany or South Korea. A *laissez-faire* façade covers a mosaic of policies that inevitably affects the competitive position of some firms and some industries more than others. Lobbying by business, labour and other interest groups focuses, not surprisingly, on matters of short-term advantage or disadvantage: surging imports of semiconductors or machine tools; tax treatment of real estate. Industry's traditional shopping list — trade protection, R & D subsidies, regulatory exemptions, tax cuts — has not changed much over the years. Businessmen quite naturally seek to exploit the opportunities that come with twists and turns in Federal policy. For their part, politicians often tend to view interest groups as tactical allies in the short run, rather than partners in an ongoing effort to develop a consistent policy. Under these circumstances, policymaking can easily devolve into a string of contests over the issues of the day. Meanwhile, changes in the world economy, in business practices and in competitive standing take their course, all too often catching government decisionmakers unaware.

Something more is needed. *Ad hoc* policymaking may have worked in the past, but today, with shrinking or vanishing technological advantages, the United States must find a new framework, as well as a new set of tools, for dealing with shifts in international competitivness and their consequences. Because these shifts are structural, reflecting deep-seated currents in the international economy, and because of the many centres of decisionmaking in the federal government, the United States' response must be systemic. This means bringing objectives related to competitiveness and structural adjustment closer to the forefront of the policymaking process. Because competitive ability can only be evaluated on a sectoral basis, it implies detailed and disaggregated analyses of the American economy. Effective policymaking must be informed by concrete understanding of how industries function, on the shopfloor as well as in the boardroom. While such analyses can only be carried out sector-by-sector, this need not imply that federal policies must or will be sectoral. As part of this process, the United States will have to rethink where its interests lie, given the interpenetration of national economies through direct investment, strategic partnerships and other forms of cross-border linkages.

Conclusion

During the 1950s and 1960s, the automobile industry symbolized American industrial might. Building cars — that was something American firms could do better than anyone else. As it became clear, around 1980, first that American production costs were not competitive and, later, that foreign firms were out-engineering Detroit, many in the United States took consolation in the mistaken view that this was a smokestack industry. Semiconductors were different; here was the outpouring of Yankee ingenuity for the postindustrial age, a case where creative engineering and entrepreneurial drive set Americans apart. By the late 1980s, it was clear that these strengths — and they do remain strengths — could not stand alone.

As the rapid competitive slide of the semiconductor industry suggests, in the 1990s, few American firms will be able to aspire to positions other than first among equals. They will have to accommodate themselves to world economic currents, react to competitors' strategies as well as initiate their own and learn to exploit the possiblities of strategic alliances as effectively as firms in Europe and Japan, where alliances originated in positions of relative weakness.

International investments and partnerships are nothing new for Detroit, but American automakers have little experience in managing business arrangements with foreign firms whose competitive postures are improving at a time when their own are in decline. In microelectronics, domestic undertakings, such as the joint production venture U.S. Memories, overshadowed collaborative arrangements with foreign manufacturers in the 1980s. Still, the larger American merchant firms clearly intended to couple participation in American-based consortia with partnerships involving Japanese firms. The failure of U.S. Memories in January 1990, illustrates how hard it is for American suppliers to forge responses that can endure among companies that have competed fiercely for years. Can American firms ultimately master such skills? Can they manage their involvement in strategic alliances so that they will learn more, and more rapidly, than foreign competitors?

The corollary follows. What sorts of policy initiatives by the United States' government could help American firms? Here the starting point must be to recognize that only when an economy is examined sector by sector will the underlying causes of competitive shifts in industries as different as automobiles and microelectronics begin to emerge. Policymakers can no longer limit their attention to macroeconomic indicators or abstract debates over antitrust. The United States' government makes decisions every day that affect the competitive environment for American firms and industries. Sooner or later, it will have to find ways of making this constant stream of decisions — some in Congress, others in executive agencies, not a few ending up on the desk of the president — yield policies with positive outcomes for American competitiveness.

Notes

1. This chapter draws on a number of studies at the Office of Technology Assessment, on which many people have worked; Robert R. Miller, of the University of Houston, deserves special mention for his contributions to the topics covered. Portions of the chapter are based on J. A. Alic, 'Industrial Policy: Politics and Economics', presented at Electro/84, Session on Technological Economic Issues and Industrial Competition, Institute of Electrical and Electronic Engineers, Boston, Mass., 15–17 May, 1984
2. See Chapter 4 in this volume.
3. See Chapter 6 and 9 in this volume.
4. For details see OTA, 1981.
5. On complementary assets, see Teece, 1987, p. 65. To justify the term 'strategic', a partnership or alliance should provide long-term support for a company's core business activities. Note that, by this reasoning, many inter-firm agreements involving R & D alone fail to qualify as strategic — for example, when firms view participation as insurance against technological surprise.

6. See, for example, Fuss and Waverman, 1986; Katz, Kochan, and Keefe, 1987, p. 685; Cusumano, 1988, p. 29; Krafcik, 1988, p. 41; Florida, *et al.* 1988, p. 3 and Shimada, 1989, p.183.
7. 'Honda's R & D Mastermind', *Automotive Industries*, November 1987, p. 52. More generally, see Takeuchi and Nonaka, 1986, p. 137; Clark, *et al.*, 1987, p.729; McElroy, 1988, p. 46; Clark and Fujimoto, 1988.
8. The 1980 estimate comes from OTA, 1981; the more recent figure from Womack, 1988, p.301. On alliances in this industry, also see Rosegger, 1989.
9. Miller and Alic, 1986, p.101. More generally, see OTA, 1983.
10. For details see Haklisch and Vonortas, 1988.
11. Kehoe, 1989, p.1; 'Mips licensing chips to Siemens and NEC', *New York Times*, 9 February 1989, p. D4; Schmitt, 1989, p. B2; Waldman, 1987, p. 8.
12. OTA, 1989.
13. Concern over the savings rate and its impacts on cost and availability of capital go back many years. See, for example, U.S. Congress, 1976. For a recent perspective, see Hatsopoulos, *et al.*, 1988, p. 299.
14. The competitive standing of a sector depends on the ability of the firms populating it to design, develop, produce and market their goods or services relative to foreign firms. For a more comprehensive treatment, see Alic, 1987, p. 1.
15. *Global Competition: The New Reality*, Volumes I and II, Washington, DC, US Government Printing office, January 1985.
16. *Defense Semiconductor Dependency: A Report of the Defense Science Board*, Washington, DC: Department of Defense, Office of the Under Secretary for Acquisition, February 1987.
17. For a more detailed discussion see Chapter 8 in this volume.

References

Alic, J.A., 1987, 'Evaluating Industrial Competitiveness at the Office of Technology assessment', *Technology In Society*, **9**, pp. 1–17.

Chandler Jr, Alfred D. (1962), *Strategy and Structure: Chapters in the History of the American Industrial Enterprise*, Cambridge, Mass: Massachusetts Institute of Technology Press.

Clark, K.B. and Fujimoto, T., (1988), 'Overlapping Problem Solving in Product Development', Cambridge, Mass Harvard Business School, Working Paper, No. 87, April.

— Chew, W.B. and Fujimoto, T. (1987), 'Product Development in the World Auto Industry', *Brookings Papers on Economic Activity*, **3**, pp. 29–39.

Cusumano, M.A., (1988), 'Manufacturing Innovation: Lessons from the Japanese Auto Industry', *Sloan Management Review,* Fall, pp. 39.

Florida, R., Kenney, M. and Mair, A. (1988), 'The Transplant Phenomenon: Japanese Auto Manufacturers in the United States', *CUED Commentary*, Winter.

Fuss, M. and Waverman, L. (1986), 'The Extent and sources of Cost and Efficiency Differences Between US and Japanese Automobile Producers', Cambridge, Massachusetts: Working Paper No. 1849, National Bureau of Economic Research, March.

Haklisch, C.S. and N.S. Vonortas, 1988, 'The U.S. Semiconductor Industry: Export Controls and The International Technical System', Rensselaer Polytechnic Institute, Center for Science and Technology Policy, June.

Hatsopoulos, G.N., Krugman, P.R. and Summers, L.H. (1988), 'U.S. Competitiveness: Beyond the Trade Deficit,' *Science* (July 15), pp. 209–307.

'Honda's R & D Mastermind,' *Automotive Industries*, November 1987, p. 52.

Katz, H.C., Kochan, T.A. and Keefe, J.H. (1987), 'Industrial Relations and Productivity in the U.S. Autombile Industry,' *Brookings Papers on Economic Activity*, **3**, pp. 685–727.

Kehoe, L. (1989), 'Motorola Sues Hitachi in US,' *Financial Times*, (January 20), p. 1.

Krafcik, J.F., 1988, 'Triumph of the Lean Production System,' *Sloan Management Review* (Fall), pp. 41–52.

McElroy, J., 1988, 'Outsourcing: The Double-Edged Sword,' *Automotive Industries*, March 1988, p. 46.

Miller, R.R and Alic, J.A. (1989), 'Financing Expansion in an International Industry: The Case of Electronics,' *International Journal of Technology Management*, **1**., pp. 101–117.

'MIPS Licenses Chips to Siemens and NEC,' *New York Times*, February 9, 1989, p. D4.

OTA, (1981), *U.S. Industrial Competitiveness: A Comparison of Steel, Electronics and Automobiles*, (Washington, D.C.: Office of Technology Assessment, July).

— (1983), *International Competitveness in Electronic* (Washington, DC: Office of Technology Assessment, November).

Rosegger, G. (1989), '*Cooperative Research and Development: The Industry–University-Government Relationship*', in A. N. Link and G. Tassey, (eds.), Boston: Kluwer.

Schmitt, H.R., (1989), 'Ruling in Intel Copyright Case Splits analysts', *Wall Street Journal*, 9 February , p. B2.

Shimada, H. (1989), 'Japanese Management of Auto Production in the United States: An Overview of 'Humanware Technology' in K. Yamamura, (ed.), *Japanese Investment in the United States: Should We Be Concerned?*, (Seattle, Society for Japanese Studies, pp. 183–205.

Takeuchi, H. and Nonaka, I. (1986),'The New Product Development Game', *Harvard Business Review*, January–February, pp. 137–146.

Teece, D. J. (1987), 'Capturing Value from Technological Innovation' in B. R. Guile and H. Brooks, (eds.), *Technology and Global Industry: Companies and Nations in the World Economy*, Washington, D.C., National Academy Press, pp. 65–95.

United States President's Commission on Industrial Competitiveness, (1986), *Global Competition: The New Reality*, Volumes I and II, Washington, DC: U.S. Government Printing office, January.

United States, (1989), 'SEMATECH: Progress and Prospects', Report of the Advisory Council on Federal Participation in SEMATECH.

US Congress, (1976), *Capital Formation*, hearings, Joint Economic Committee, Congress of the United States 9 June, 1976, (Washington, DC, US Government Printing Office.

US Department of Defense (1987), *Defense Semiconductor Dependency: A Report of the Defense Science Board*, Washington, DC, Department of Defense, Office of the Under Secretary for Acquisition, February.

Waldman, P. (1987), 'Advanced Micro Asks $1 Billion in Intel Lawsuit', *Wall Street Journal*, 19 May, p. 8.

Womack, J.P. (1988), 'Multinational Joint Ventures in Motor Vehicles' in D. C. Mowery (ed.), *International Collaborative Ventures in U.S. Manufacturing*, Cambridge, Mass, Ballinger, pp. 301–48.

8 Strategic partnerships in telecommunications: the role of states in determining comparative advantage

Barbara Jenkins

Introduction

As in many other high technology industries, strategic partnerships have swept the global telecommunications industry. Spurred by deregulation and the overlap of telecommunications and computer technologies, corporate alliances, joint ventures and acquisitions have become an important tool for telecommunications companies trying to stay afloat in what has become a fiercely competitive industry. This chapter reviews the partnership patterns of firms in the telecommunications industry and seeks to explain the choices companies make among these various forms of investment. Because of the highly politicized nature of the industry, however, and because a strong position in the domestic market provides a crucial backdrop for a firm's strategic positioning internationally, the role home governments play is also critical to a company's international success. Strategic partnerships alone will not guarantee the global competitive advantage of a country's domestic telecommunications industry.

This chapter thus focuses on two levels of competitive strategy: firm-level efforts such as alliances, joint ventures and acquisitions that are part of a company's corporate strategy, and macro-level factors such as government policies that affect domestic telecommunications companies. These two levels of competition roughly correspond to what Pierre Musso has characterized as a 'war of movement', in which firms seek competitiveness on the international level through strategic partnerships, and a 'war of position', in which the national market is used as a backdrop for international deployment. (Musso, 1988)

The war of movement, strategic positioning in the telecommunications industry

Changes in the regulatory and technological environment of the telecommunications industry have placed new demands on producers of telecommunications goods and services. In the regulatory sphere, the deregulation of various national networks has created new market opportunities for producers from abroad. This is particularly true for the United States, whose large telecommunications markets and open regulatory policies make it especially appealing to foreign producers. Consequently, numerous foreign firms have entered into partnerships with U.S. firms in order to gain market access.

American deregulation spurred a series of alliances in the industry in another sense as well. In 1980, the Federal Communication Commission's (FCC) Computer Inquiry II ruled that AT&T would be allowed to provide computer-related products and services after 1983, provided that it did so through an arms-length subsidiary. In 1982, the government abandoned its antitrust suit against IBM, freeing it to compete with AT&T in computer-driven telecommunications systems. These changes placed AT&T in direct competition with IBM, a rivalry which resulted in a series of arrangements and rearrangements of partners world-wide as each company entered and exited various product markets and other firms responded to their manoeuvres.

For example, IBM entered the long distance market in 1977 through its partnership with Satellite Business Systems and further consolidated its position in the market in 1985 by selling SBS and acquiring a 16 per cent share of MCI. In 1983, it purchased a minority interest in the PBX manufacturer Rolm, which it fully acquired in 1984. AT&T took a minority share in the Italian company Olivetti and entered into an agreement with it for desktop computers. It also formed an alliance with EDS in 1985 for system integration of special communications systems and began talks for the acquisition of the computer company DEC. Both firms also entered alliances with Japanese partners. Recently, however, each company began to recentre its activities on its core business and the stimulus for partnering emerging from this rivalry has subsided. AT&T has shifted from computer manufacturing to data networking and its agreement with Olivetti is floundering.[1] Similarly, IBM sold its shares back to MCI and its PBX subsidiary Rolm to Siemens in 1988.

Technological changes also pushed firms toward corporate alliances. First, the merging of computer and telecommunications technologies means that products that are connected to a network, like PBXs and local area networks (LANs), have to be consistent with the protocols of computers or other peripherals integrated into the network. Therefore, computer and telecommunications firms often work together to ensure compatibility between various aspects of network systems. Second, the merging of the two technologies led to a spurt of innovation in equipment, software and integrated circuits. Since keeping up with these new technologies is extremely difficult for any single firm, companies may collaborate to obtain complementary technologies (Pisano *et al.*, 1988).

Third, technological innovation in the industry has increased so rapidly that R & D costs in some product areas have become extremely high. For example, costs for the development of a digital central-office switch are estimated to be between $1.5–2 billion. With product turnover times anywhere from five to ten years, such investments are extremely risky. Given the high development costs in the switching industry, it is estimated that a firm needs approximately a 10–15 per cent share of the global industry in order to survive. This means that of the eight to ten largest switch producers world-wide, only five will be around in the 1990s. The mergers, acquisitions and joint ventures taking place in this area of the industry are thus part of a shakeout, as firms attempt to stabilize an uncertain environment and position themselves strategically.

Alongside the more traditional forms of investment taking place in the central-office switching market, telecommunications companies have also pursued novel strategies such as non-equity cooperative agreements and minority equity involvements. Table 8.1 presents data for several of the major telecommunications agreements signed in the period 1985–9. No discernable pattern in the preferences of firms for equity versus non-equity arrangements emerges from this table. Other more comprehensive studies, however, suggest that a relationship between the function of an agreement and its organizational form does exist.

Using data on 117 agreements in the telecommunications industry drawn from the FOR database, Pisano *et al.* found that agreements involving two-way R & D flows and technology transfer were more likely to be structured around contractual or non-equity forms of 'governance structures'. In contrast, they found that one-way technology agreements were more likely to involve equity investments. Using a modified form of transaction cost analysis, they argued that this could be explained by two factors. First, technological collaboration is often carried out on a project-by-project basis and this reduces the need to have a 'specialized governance mechanism' to conduct such projects. Second, if the companies involved are swapping technology, there is less risk of opportunism since both are contributing and are not using any other capital (Pisano *et al.*, 1988: 60). When R & D collaboration was combined with other functional objectives such as production or marketing, however, it was more likely to be organized in an equity form of collaboration. This, they argued, was due to the fact that multifunctional agreements involved the partners in more communication and coordination matters which were better organized through hierarchical or more formal channels. (Pisano *et al.*, 1988: 62)

The study also found that agreements involving production alone were more likely to be organized in traditional equity forms of investment. When they tested to see whether multifunctional agreements involving production were disproportionately driven towards equity forms, however, they did not obtain statistically significant results. Finally, they hypothesized that agreements involving marketing and distribution would be more likely to involve equity investment. They argued that because these arrangements often involved 'transaction-specific' investments such as specialized knowledge, after-sales service or rapid product innovation, they increased the burden of information flows between the supplier and distributor. However, they found no statistically significant trend in firms' choices between equity or non-equity forms of investment in this area (Pisano *et al.*,1988: 64–5).

These data provide only partial support for an explanation of the alliance phenomenon based on transaction cost arguments. While the argument did apply to R & D agreements, it was less successful in explaining the

Table 8.1: Selected alliances in telecommunications

1989	— DEC, Northern Telecom and Nynex form a data-networking joint venture.
	— DEC and Siemens form a joint venture in packet-switching gateways.
	— Olivetti agrees to distribute Northern Telecom's SL/1 PBX line in Europe.
	— AT&T and STET/Italtel form joint venture to manufacture equipment in the Italian market.
	— Siemens buys Britain's GPT.
	— Ericsson and General Electric form joint venture to sell cellular telephones in North America.
1988	— IBM sells Rolm to Siemens, maintaining 3.9 per cent share.
	— AT&T takes 10 per cent share in Sun Microsystems for joint product development.
	— AT&T enters into a joint venture with Amper SA (Spain) in micro-electronics and increases share in APT joint venture with Philips to 60 per cent.
	— Nokia buys Ericsson's computer business.
	— IBM sells its share in MCI.
1987	— Bosch buys 35 per cent of Jeumont-Schneider Telecommunications.
	— Northern Telecom buys ITT's holdings in STC of Britain.
	— GEC/Plessey merger in Britain creating GPT.
	— Matra-Ericsson Telecommunications is created to buy the French company CGCT.
	— CGE/Alcatel buys ITT's European telecommunications establishing Alcatel N.V.
	— IBM forms joint ventures in VANs with (a) Paribas, Sema Metra and Crédit Agricole (France), (b) Fiat and STET (Italy) and (c) Telefonica (Spain) and Sema Metrá in Spain.
1986	— Siemens buys GTE's Belgian and Italian business.
	— AT&T forms partnership with eighteen Japanese companies in VANs consortium in Japan.
	— IBM forms joint venture with NTT for network systems and services in Japan and marketing and R & D joint ventures with Mitsubishi in Japan for PBXs.
1985	— IBM buys 16 per cent share of MCI.
	— AT&T forms strategic alliance with EDS for system integration special communications systems.
	— British Telecom acquires 51 per cent of Mitel Canada.

Source: *Communications Week; Telecommunications*, various issues

organization of marketing and distribution agreements. Pisano *et al's* findings on R & D agreements, however, do corroborate Mytelka's argument that in periods characterized by increased knowledge intensity of production and rising uncertainty, non-equity R & D agreements provide firms with greater flexibility (see Chapter 1). She argued that in periods of rapid technological change, a firm's need to have a window on technological change but to do so flexibly was a key motivation for the formation of strategic partnerships. Several other factors bolster the flexibility hypothesis. R & D agreements, for example, are likely to be temporary once research on a particular project is completed. Since a single company in search of economies of scope may be involved in several such alliances, equity investments would be costly and probably unnecessary. Similarly, agreements which focus on discrete projects or functions such as interconnecting a particular product to a network or marketing and distribution arrangements may also not merit equity investments.

Multifunctional agreements, however, are more likely to be organized in the form of a joint venture or majority investment when they represent a decision by the firm to enter into a product area on a permanent basis. Because such agreements represent a greater commitment on the part of the firm, equity investments may be more appropriate. Joint production partnerships based on a similar commitment to enter a particular product market would also tend to be organized on an equity basis.

To test the flexibility argument, I looked at 130 telecommunications agreements drawn from the CEREM data base.[2] These agreements, signed over the years 1980 through 1987, all involve at least one European firm. The CEREM data base covers agreements in network services such as value-added networks (VANs) in addition to those involving central-office switches, private exchanges and other telecommunications equipment. It is thus slightly broader in its coverage than the data base used by Pisano *et al.*

If the flexibility hypothesis is correct, one would expect to see non-equity cooperative agreements predominate in R & D collaboration, interconnection arrangements and marketing and distribution agreements. Conversely, more traditional equity investments such as joint ventures, mergers and acquisitions would be more common in multifunctional agreements and in those involving joint production only.

The data bear out these hypotheses to some extent. For example, 76 per cent of the R & D agreements examined did not involve equity investments. Similarly, 60 per cent of the marketing and distribution agreements were either in the form of non-equity investments or minority investments. Finally, all of the interconnection agreements were organized through non-equity agreements. In contrast, 89 per cent of the agreements involving more than one function had equity investments. Of these, 66 per cent involved greater than 50 per cent participation. In terms of production alliances, 62 per cent of the arrangements involving joint production involved some equity investment. If minority investments are excluded, 50 per cent of the joint production arrangements were either joint ventures, majority equity holdings or mergers and acquisitions.

The transaction cost and flexibility hypotheses, however, go only part of the way to explaining a firm's investment decisions. Both frameworks have difficulties explaining changes in investment patterns over time. Transaction-cost arguments in particular are concerned with a relatively narrow universe of events — why a firm chooses a contractual (that is, non-equity) as opposed to an equity investment at a particular time. Thus, it cannot explain why a firm would be satisfied with a contractual marketing or distribution agreement at one point, then move to a merger or acquisition later on.[3]

A different way to look at this question is to consider mergers and acquisitions, joint ventures and non-equity cooperative agreements as alternative methods to stabilize rapidly changing market situations. From this perspective, the market conditions that firms confront will affect their choice of how to organize an investment. As those conditions change, so, too, will the preference for one strategy over another. A company wishing to expand its market access in order to amortize high R & D or production costs or to gain economies of scale could simply do so by entering a marketing and distribution alliance with another company. This was the pattern followed by many producers of customer premises equipment such as PBXs throughout most of the 1980s.

But in an industry such as central-office switching, this solution would not fully resolve the problems facing a firm. As noted above, the enormous expense involved in developing and producing a digital central-office switch means that all firms in this sector must expand their market share to 10–15 per cent of the global market. In a sector where total market growth is slowing down, competition for market share is a zero-sum game. To survive, a company must not only expand market share but eliminate potential competitors. In this respect, the economics of central-office switching are similar to those in the jet engine and aircraft industries discussed by Mowery in Chapter 4. As a result of these market considerations, a series of mergers and acquisitions took place in the 1980s as firms tried to buy a position in foreign markets while at the same time reducing competition in the market by at least one. Examples of this include CGE's acquistion of ITT's telecommunciations operations, the Siemens–GEC–Plessey deal and the AT&T and Philips joint venture APT.

Looking at the question from a market perspective means that investment patterns in any product sector could change over time. For example, as barriers to entry in the PBX market dropped in the mid-1980s, a number of smaller firms entered the market. Many of them entered into distribution agreements with other companies to obtain a share of what was then a rapidly growing market. Since that time, conditions in this market have changed. The growth in the PBX market has slowed as many customers opt to merge voice and data networks through T1 multiplexers rather than PBXs. In addition, the vast number of firms entering the industry led to a flurry of price-cutting as competition heated up, resulting in rather slim profit margins. Consequently, the PBX market appears to be entering a shake-out period similar to that in central-office switching.[4] One of the first signs of this was IBM's sale of its PBX subsidiary Rolm to Siemens in 1989.[5] PBX manufacturers are also increasingly purchasing interconnection distribution companies in an attempt to consolidate their market share. (*Telecommunications*, 1989)

Similar patterns may emerge in network services such as value-added networks (VANs) and to a lesser extent in mobile telephone networks. Currently, a number of joint ventures and consortia are emerging in the United States, Europe and Japan to supply VANs to private customers. However, most analysts expect that a single dominant supplier will emerge in many markets since subscribers to the network will find the operator with the largest customer base the most attractive. As more customers switch over to this operator, it will benefit from greater economies of scale. As a dominant supplier it can also charge higher prices, thereby receiving higher profit margins. A similar phenomenon may occur in mobile telephone networks, if one network operator is more successful at attracting customers than its competitors. This is more likely to occur in countries such as Britain, where due to liberal regulatory policies, a number of personal communicator networks (PCNs) have been set up.

The form agreements take in the telecommunications sector thus appears to depend as much upon flexibility considerations as it does upon conditions in the market. From this perspective it is essential that we consider the role states play in altering market conditions which shape the strategic choices of firms and ultimately affect their competitiveness.

The war of position, states and corporate competitiveness

There is no question that the internationalization of the telecommunications industry has changed the role states can play in ensuring the welfare of national firms. Gone are the days when a monopolistic network operator could ensure an equipment supplier's economic viability through national procurement policies. Telecommunications companies can no longer rely on their domestic markets alone – now they must venture abroad into markets where automatic procurement contracts can no longer be taken for granted. Although the role of the state in the industry may have changed this does not mean it is no longer relevant. Indeed, states have an important impact on corporate strategies in the industry and on corporate competitiveness in at least three ways.

First, they can affect the shape and content of strategic partnerships themselves. As Mowery noted with respect to the aircraft industry, trade policies and regulatory policies in telecommunications can affect a company's choice of partners in a foreign market. Because telecommunications, like the aircraft industry, is considered strategic, most governments guard access to their domestic markets carefully.

Second, the relative openness of a market can affect the global competitiveness of national firms. Because economies of scale are so important in many branches of the industry, a strong base in the domestic market is basic to a company's international success. Openness can be measured by the relative liberalness of various regulatory or trade policies or by the closeness of the relationship between the network operator and supplier firms in the domestic market. More generally, the openness or closedness of the national market affects the ability of the state to offer a 'springboard' from which firms can successfully be launched into the international market, in the sense discussed by Delapierre and Zimmermann in Chapter 5.

Third, states can help firms acquire economies of scale by creating common standards across markets so companies can sell their products abroad. This issue is particularly important in Europe, where the fragmentation of national markets has hampered the progress of European firms in the past. In all three cases, failure by states to protect the interests of domestic firms can have major implications for a company's international competitiveness. In what follows, I will examine each of these points in greater detail.

State policies affecting partnership decisions

All telecommunications companies recognize that states regard their domestic industries as strategic in nature, both in a military and an economic sense. Frequently, companies seeking to enter a foreign market will take on a local partner to give them a national 'cloak'. There are two ways to do this; the first is a blanket approach where a company takes on a partner that is already present in a number of the markets it wishes to enter and thus is considered to be part of the local industry. This was the strategy followed by AT&T in its joint venture with the Dutch company Philips, a company with a position in many European markets. The second way is to take on a different partner in each market, whose home base is located in the country being targeted. This is the strategy generally pursued by Ericsson and Siemens.

The second strategy tends to be more successful because states often have very specific demands as preconditions for a foreign firm entering their market. Frequently, one of these demands is taking on a partner of their choosing. In addition, with the exception of the United States and Britain, most countries demand reciprocal access to foreign markets in return for access to their own. Combined with their desire to match up foreign entrants with their favoured local partners, this policy makes strategic partnering a highly political process.

An example of this is the political battles that raged around the sale of the small French telecommunications company CGCT. At first, it appeared that AT&T's acquisition of CGCT was a *fait accompli*. However, under pressure from the EEC and internal forces to sell the company to a European company, France re-opened the bidding in 1986. Three finalists quickly emerged — Siemens of Germany, Ericsson of Sweden and AT&T of the United States. The situation was further complicated by the French firm CGE's acquisition of ITT's telecommunications division in 1987. The acquisition gave CGE a strong position in the German market via the former ITT subsidiary SEL. In return, the German government demanded that the French give Siemens reciprocal access to the French market by allowing it to purchase CGCT.

In the end, Ericsson was allowed to purchase the company through a joint venture with the French company Matra. While political considerations were obviously paramount in this situation, many observers argued that the key to Ericsson's success was its choice of Matra as a partner. This, too, was a decision of considerable political significance in part because Matra had previously been involved with CGCT, but more importantly because it had recently been denied a partnership in the area of cable television. The French government thus had a strong preference that Matra be taken on as a partner.[4]

The close involvement of the French and German governments in partnering issues can be contrasted with the approach of the United States. Angered by AT&T's exclusion from the French market, former FCC chair Mark Fowler issued a Notice of Inquiry and Proposed Rulemaking in 1987 to 'comment on whether we can, and should, consider proposing actions that might include, among other things, limitations on access to U.S. markets for foreign-owned carriers, enhanced service providers, terminal equipment manufacturers, and core equipment manufacturers from jurisdictions that are "closed" to U.S. telecommunications service providers and equipment manufacturers. (FCC, 1986a). Such 'limitations' included making foreign producers subject to the same information disclosure requirements as AT&T.

The FCC initiative elicited a forceful response from other bureaucracies involved in telecommunications trade issues. A response coordinated by the Department of Commerce on behalf of the Office of the United States Trade Representative (USTR) and other executive branch agencies, argued that: 'The FCC is an independent regulatory agency and its statutory jurisdiction does not include the independent formulation or implementation of U.S. trade policy . . . The FCC has no greater authority to develop or implement U.S. trade policy, however, than it has with respect to antitrust policy, foreign policy, and national defense policy' (FCC, 1986b).

The document further maintained that the information reporting requirements that the FCC proposed imposing on foreign firms abrogated American obligations to comply with national treatment principles. As defined by the OECD, national treatment refers to the 'most' favoured firm in the domestic market. The executive branch argued that the proposed information disclosure requirements were equivalent to those placed on AT&T, which was in fact the 'least' favoured firm in the market (FCC, 1986b, 7–8). It is difficult to imagine a European or Japanese government official arguing that a foreign company should enter their domestic market on terms better than their strongest national competitor.

Another interesting incident in this regard was the response to a suggestion by the National Telecommunications and Information Administration (NTIA) that if manufacturing restrictions on the Regional Bell Operating Companies (RBOCs) were dropped, these companies' partnerships with foreign firms should be monitored. Under the terms of the 1982 Consent Decree, the RBOCs are prohibited from producing a variety of goods and services domestically, although they are allowed under certain circumstances to manufacture such goods abroad. The Justice Department recently recommended that such restrictions be dropped since they were reducing the overall production potential of the United States. However, NTIA argued that if these restrictions were dropped in areas such as the manufacture of central-office switches, it might risk adverse trade effects.

In order to mount an adequate challenge to large competitors such as AT&T, the RBOCs would have to enter into joint ventures with foreign companies. Unless these joint ventures were closely monitored, foreign companies could gain a large share of the American market at the expense of domestic firms, with no guarantee that reciprocal access would be granted elsewhere. The report concluded that in the absence of appropriate safeguards, such joint venturing would likely cause significant harm to American competitive technology and trade positions, and could pose the threat of destroying this country's indigenous central-office equipment manufacturing capacity'. (US Department of Commerce, 1987, iv). This recommendation was vociferously opposed by the RBOCs and if it is brought forward through legislation it would likely be opposed by the USTR and the executive branch since it does not grant foreign companies national treatment.[7] Since a 'free the Regionals' bill was introduced to Congress in April 1989 by Representatives Swift (Democrat, Washington) and Tauke (Republican, Iowa), this issue could soon become prominent in U.S. debates on this issue.

The openness of national markets

Because of the importance of economies of scale in the industry, a large market share in the domestic market provides a critical backdrop from which firms can 'spring' out into the international economy. As Borrus notes, this is an old and consistently successful strategy of Japanese companies. Because they can obtain scale and learning economies in their protected domestic economy, Japanese firms are able to recoup R & D expenses at home which gives them an advantage abroad. In addition, guaranteed procurement contracts at high prices at home means that they can use domestic receipts to subsidize sales abroad (Borrus, 1985).

In telecommunications, the relative openness or closedness of markets is often determined by regulatory policies. If the market is deregulated, with one or more network operators allowed to purchase from competing suppliers, the market tends to be more open. This is not always the case, however. In 1985, for example, Japan decided to privatize its national telecommunications firm NTT and divide it into central and local companies, along the lines of the divestiture of AT&T. Despite this apparent opening of the industry, in 1989 American companies were still complaining that the Japanese market remained largely closed to them.

One of the reasons for this is the close network of relationships among Japanese companies themselves and between these firms and the state. As Levy and Samuels showed in Chapter 6, Japanese firms have a long tradition of cooperating with each other. Because these established relations have worked very successfully for them, they have little incentive either to buy from American firms or to enter into partnerships with them in the domestic market. Perhaps more importantly, the developmental role that the network operator NTT has traditionally played in the industry left a legacy of close relations between the state and individual suppliers.

For decades, NTT helped to finance and develop joint R & D and production projects among private firms. Plans for its Information Network System project, designed to provide a fully integrated digital communications network by the year 2000, indicate that it intends to continue this role in the future. Since the project began, NTT has worked almost exclusively with Japanese companies to develop the switching and transmission technologies necessary for this network, estimated to be worth $80–120 billion in investment (Borrus, 1985, 26). In addition, although Japan has opened up its VANs market to foreign firms, the Ministry of Posts and Telecommunications (MPT) retains strict control over access to the market. All potential market entrants must register with the MPT, who then decides which firms will be allowed to enter the market and under what conditions. (Borrus, 1985: 33).

A similar situation exists in France, where strong ties link the network operator France Télécom, its research affiliate CNET, and French supplier firms such as CGE's Alcatel. France Télécom has used its relationship to develop one of the most advanced telecommunications systems in the world, with digital switches comprising 45 per cent of the lines subscribed in 1986. This is due primarily to the fact that Alcatel was one of the world's first producers of a completely electronic digital switch, the E10. This in turn was the result of the central role CNET played in working closely with Alcatel engineers to develop the switch, and to provide approximately 70 per cent of the R & D costs involved over the period 1970 and 1975. (Ergas, 1983, 13)

One result of this joint development was the construction of close, direct ties between France Télécom, CNET and CGE/Alcatel. This trio works closely together on a regular basis even today, a large percentage of Alcatel's R & D is financed by the '*credits d'études*' granted to it by CNET, and Alcatel's product lines are tailored directly to fit France Télécom's needs. In addition, there is a constant flow of personnel among these agencies, with engineers and managers moving frequently between France Télécom, CNET and Alcatel. Because of these closely-knit ties, an environment of mutual reliance pervades the industry.

Given this relationship, it is clear that Alcatel will continue to be France Télécom's preferred supplier. Even the changes advocated by the EEC's Green Paper on Telecommunications are unlikely to result in any radical changes in this relationship. First, while technically direct subsidies to firms would be disallowed under the Green Paper recommendations, French industry officials have indicated that there is no question that CNET's *crédits d'études* will stay, reinforcing the ties between Alcatel and France Télécom. Second, while new procurement regulations are to be enforced, the French and West German position on the opening of procurement policies is that access to markets should be negotiated according to reciprocal access criteria. While this option is strongly opposed by the British and the Dutch, it is probable that in practice negotiated access will prevail. It is unlikely that telecommunications authorities who are used to dealing with domestic suppliers that know the intricacies of their networks will freely give up their purchases to open-bidding processes.

Even on a regulatory level, France is far from opening its telecommunications market. In 1987, two '*chantiers de liberté*' were opened up to competition: (1) mobile cellular telephone networks and car paging and (2) VANs. As a result of these moves, private firms, both foreign and domestic, are now running telecommunications networks. This is a first for France, where the network had been run by a public administration since 1889 with private companies restricted to roles as suppliers. As a result of liberalization policies, alliances have developed between IBM, Crédit Agricole, Paribas and Sema-Metra in VANs and between Alcatel, Nokia and Compagnie Générale des Eaux in cellular telephones.

Despite these moves toward opening up the French market, it is unlikely that any major liberalization of the industry will take place. France Télécom still jealously guards its role as the primary network operator in both local and long-distance services. It strictly monitors any attempts to bypass this network — even the installation of PBXs is watched carefully by the telecommunications authority. And as the CGCT case showed, entry to the market by foreigners is still a highly sensitive issue.

The situation in Japan and France can be contrasted with that of the United States, which claims to have the most open market in the world. Foreign companies that have attempted to enter the American market would contest this claim, arguing that Bellcore's stringent testing standards make adapting to the American network onerously time-consuming and costly. They also note that the relationship between AT&T and its manufacturing subsidiary Western Electric means that much of AT&T's equipment procurement is done in-house. In addition, despite the fact that the 1982 Consent Decree cut the umbilical cord between the network operators (the RBOCs) and the major American equipment supplier (AT&T), the RBOCs still prefer to buy AT&T goods.

All of this notwithstanding, the United States can point to its $2 billion trade deficit in telecommunications (estimated to be $7 billion by 1995) to illustrate the relative openness of its market. After the Canadian-based Northern Telecom, the German firm Siemens seems to have established itself as the third central-office switch supplier and Ericsson is also making progress in cellular telephone networks. While the infiltration of foreign companies has not seriously damaged the position of the United States' 'national champion' AT&T to date, there are signs that challenges could be brewing in the future, particularly if the RBOCs acquire manufacturing capacities in areas such as central-office switching through joint ventures with foreign companies. Such a scenario is entirely possible in view of the conflictual relations that exist between the RBOCs and AT&T.

The conditions of the Consent Decree put AT&T in the contradictory position of having the RBOCs as both its biggest customers and its biggest suppliers (in terms of supplying access to local-exchange networks.) This has resulted in great difficulties for AT&T: while divisions such as Network Systems are anxious to maintain good relations with the RBOCs in order to sell AT&T equipment to them, other divisions concerned with regulatory affairs are determined to push the RBOCs into greater concessions in terms of access charges.

Further conflicts have arisen between the Centrex services offered by the RBOCs and the PBX systems offered by AT&T. While Centrex services provide many of the same systems as PBXs, they are integrated into a central-office switch. The RBOCs and AT&T are thus competing in an area where the product of one — Centrex — was effectively supplied by a central-office switch manufactured by the other company. The RBOCs accused AT&T of focusing on the development of functions for its PBXs instead of enhancing Centrex capabilities in order to boost PBX sales.

The RBOCs and AT&T also compete to acquire government contracts. In a 1988 scandal, the Senate Government Affairs Committee and the General Services Administration investigated whether three Bell companies cheated in their attempts to gain government contracts. The investigation was prompted by AT&T's complaint that the GSA leaked confidential information to the 'Baby' Bells about AT&T's bid. With AT&T constantly providing information to implicate the RBOCs, customer relations were hardly smooth. In addition, AT&T has consistently opposed the RBOCs' efforts to obtain deregulation in manufacturing and information services because of the obvious harm it would do to its business.

These conflicts have caused a decided rift in relations between AT&T and the RBOCs. As Executive Vice-President for External Affairs Al Partoll said, 'If we permit our relationship to be determined by the fact that both of us fear each other, it would paralyze the industry'. (*Wall Street Journal*, 1988). Partoll's concern is justified. It is estimated that the RBOCs bought $5 billion of AT&T's $6.2 billion in equipment sales in 1986. Already, RBOC purchases from AT&T have fallen from 92 per cent of total procurement in 1982 to 57 per cent in 1986 (Deptartment of Commerce, 1987: 21). Unless AT&T recoups these lost sales in foreign markets, it could be headed for difficulties.

Developing standards

Standards can also be used to open or close domestic markets to foreign firms. By adopting a different standard for its domestic market, a country can create a major barrier to the entry of future foreign competitors. At the same time, however, it may be denying domestic firms the economies of scale they might achieve if they were able to sell equipment designed for the local market abroad. The division of national markets because of different standards is particularly troublesome in Europe, where no single market is large enough to support a digital central-office switch producer. Obviously, only states can remedy a situation where publically owned PTTs are responsible for setting these standards.

One of the few things all EEC members could agree on in the EEC Green Paper was the need to set common standards. While movement in this direction is taking place in international organizations such as the CCITT and the ITU and European-wide organizations such as CEPT, one of the most important standard-setting endeavours is taking place through the EEC's RACE programme. RACE (Research for Advanced Communications in Europe) is a joint European project designed to introduce Integrated broadband communications across Europe by 1995. Created in 1987, RACE is also encouraging standards work in broadband technologies with a view to the provision of advanced telecommunications services in Europe by 1992.

In March 1989 RACE members agreed to prepare a memorandum of understanding on intra-European broadband links by 1990 and to establish a schedule for work in the area of standardization by the end of 1989. However, while some progress has been made, a number of major hurdles must be overcome before any meaningful results emerge from this project. Delicate regulatory issues regarding the integration of telecommunications and broadcasting have yet to be resolved. Also, it is estimated that $570 billion will have to be invested by public and private investors if RACE's goals are to be achieved (*Communications Week*, 6 March, 1988). Whether or not Europe can resolve these problems will have a major impact on the future competitiveness of its firms. Currently, the fragmented nature of European markets is considered to be one of the most significant barriers to the international competitiveness of European telecommunications firms. As to the pattern of alliances, while programmes such as RACE do not technically exclude non-European firms from participation in the process of standard-setting, they have tended to encourage European firms to look towards each other as potential partners.

Conclusion

Telecommunications firms have adapted to a rapidly changing technological and regulatory environment with a variety of investment forms. Through cooperative agreements, joint ventures and mergers and acquisitions companies have sought to stablize a market situation marked by high levels of uncertainty. In the absence of support on a domestic level from their respective governments, however, firm-level initiatives such as these will not ensure the international competitiveness of any company. By making possible greater economies of scale in the domestic market and by creating common standards across national markets, states can and do provide the support necessary for firms to become internationally competitive. Through such policies, moreover, states are altering the parameters within which firms chose among partners and investment forms. In a strategic industry such as telecommunications, politics and markets continue to be major factors shaping the partnering activity of nationally-based firms.

Notes

1. See Chapter 3 of this volume.
2. For a description of this data base see Chapter 5 of this volume.
3. For a more in-depth critique of transaction cost analysis, Chapter 3.
4. See *Communications Week*, 'Roundtable on PBXs', 24 July, 1989 for further details.
5. IBM retained a 3.9 per cent share in Rolm.
6. For a more detailed description of the CGCT affairs see Jenkins and Lodge, 1988.
7. It seems ironic that the NTIA is actually a branch of the Department of Commerce, which opposes abrogation of national treatment principles. It will be interesting to see the position of the Department of Commerce should such a recommendation be proposed as legislation.

References

Borrus, Michael (1985), 'Telecommunications Development in Comparative Perspective: The New Telecommunications in Europe, Japan and the U.S.', BRIE Working Paper No. 14.

Communications Week (1989), 6 March, and 24 July.

Ergas, Henry (1983), 'Industrial Policy in France, the Case of Telecommunications', (mimeo).

FCC (1986a), *Notice of Inquiry and Proposed Rulemaking*, CC Docket 86–494.

— (1986b), *Petition for Reconsideration* before the Federal Communications Commission in the Matter of Regulatory Policies and International Telecommunications, CC Docket No. 86–494.

Jenkins, Barbara and Lodge, George (1988), 'French Telecommunications in the 1980s' (A) & (B), Cambridge, MA. Harvard Business School.

Musso, Pierre, (1988), 'Télécommunications en Europe, politiques éclatés dans un espace unifié', *Médiaspouvoirs*, October, November, December.

Pisano, Gary, Russo, Michael V. and Teece, David J. (1988), 'Joint Ventures and Collaborative Agreements in the Telecommunications Equipment Industry' in David C. Mowery (ed.), *International Collaborative Ventures in the United States*, Cambridge, Mass., Ballinger.

Telecommunications, (1989), June.

US Department of Commerce (1987), National Telecommunications and Information Administration Trade Report, *Assessing the Effects of Changing the AT&T Antitrust Consent Decree* Washington DC.

Wall Street Journal, (1988), 9 March.

9 States, strategic alliances and international oligopolies: The European ESPRIT programme

Lynn Krieger Mytelka[1]

As large Japanese firms accelerated their investment in product development and in process engineering and began to experiment with new forms of industrial organization and new management systems, relatively smaller European companies remained cloistered within national markets. Lacking economies of scale and slow to move towards economies of scope, European firms in knowledge-intensive industries were rapidly becoming less competitive (Richonnier, 1984). Over the years 1963–80, for example, the European Commission's index of 'technological specialization' based on the share of high technology products in a country's total trade in manufactures showed relative stability for the United States, a substantial increase for Japan and a sharp decline in the case of Europe (Carli, 1983: 102). Replicating that index for trade in information technology products, produces similar disheartening results in so far as European competitiveness is concerned (See Table 9.1).[2]

European R & D efforts, moreover, lagged behind those of their Japanese and American rivals (see Tables 1.2, 1.3 in Chapter 1) as did the rate of technology diffusion in European industry — a *per capita* consumption of electronics components that is two to three times lower in Europe than in the United States or Japan, for example (Carpentier, 1987: 92). To the extent that technology diffusion is a key factor in the international competitiveness of firms and indeed of whole industrial sectors (Vickery, 1987; Ergas, 1987), the relatively low levels of R & D and the slow pace at which technology was diffusing did not augur well for the future.

Equally worrisome were indications that European firms, having experienced failure in earlier efforts at cooperation[3] were turning outwards in their search for new partners. In a survey of 497 agreements, culled from public sources and covering the five-year period 1980–85, the Centre d'Etudes et de Recherches sur les Entreprises Multinationales (CEREM) found that, insofar as the aerospace, biotechnology, information technology and the materials industries were concerned, on average only one quarter of the agreements involving a firm based in the European Community (EC) were concluded with other EC firms. In well over half the cases, the European firm's partner was an American company (LAREA/CEREM, 1986b: 14).

Other studies confirmed these findings. Intra-EC agreements, for example, made up only 14 per cent of the 974 agreements covered in the FOR data base. EC–United States agreements, in contrast, accounted for 26 per

Table 9.1: Index of technological specialization in information technology products*

	1971	1975	1979	1983	1987
USA	1.54	1.27	1.20	1.56	1.49
Japan	2.12	1.44	1.74	1.84	1.80
EC	1.04	0.88	0.83	0.80	0.84
OECD	1.00	1.00	1.00	1.00	1.00

*the share of 'information technology products' in total trade in manufacturers.

Source: calculated from the OECD Industrial Outlook data base (January 1989)

cent of the total. Intra–American agreements made up a further 24 per cent, United States–Japan agreements 13 per cent, EC–Japan agreements 8 per cent and all other possible combinations came to only 15 per cent of the total. Thus American firms were partners in 63 per cent of the agreements surveyed (OECD, 1986: 24). Similarly, a recent paper by G. Cainarca *et al.* (1988) revealed that agreements between Europe and the rest of the world represent 74 per cent of the 2,014 semiconductor, data processing and telecommunications agreements they surveyed over the years 1980–6. Indeed· in the information technology industry not only did intra-EC agreements constitute on average less than one third of all agreements signed by EC firms (LAREA/CEREM, 1986b), but with the exception of Siemens and ICL, other major German and British information technology firms–AEG, Nixdorf, GEC and Plessey — appeared reluctant to enter into cooperation agreements at all (see Table 9.2).

The global scope of the information technology industry, the technology based strategies for competition within it and the extensive use being made of cross-national inter-firm collaborative agreements thus appeared to be eroding the fragile autonomy of Europe's information technology industry (*International Herald Tribune*, 20 November 1984; *Le Monde*, 24 October 1984; Commission, 1983). Through their impact on the structure and organization of domestic technological capacities, inter-firm alliances would also shape patterns of technological specialization and hence economic growth (Chesnais, 1988). The need to ensure the coherence and dynamism of a European information technology industry thus became a central policy consideration.

The emergence of ESPRIT

By the early 1980s a small number of European firms within the information technology industry had begun to cooperate among themselves. The nucleus of this group included several former antagonists and competitors — Bull, Siemens, Philips and Compagnie Générale d'Electricité (CGE) (Mytelka and Delapierre, 1987: 242). When dissagregated by

Table 9.2: Twelve top European information technology firms: distribution of their non-ESPRIT agreements by partner, 1980–5 (By no. of agreements and % of total)

	Intra–12		other EEC		USA		Japan		Other		Total
	No.	%	No.	%	No.	%	No.	%	No.	%	No.
Siemens (FRG)	10	42	3	13	7	29	4	17		—	24
AEG (FRG)	2	67	1	33		—		—		—	3
Nixdorf (FRG)	2	67	1	33		—		—		—	3
Plessey (UK)	4	44	2	22	3	33		—		—	9
GEC (UK)	2	67		—	1	33		—		—	3
ICL (UK)	4	25	6	38	3	19	3	19		—	16
Philips (Neth)	11	40	1	4	14	52	1	4		—	27
CGE (F)	12	35	11	33	9	26	1	3	1	3	34
Thomson (F)	5	26	4	21	8	42	2	11		—	19
Bull (F)	11	41	9	33	5	19	2	7		—	27
Olivetti (I)	5	14	9	25	15	42	5	14	2	6	36
Stet (I)	3	23	3	23	6	46	1	8		—	13

Source: Mytelka and Delapierre, 1987: 241

function and by partner, their intra-EC alliances, moreover, showed an important difference from the general trend: they were orientated far more towards knowledge production than were their agreements with EC or American firms (LAREA/CEREM, 1986b: 30). While there were grounds for thinking that such differences might be built upon to strengthen the European information technology industry, how this could be done and by whom remained elusive.

Inspired by the Japanese experience with inter-firm research consortia and empowered by Article 235 of the Rome Treaty to promote the competitiveness of European industry, Etienne Davignon, then commissioner of industry in the European Community, seized upon the difficulties facing European firms and in 1980 invited Europe's twelve largest information technology firms to draw up a work programme for their industry. The European Strategic Programme for Research and Development in Information Technology (ESPRIT) which resulted, has as its objectives (1) to promote intra-European industrial cooperation in R & D in five main IT areas—advanced microelectronics, software technology, advanced information processing, office systems and computer integrated manufacture; (2) to furnish European industry with the basic technologies that it needs to bolster its competitiveness through the 1990s; and (3) to develop European standards (Cadiou, 1986: 3; Commission, 1987b: 1). A total of 750 Million European units of account (Mecu) were committed to ESPRIT I.

In 1987, the ESPRIT programme was renewed for another four year-period and the financial committment was increased to 1,600 Mecu (Commission, 1987, O–22). In contrast, the United States' Defense Advanced Research Projects Agency (DARPA) funds research at the level of over 1,000 Mecu annually (Bellon, 1986: 117).

ESPRIT I consisted of a pilot phase in 1983, during which thirty projects were initiated, followed by a first, second and third call for projects in 1984, 1985 and 1986 respectively. A first call for projects under ESPRIT II was made in 1988. A total of 225 projects were in operation at the end of the first phase of ESPRIT and a further 153 projects were accepted under ESPRIT II.

ESPRIT's rules of operation require that each project associate a minimum of two firms located in at least two different EC countries. Although there is no obligation to include university laboratories, public or private research institutes as partners, of the 225 ESPRIT-I projects, 71 per cent included at least one research organization (RO) among its participants, some as partners and others as sub-contractors. A number of important positive consequences have resulted from the promotion of R & D collaboration between ROs and firms, and these will be briefly mentioned below. The discussion that follows, however, will primarily draw on data concerning the participation of firms in the ESPRIT programme. It is based upon two sources: the CEREM ESPRIT data base compiled from the ESPRIT Project Synopses published annually by DG-XIII of the Commission of the European Communities (1986, 1987, 1988, 1989) and a recently completed study of cooperation in R & D between French firms, ROs and their European partners.[4]

From the outset enthusiasm for the ESPRIT programme has been high, with project proposals outnumbering projects retained by a ratio of five to one (Interviews with EC officials, Brussels, December 1987). Firms account for the vast majority of the participants in the larger EC countries. In France, for example, sixty-four firms and twenty-four research organizations ROs participate in a total of 154 ESPRIT-I projects. In smaller countries the proportions are more variable. Although Belgian participation in the ESPRIT-I programme is higher than that of Denmark (see Table 9.3), 77 per cent of the thirty-one Danish participating organizations are firms but only 64 per cent of the thirty-six Belgian participants are. In the first year of the ESPRIT-II programme, the rate of participation by Belgium firms rose to 70 per cent of the participating Belgian-based organizations, but it was still below the level of participation attained by Danish firms — 79 per cent of the twenty-four participating organizations.

All of the EC's older member–countries are major participants in the ESPRIT programme and their rates of participation appear to vary largely in relation to the size of the national information technology sector and to a lesser extent in relation to their overall participation in inter-firm cooperative agreements. But this tells only part of the story. For while firms based in France, the United Kingdom and West Germany engage in many inter-firm cooperative agreements outside of ESPRIT, the relative importance of their participation does not parallel that found within the ESPRIT pro-

Table 9.3: Participation by nationality

	ESPRIT 1		ESPRIT 2	
	No. of projects	% of total projects	No. of projects	% of total projects
United Kingdom	154	68.4	121	79.1
France	154	68.4	116	75.8
West Germany	127	56.4	108	70.2
Italy	96	42.7	77	50.1
Netherland	49	21.8	57	37.0
Belgium	49	21.8	33	21.6
Denmark	31	13.7	25	16.3
Greece	22	9.8	42	27.3
Spain	15	6.7	72	46.8
Portugal	6	2.7	28	18.2
Ireland	3	1.3	31	20.2

Total No. of Projects
ESPRIT 1 225
ESPRIT 2 153

Source: ESPRIT data base

gramme. Thus Hergert and Morris (1988: 103) report that among European countries, French firms are by far the most intensely engaged in inter-firm collaboration — 250 agreements over the period 1979–85. This contrasts with 200 agreements for British firms and, despite the size of its industrial sector, only 150 agreements for West German firms over the same period. Considerable promotion of European programmes and of European cooperation in general by the French government must thus be taken into account in explaining the high level of participation by French firms and research organizations.

ESPRIT and its critics

A discussion of participation rates within ESPRIT cannot avoid dealing with an earlier critique of EC programmes designed to promote cooperation among European firms — the market distorting and ultimately self-defeating nature of such efforts (Sciberras, 1987: 15). Data on the evolution of strategic partnering activity by European firms over time, however, does not bear out such criticism. Thus, despite a small increase in the intensity of partnering activity among European firms that may be attributable to the launching of ESPRIT and a number of other European programmes,[5] Hergert and Morris found in their survey of 839 agreements that it was the rate of increase in American-EC alliances over the years 1979–85 that accelerated most markedly (1988: 101). Similarly Cainarca, *et al.* argue on the basis of over 3,000 agreements between firms in the information technology industry that although

> agreements across European frontiers show a strong upward trend with their quota almost doubling from 9.8% in the period 1980–83 to 18.3% in the period 1983–86, this has been at the expense not only of extra-European agreements which fell from 78.6% to 72.2% but also of those within the same country, the latter suffering the most dramatic contraction over the period, falling from 11.7% to 9.5% (–18.8%). . . . Industrial cooperation among European firms is thus acquiring greater importance, though it remains firmly in second place behind agreements with the other areas of the world market. [Cainarca, *et al.*, 1988: 13]

Equally revealing are differences in the directionality of partnering activity for companies based in the major EC countries. French-based firms, for example, despite a history of nationalism in that country, have a higher propensity to engage in strategic alliances with American companies than do their European counterparts (See Chapter 5). Similarly, Hergert and Morris found that although French companies were the most active of the Europeans in inter-firm cooperative agreements, slightly more than half their agreements are with non-EC partners. West German firms were more Europe-orientated in their collaborative agreements outside of ESPRIT, with intra-European agreements constituting 57 per cent of their total (Hergert & Morris, 1988: 104). This variation across countries suggests that ESPRIT may be playing a number of different strategic roles for European firms. From the microperspective, casting participation in European programmes as simply a distortion in the process of partner choice obscures more than it reveals about the complexity of strategic partnering activity.

Accusations of anti-competitive behaviour have also dogged efforts to promote inter-firm cooperative agreements in R & D (Woods, 1987: 85–87). Concerned lest the move towards inter-firm collaboration be interpreted as a step towards the creation of a European oligopoly of 'national champions' in the information technology industry (Sharp and Shearman: 1987), considerable emphasis was placed at the outset on the pre-competitive nature of the R & D activities to be undertaken through ESPRIT. A classification of ESPRIT-I projects by function, however, reveals that over one-fifth of the projects were designed to produce working protypes with immediate market application, and that the share of these application-specific projects rose from 13 per cent in the pilot year 1983 to an average of 20 per cent in 1984 and 1985, reaching over 40 per cent in 1986 (See Figure 9.1). A further 12 per cent of the total, moreover, were standardization projects with direct market relevance, while as many as 15–20 per cent of the projects classsified as 'pre-competitive' research involved the development of products and processes which could potentially reach the market within one to two years after the project's completion (interviews with participating firms, 1988).

Within a few years of its launching, a different sort of criticism, however,

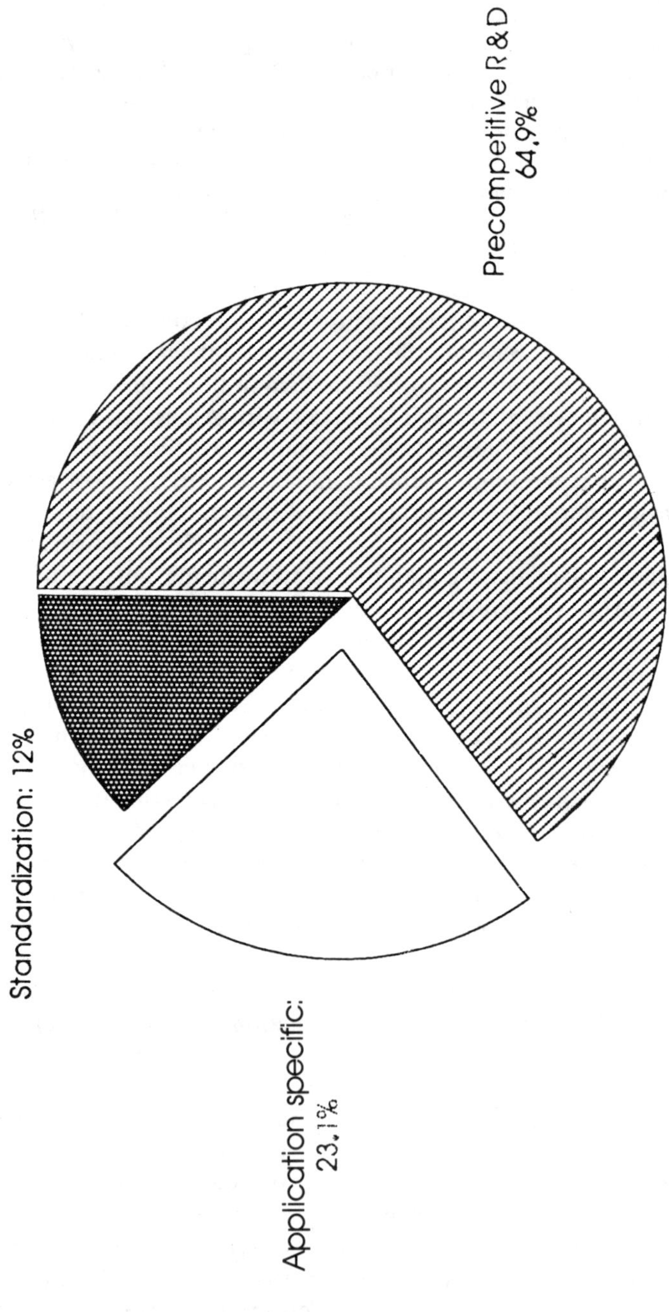

Figure 9.1 Distribution of Esprit 1 projects by function

had gained prominence. It centred on a growing concern that pre-competitive research was too far removed from the market to provide the basis from which European firms could compete internationally. The contrast between ESPRIT and the newer EUREKA programme was particularly telling. Launched in 1985 by the twelve EC and six EFTA countries on the initiative of President François Mitterand of France, and later joined by Turkey, the EUREKA programme fosters inter-firm cooperation in research but more specifically in development activities leading to marketable products in all areas of industrial technology. Unlike ESPRIT, neither the EUREKA secretariat in Brussels nor a steering committee of major European firms guides the choice of fields or themes for R & D. Since firms can initate projects dealing with any technology-related industrial problem, the EUREKA structure may permit a more flexible and rapid response to changes in the market.[6]

By 1987, the European Commission thus appeared to be more on the defensive against charges that ESPRIT projects lacked commercial significance than concerned about their possible anti-competitive effects. Although most ESPRIT projects were barely a quarter of the way into their research programme, the annual report on ESPRIT of that year stressed that some 108 of the ESPRIT projects had already 'produced a total of 143 results of industrial significance'. Of this total

> 27 have contributed directly to products or services currently on the market . . . [a further] 44 have contributed directly to products or services being developed for the market but not yet commercially available [and] 44 are being used outside the ESPRIT project, either within the company concerned or in another company . . . [Commission, 1988: 3].

ESPRIT II carries this trend towards a market-driven 'Springboard Europe' strategy still further by focusing on 'those sectors which offer the best potential for business opportunities or provide the basic technologies needed for establishing a competitive position in the most promising market segments' (Commission, 1987a, 0–2). It thus pays less attention to the design, manufacture and testing of DRAMs, SRAMs and EPROMs, where the scale of production, marketing and the ability to withstand the cyclical swings characteristic of the semiconductor industry are paramount and promotes instead the development of ASICs, where higher value added and lower volumes are possible and where closer cooperation between system manufacturers and semiconductor suppliers provide European firms with an advantage (Commission,1987a, 0–4). ESPRIT II also places considerable emphasis on expert systems and on application technologies in the field of office and business systems, notably in the development of workstations, networks and other forms of integration and in computer integrated manufacturing (Commission, 1989a, 0–2). The distribution of ESPRIT-II projects by function reflects this shift. Barely 50 per cent of the projects now fall under the heading 'precompetitive R & D', while over one-third can be classified as application specific and a further 13 per cent as standard-setting projects (See Figure 9.2). Responding to the need for flexibility, the

ESPRIT-II work programme, moreover, is being updated annually and it leaves unspecified a number of possible research topics within broadly defined technology domaines (Commission, 1987a, 1989a).

Critics have also challenged ESPRIT's funding policy, charging that with 50 per cent of the project costs borne by the Community, ESPRIT merely constitutes a 'European' subsidy for 'national champions' that have a history of dependence upon public financing (Wood, 1987: 94–7). Others have gone further, suggesting that this subsidy is of particular benefit to big European capital — in this instance the twelve European IT 'majors' (Braendgaard, 1987).

To a certain extent, EC data covering the first phase of the ESPRIT programme support such charges. Over the years 1984–8, fully 50 per cent of ESPRIT's budget was allocated to the Big twelve firms. The remaining 50 per cent was divided among small and medium-sized enterprises (SMEs), 14 per cent, other large firms 14 per cent and research organizations (universities, public and private research institutes) 21 per cent (Commission, 1989d, 17). Other data, however, make it possible to analyse the differing importance of these funds to the R & D budgets of the large and small firms that participate in ESPRIT.

In 1985, the EC created an independent review board to undertake a mid-term evaluation of the ESPRIT programme. In response to a questionnaire sent to participating organizations[7] the Board found that when university faculties are excluded only 6.7 per cent of the respondants reported that ESPRIT project funding accounted for more than 25 per cent of their total R & D budget, A further 18.4 per cent said that it accounted for between 5 and 25 per cent while 49.1 per cent said it accounted for less than 5 per cent of their total R & D expenditures (Commission, 1985: 64).

Interviews with French firms confirm these results and permit us to distinguish among the firms within these categories. Thus only in the case of small firms with limited R & D resources did we find that participation in two or three ESPRIT projects supplied the financing for 25 per cent or more of their R & D budget. For these small firms, ESPRIT projects had the added advantage of providing access to the research services of university laboratories for which they would otherwise not have been able to pay.

For larger firms ESPRIT funding barely accounted for 5 per cent of their R & D budget. Bull is a case in point. Over the period 1984–86 Bull participated in thirty-two projects with a total budget of 321.5 million ECU. Of this amount, half was paid by the EC. Assuming that in each of these projects the EC's half was shared equally among the partners, the per partner receipts over this four year period would have come to 55.7 million ECU which is equivalent to FF97.7 million per year or just over 5 per cent of Bull's 1986 R & D budget (Bull, 1986).

While ESPRIT funding did not represent an important 'subsidy' for Bull, the total cost of the thirty-two projects in which Bull was a participant came to just over 21 per cent of the total ESPRIT-I budget of 1.5 billion ECU. Bull, therefore, helped to shape over one-fifth of all ESPRIT spending. We will look further at the consequences of this below.

The impact of ESPRIT

In addition to the sharing of risks and costs, participation in ESPRIT projects has brought a number of other benefits to Europe's IT firms. First, by building inter-sectoral links through ESPRIT, the range of applications for existing or new technologies has been extended. Second, linking firms in five year long research projects with market objectives provides both large and small firms with an opportunity to observe the future shape of the market and contributes to a reduction of uncertainty in an industry undergoing rapid technological change (see Chapter 1). Third, networking through ESPRIT also promotes critical mass in research and development by enabling larger European firms to secure complementary technological assets from a range of different project partners. This has enhanced the ability of these companies to respond flexibly to change without adding to the inertia of the firm.

These points are well illustrated by data on the partnering activity of firms through ESPRIT. In the case of Bull, Philips and Siemens, for example, partner/project ratios show an important networking multiplier effect (See Table 9.4), with a dramatic rise in the ratio for ESPRIT II projects as compared to ESPRIT 1.[8] Thus Bull established links to 134 different firms through its 22 ESPRIT-II projects, a partner/project ratio of 6.09 as compared with 1.96 in ESPRIT I. For Siemens the ratio rose from 1.92 in the first phase of ESPRIT to 4.62 in the second phase, while in the case of Philips a higher initial ratio of 2.6 in ESPRIT I increased by a far small amount, to 3.85 in ESPRIT II. Similar results are obtained for small and medium-sized firms and they have been confirmed by interviews in the case of French companies.

Partners, moreover, came from a wide range of different and hitherto unrelated industrial sectors. These included major telephone operating companies in Denmark, Sweden, Italy, Belgium, the Netherlands and the United Kingdom; many of Europe's principal airlines and aircraft companies — British Airways, Aerospatiale (F), MBB (D), Aeritalia, Construciones Aeronauticas (E); automobile manufacturers — BMW, VW, Peugeot, Renault, Rolls Royce, Fiat, Mercedes Benz, DAF, SAAB, Porche, Ford and Audi; machinery and robotics firms—Dornier (D), Comau (I), Bertin (F), Matra (F), Electrolux Mecatronik (S), Robotiker (E), Bosch (D), Mannesmann (D), Krupp (D); chemicals and plastics companies — BMP (D), Pirelli (I), Basf (D), Hoechst (D), Elf (F), Montefibre (I), Solvay (B), Akzo (NL) as well as Banks, Health care centres and other service sector firms.

The ESPRIT programme has also produced a new openness towards Europe for firms and research organizations. This is particularly important given the earlier reluctance of European firms to cooperate. Nearly all of the over 200 firms and research institutes responding to the EC's mid-term evaluation, for example, characterized their collaboration within ESPRIT as either good (54.2 per cent) or very good (42.8 per cent). Fifty-seven per cent reported a total absence of conflicts and only 0.4 per cent noted that conflicts among the partners were 'frequent'. The vast majority of respond-

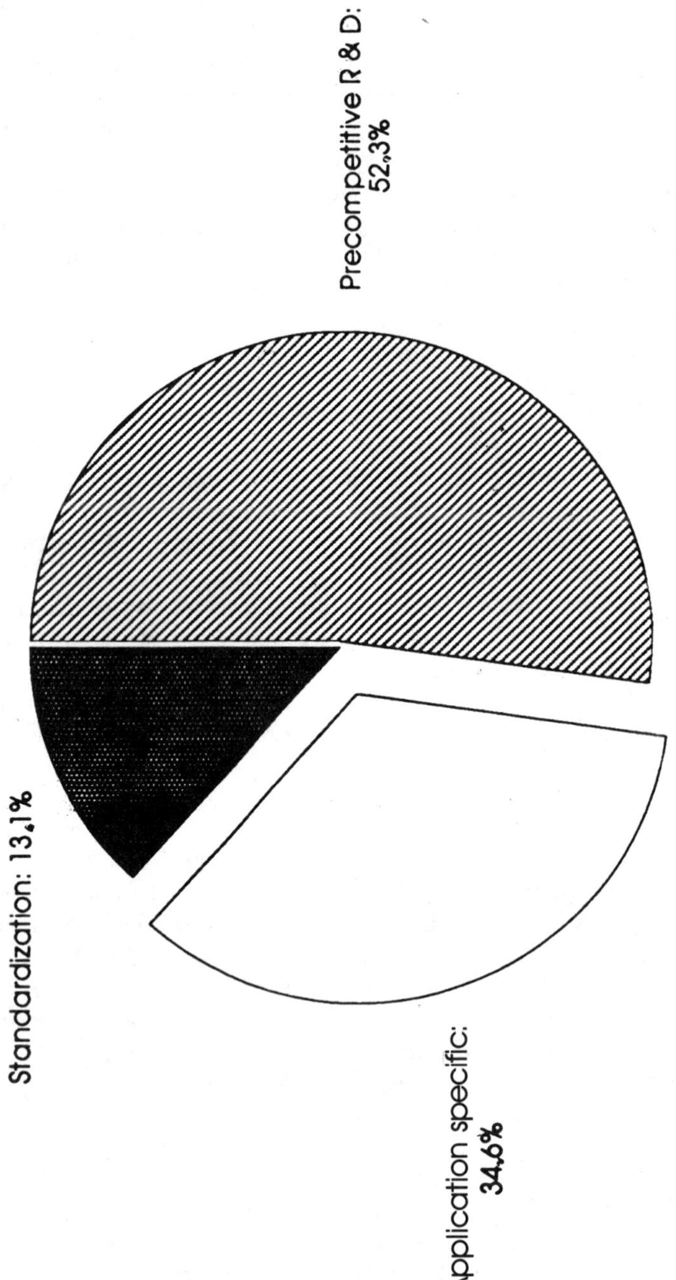
Precompetitive R & D:
52,3%
Standardization: 13,1%
Application specific:
34,6%

Table 9.4: Bull, Philips and Siemens range of partnering activity within ESPRIT

		Total projects	Total partners	F	D	UK	I	B	NL	DK	IR	E	GR
				Distribution of partners[a]									
Bull[b]	E1	32	63	15	13	10	12	6	2	3	0	2	0
	E2	22	134	25	20	14	29	5	9	2	3	12	10
Philips[c]	E1	25	65	15	9	12	16	4	2	3	2	2	0
	E2	27	104	16	17	19	18	4	4	4	4	9	4
Siemens[d]	E1	25	48	10	11	8	9	4	1	4	1	0	0
	E2	27	125	20	28	22	20	3	5	4	3	7	5

Notes: (a) includes only firms from France (F), Germany (D), United Kingdom (UK), Italy (I), Belgium (B), Netherlands (NL), Denmark (DK), Ireland (IR), Spain (E) and Greece (GR)

(b) in ESPRIT 2 Bull also had links to 3 Portuguese, 1 Swedish and 1 Finnish firm.

(c) Philips had links to 3 Swedish, 1 Finnish and 1 Norwegian firm through ESPRIT 2.

(d) Siemens had links to 5 Swedish, 2 Norwegian and 1 Finnish firm through ESPRIT 2.

Source: ESPRIT data base

ing firms and research institutions, moreover, felt that the exchange of information among partners was either good (59 per cent) or excellent (34.1 per cent). With regard to the broader issue of intra-European cooperation, 97.5 per cent of the respondants thought ESPRIT was stimulating such cooperation, and 45.5 per cent assessed this development as 'very' favourable for their organization while a further 45.9 per cent rated trans-European cooperation as 'moderately' so (Commission, 1985: Annex C).

A second EC evaluation carried out through face-to-face interviews with 210 participating organizations as a complement to 949 returned questionnaires produced similar favourable assessments. With regard to 'how well collaborative research worked with partners from other countries', 30 per cent responded 'well', 60 per cent 'adequately' and less than 10 per cent rated it 'poorly' (Commission, 1989d).

The impact of the ESPRIT programme on the behaviour of French firms and research organizations has been even more remarkable than the above figures would indicate (Delapierre *et al.*, 1988). Prior to ESPRIT, French firms were primarily engaged in partnerships with other firms, universities and research institutes based in France. Three factors account for this: first, participation by these firms in national programmes such as the Plan Calcul, second, the mission to transfer technology to National industry assigned to public research bodies such as CNET and INRIA and last, government procurement policies in defence, telecommunications and other high-technology sectors. When not involved with the state or each other, French firms licensed technology and signed distributional agreements with a number of American firms, but with the exception of Bull and CGE, they rarely had intra-European ties and almost never with a university or research institute.

Similarly, French research organizations had few contacts with foreign firms, and collaborative ventures were excessively rare. This, in the case of public ROs, was partly due to their mandate which orientated their activities towards the development of national technical capacity and the transfer of technology to national firms. Contacts with other research organizations were far more frequent, especially through scientific congresses but they did not usually involve collaboration.

ESPRIT was to alter this pattern quite radically. For many of the French firms and ROs that we interviewed, ESPRIT has had five important significant consequences for inter-firm and firm/RO cooperation. First, ESPRIT prompted these firms to look beyond national frontiers for their markets. The software industry, which had been heavily engaged in work for captive markets, frequently involving military applications, for example, was described by one respondant from the industry as singularly 'non-innovative.' This attitude, however, is changing as these firms, through their ESPRIT projects, begin to compete in the wider European market.

For small, relatively new firms the opportunities that this openness offers are particularly important since a close relationship between the state and large firms in France had earlier constituted a serious barrier to entry in the domestic market for these firms. Such firms, however, have not been alone in taking advantage of the ESPRIT programme. By cementing ties between technology suppliers and their clients ESPRIT projects enable SMEs from all European countries to widen their access to markets for new products and processes.

Second, participation in ESPRIT I has provided both French firms and ROs with a cachet of quality in research and development. This has led subsequently to invitations to join projects being developed under ESPRIT II and other European programmes and to enter into collaborative ventures outside of ESPRIT with partners with whom they have worked in the context of ESPRIT. Indeed only in rare instances did respondants from the firms and research organizations in which we interviewed feel that cooperation with all present ESPRIT partners would not be possible in the future.

Once again the experience of these French firms and ROs is not unique. Data on the alliance pattern of Big-twelve firms shows a similar willingness to engage in repeated alliances with ESPRIT partners. In the case of Siemens, for example, 50 per cent of the 48 firms with which it had collaborated in ESPRIT I were chosen as partners in ESPRIT II. Similarly, 43 per cent of the sixty-three firms with which Bull had collaborated in ESPRIT I and 38.5 per cent of the sixty firms with which Philips had worked in the first phase of ESPRIT were among the ESPRIT II partners of these firms.

Several groups of firms have also gone on to do new projects together in ESPRIT II. A typical case is a four-year project designed to develop a dynamic scheduling system for factories based on knowledge-based system

(KBS) techniques (Project 932). The project began in January 1986 and moved rapidly from design to development. By 1987, the first KBS was introduced into the Pirelli factory and a year later piloting of work-cell controllers began in a Philips computer-integrated-manufacturing (CIM) line for short-term production planning. By 1989 'the general system design had been finished for the dynamic planning task at Pirelli and BICC. The diagnosis KBS had been programmed for Pirelli . . . (and) demonstrations (were) . . . available for . . . diagnosis KBS at ARS, planning KBS at BICC (and) AEG . . . [and the] knowledge acquisition tool at Politecnico di Milano' (Commission: 1989b, vol. 6: 50).

Even before that data, however, most of the same partners joined forces to develop 'knowledge-based real-time CIM controllers for distributed factory supervision' (project 2434) and to test this system in a car-radio factory, a tyre-manufacturing plant and a cable-manufacturing plant. The second project which began in January 1989, has a three-year duration (Commission: 1989b, vol. 6: 116).

That there have been numerous 'iterative games' played through the ESPRIT programme, should not be taken to imply that all partnerships work equally well. Partnering requires considerable human intervention and the role of the prime contractor in managing the project is a major factor in its success. In addition, project size and project management techniques have a bearing on success.

Optimal size, for example, will differ with project type and the number of tasks to be undertaken. In the case of standardization projects, efforts to extend the range of potential users has led to projects with upward of fifteen participating organizations. Since complex techniques such as those being developed in ESPRIT tend to move rapidly up a learning curve as they are used, the more quickly and frequently they can be put to use, the more rapidly problems will be solved and the stronger the techniques become *vis-à-vis* their rivals (Arthur, 1985; Cowan, 1988). Thus, expanding the number of participants is particularly important in standardization projects where there are likely to be increasing returns to the use of new techniques. Application-specific techniques may also benefit from immediate trials in multiple domains and this, too, requires a wider range of partners to cover each of these domains.

Several French respondants, however, suggested that the relationship between the ease of cooperation and the number of partners was characterized by a 'U'-shaped curve — with cooperation easier to manage when there were fewer than four or more than eight partners. In the former case, cooperation was facilitated by small working sessions and greater coherence of interests. A larger number of partners, however, permitted a division of labour that replicated this small group environment. 'Distributed cooperation' (see Chapter 6) of this type is being practiced within ESPRIT II in the new large scale technology integration projects (TIP) aimed 'at meeting ambitious, well defined industrial targets' (Commission, 1987: O–83). During the first call for projects eleven TIP projects were approved, all of which have several of the European major IT firms as partners along with a relatively large number of other firms (Commission, 1989b).

Third, as one French industry respondant put it 'ESPRIT created an awareness of the technological potential that existed in other European countries' and this has stimulated the growth of inter-firm and firm/RO ties across Europe. But the point was also made by directors of several French research institutes when they noted that ESPRIT enabled them to bring together scientific and technical competences that were not easily found at the national level. As respondants from both industry and research argued, only by pooling their technological strengths can European firms and ROs attain the critical mass needed to compete in the global economy. It is clear from these interviews that even if these firms and ROs had not originally shared the view that ESPRIT was needed to promote European competitiveness, they have since come to articulate it as their own.

Fourth, ESPRIT I has encouraged some firms to engage in longer term (four to five-year) research projects, thus increasing the likelihood that they will establish ties with universities and research institutes. While ESPRIT II continues the practice of encouraging long-term projects, the shift away from basic and towards applied research and development may reduce the stimulus to engage in research on the frontiers of technological change.

Finally, within a number of French firms, ESPRIT served to enhance the importance of R & D decisions in the overall planning process. While it may not have transformed directors of research into the close confidents of CEOs, in every French company in which we interviewed, participation in ESPRIT projects was described in strategic planning terms. This was particularly true with respect to the role that precompetitive research can play in setting standards. We will return to this point later.

Building a European oligopoly

From a European perspective there are grounds for arguing that the ESPRIT programme has contributed both to the preservation of competition within Europe and internationally, while at the same time it has laid the bases for a future reduction in competition and the strengthening of an information technology oligopoly on a world scale. The ESPRIT programme, for example, has strengthened the European information technology industry as a whole by encouraging firms to establish European standards and harmonize interfaces in such a way as to overcome the disadvantages associated with the relatively smaller size of European firms as compared with their American or Japanese competitors. Conceptualized as a *post-hoc* product-related process, standard setting, however, has always played a strategic role in national economic planning, serving mainly as a device to protect national markets. Today it is becoming a competitive weapon in the arsenal of large IT firms as well.

Through the literature on technological regimes and national trajectories (Nelson and Winter, 1982) or technological paradigms (Dosi, 1982), it is possible to rethink the way in which the large numbers of product designs and approaches that coexist during the initial period in the evolution of new technologies is replaced by a dominant design or approach (Abernathy and Utterback, 1975). From our interviews with firms' participating in the ESPRIT programme it is evident that one of those ways is through the process of standardization. Thus firms in dynamic knowledge-intensive industries, see the need to develop standards at a far earlier stage in the production process — at the research phase itself. Collaboration in precompetitive R & D of the sort promoted through ESPRIT has a particular advantage in this respect because it ensures an early approach to the harmonization of technical solutions — environments, architectures, interfaces. At a latter stage in the investment process, common standards enable firms to develop compatible products and this, it is argued, is a prequisite to the creation of new markets in these dynamic sectors.

Standard-setting through broad-based networks can also lead to the creation of new barriers to entry.[8] The European IT majors have clearly recognized the role that standardization plays in international competition today. Their propensity to participate in standard setting projects is twice the average recorded in Figure 9.1. Scibberas, however, misses this point when he writes 'if standardisation is a problem, then schemes designed specifically to encourage collaborative design and development to achieve international standards are needed, not broad technical development schemes such as ESPRIT' (Sciberas, 1987: 21).

Although the process of imposing standards is necessarily long, progress on this front has already been substantial. One of the first projects undertaken within ESPRIT was the 'Basis for a Portable Common Tool Environment' (PCTE). The PCTE 'kernel' developed through this project consisted of basic mechanisms for process control — interprocess communication and an object-management system — user inter-face mechanisms and distributed facilities such as LAN interface and higher-layer protocols. This environment was developed in UNIX and Ada-based versions by the six partners: Bull, GEC, ICI, Nixdorf, Olivetti and Siemens. In France, through the National Software Engineering Plan, three firms — Eurosoft, Syseca and Bull — were also working on an environment for software engineering, Emeraude. By making Emeraude compatible with PCTE, it was transformed from a French project into a European standard. Within ESPRIT there are projects to port PCTE/Emeraude to other machines — VAX and SUN (PAVE, SAPPHIRE), to develop software engineering environments using the PCTE norm with Emeraude (ALF, PROSPECTRA, SFINX) and to link the British ALVEY project with Emeraude (SAPPHIRE). In total some seventy projects are currently using PCTE/Emeraude. As a result of the joint research leading to the establishment of this standard, it has been suggested in interviews with participating firms (Paris, February 1988) that the European software industry has gained a one-to-two-year lead over its American and Japanese competitors in software engineering.

The ESPRIT programme has also strengthened competition within

Europe by enabling small firms to work with large firms in a contractual environment that insulates them to some extent from takeovers by larger firms. In the first five years of operation and over 200 projects there was no instance of such a takeover. Even more importantly, under ESPRIT I, all partners had access to research results on an equal basis. Unlike more hierarchical forms of networking, therefore, the first phase of ESPRIT permitted considerable latitude for small firms to accumulate knowledge beyond that generated by the firm itself. Interviews with small firms in France support this generalization. Braendgaard also reports that 'some Danish ESPRIT participants say that they have reaped immense benefits in terms of speedy access to a wide range of new technologies and giant moves up the learning curves of high technology and international management' (1987: 196). ESPRIT II, however, will likely change this. Only 'contractors' will now '. . . have full exploitation rights to all project results', while 'associated contractors and 'subcontractors' who are not signatories to the contract with the Commission but conclude a bilateral contract with one of the contractors will have access only to their own work (Commission, 1989e, 4). Because 'associated contractors' do not bear their full share of the project's costs, this arrangement is particularly attractive to small firms.

Through ESPRIT, small firms from small countries have established contacts with partners in other EC countries who are potential suppliers and/or clients. In the case of Denmark, for example, twenty-four Danish firms participate in some thirty-one ESPRIT-I projects. Through these projects Danish firms have established links to forty-nine other European firms: thirteen French, eleven German, nine British, nine Italian, two each from the Netherlands, Belgium and Ireland and one from Greece. Among the forty-nine firms are all but one of the European IT majors as well as many of Europe's top aerospace, automobile and software engineering firms. In its twenty-five ESPRIT-II projects, Danish firms have established contacts with eighty-one European firms, fourteen French, eleven German, twenty-one British, ten Irish, eight Spanish, four each from Belgium and Ireland, three from the Netherlands, two each from Greece and Sweden and one each from Finland and Norway. This level of participation by Danish firms is all the more remarkable since Denmark is the only EC country involved in a parallel regional grouping, the Nordic Community, which has had its own fund for the promotion of inter-firm cooperation in R & D since the mid-1970s (Launet, 1988: 12). Danes, moreover, barely accepted the Single European Act in a 1986 referendum and remain, according to recent opinion surveys, least favourable to the integration effort (Launet, 1988, 13–14).

Once again, however, the impact is dialectical. Thus closer ties to firms in other EC countries are not without their costs for firms in small countries and by extension for the development of technological capacity in the economy more broadly. This occurs, Walsh has argued first because

> the nature of the science and technology developed by a small country may well be decided by the existence of a technological paradigm established outside that

country . . . Decisions about where to invest R & D funds and at what level, may therefore be imposed on the small country, and may not always correspond exactly to what is most appropriate for that country.

Secondly, to be competitive at all, the small country may have to spend a relatively large share of its resources on the development of these core technologies because a minimum level of R & D activity is likely to be necessary to ensure a sufficient degree of competence in the area. . . . [it will thus] have very little room for manoeuvre; . . . unless it has the considerable R & D and capital investment resources necessary to be the first in the world to establish a new technological paradigm. [Walsh, 1987: 92].

To the extent that the European IT majors, all of which with the exception of Philips are domiciled in the large European countries, exercise a predominant influence in shaping priorities in precompetitive research, then scarce R & D resources in these small countries leave little room for the generation of new knowledge relevant to domestic needs there. This Braendgaard argues, is increasingly the case in Denmark today (Braendgaard, 1987: 196). Data from the ESPRIT data base support his argument on the dynamics of involvement in the ESPRIT programme. Thus 51.6 per cent of the ESPRIT-I projects in which Danish firms and research organizations were participants included at least one of the large twelve firms and this figure rose to 56 per cent of the projects with Danish participation in ESPRIT II.

To appreciate fully this structuring effect, a more detailed analysis of the pattern of partnering through ESPRIT is needed. Table 9.5 presents data on the form of participation in ESPRIT projects through 1989. It gives considerable support to the argument that the European majors have played an important role in shaping technological trajectories through the ESPRIT programme. It also provides evidence of the importance of ESPRIT for SMEs.

Three types of participation are identified in Table 9.5. Type 1 are projects that involve only the European IT majors in partnership with each other or with research institutes and/or universities. Type-2 projects include partnerships between the majors and other firms with or without participation by research organizations. Type-3 projects involve only non-majors either in partnership with each other or with ROs.

Over the years 1983–9, several important changes took place in the pattern of networking through ESPRIT. One of the most salient is a decline in the use of ESPRIT projects as a means of networking exclusively among the European majors (Type 1). During the pilot year, 1983, more than a quarter of all ESPRIT projects had involved collaboration between the European majors to the exclusion of other European firms. This fell to an overall average of 11.6 per cent for all ESPRIT-I projects and the decline in this form of networking among the Big-twelve firms was confirmed in ESPRIT II.

The relatively small proportion of collaborative projects that involve only Europe's major IT firms, however, has in no way diminished the intensity of participation by the Big twelve in the ESPRIT programme nor has it

Table 9.5: Configuration of participation types in ESPRIT I and II

	Types (1)	(2)	(3)	Total number of projects
1983	8	11	11	30
%	26.7	36.6	36.6	100.0
1984	12	40	23	75
%	16.0	53.3	30.6	100.0
1985	2	52	28	82
%	2.4	63.4	34.2	100.0
1986	4	11	23	38
%	10.5	29.0	60.5	100.0
ESPRIT 1				
Total	26	114	85	225
%	11.6	50.7	37.7	100.0
ESPRIT 2				
1988/9	10	87	56	153
%	6.5	56.9	36.6	100.0

(1) projects involving the 12 European majors in partnership with each other or ROs
(2) majors with non-majors and/or with ROs
(3) non-majors with each other or with ROs

reduced their structuring effect. But it does indicate a change in strategy over the 1980s. We can begin to assess this change by looking at overall participation rates and at differences in the intensity of participation and in linkage patterns among the large twelve firms through ESPRIT.

By combining the figures for Type 1 and 2 projects, it is possible to estimate the overall involvement of the large twelve in ESPRIT. Far from a decline in their participation within ESPRIT, these figures show a slight rise, from 62.3 in ESPRIT I to 63.4 per cent in ESPRIT II, in the share of projects in which at least one firm is involved. Not all of the Big twelve firms, however, have increased their participation in ESPRIT [Table 9.6]. There is, in fact, considerable variation in the intensity of participation in the ESPRIT programme among the European IT majors and more importantly, a significant change in that intensity has occurred over the six year period.

While a comparison of Tables 9.2 and 9.6 suggest that there is a propensity for firms that engage heavily in inter-firm collaborative agreements — Philips, Bull and Siemens — to participate actively in ESPRIT and those with limited experience in alliance formation — AEG, Nixdorf and Plessey — to participate less actively in ESPRIT, there are several notable exceptions. GEC, which had relatively few partnerships outside of ESPRIT, intensified its collaborative relationships within Europe and is

Table 9.6: Participation by the European IT majors in ESPRIT I and II

	ESPRIT 1 No	ESPRIT 1 %	ESPRIT 2 No	ESPRIT 2 %	TOTAL No	TOTAL %
GEC	41	18.2	16	10.5	57	15.1
Thomson (SGS)	38	16.9	43	28.1	81	21.4
Bull	32	14.2	22	14.4	54	14.3
Philips	26	11.6	27	17.6	53	14.0
Siemens	25	11.1	27	17.6	52	13.6
Olivetti	24	10.7	10	6.5	34	9.0
ICL	24	10.7	8	5.2	32	8.5
AEG	22	9.8	17	11.1	39	10.3
CGE (Alcatel)	17	7.6	20	13.1	37	9.9
STET (CSELT)	16	7.1	8	5.2	24	6.3
Plessey	15	6.6	8	5.2	23	6.1
Nixdorf	12	5.3	7	4.6	19	5.0
Total projects	225		153		378	

second only to Thomson in the total number of projects in which it is a participant. In contrast, Olivetti, which had engaged in the largest number of alliances outside of ESPRIT, has significantly reduced its participation within ESPRIT over time in line with its overall R & D and marketing strategy (see Chapter 3).

From the data in Table 9.6, a pattern of concentration among the Big-twelve also emerges. A comparison of the linkages among these twelve firms through ESPRIT I (See Figure 9.3) and ESPRIT II (See Figure 9.4) moreover, shows a division within the Big-twelve into core and periphery members of a European information technology oligopoly.

Not only are some of the European IT majors active participants in ESPRIT, but as these two figures show, the linkages between them are particularly strong and among a small group of Big-twelve firms, these links are intensifying. Siemens, Philips and Bull, for example, have a history of cooperation among themselves and participation in ESPRIT I reinforced those links. BULL participated in six projects with Philips and eight with Siemens while Siemens and Philips participated in nine projects together. In addition, Bull participated in twelve projects with ICL, ten with Olivetti, nine with Nixdorf, eight with GEC, six with Thomson and five with CGE. Several other Big-twelve firms were important networkers within the Big-twelve in phase one of ESPRIT. GEC had intense linkages (participation in over five projects together) with seven of the Big-twelve firms, Thomson with six and Siemens and Olivetti with five. Even firms with far more limited overall participation, AEG and Nixdorf, for example, maintained intense linkages with several of the European majors.

Under ESPRIT II, however, the pattern of participation by the European majors and the linkages they established among themselves have changed.

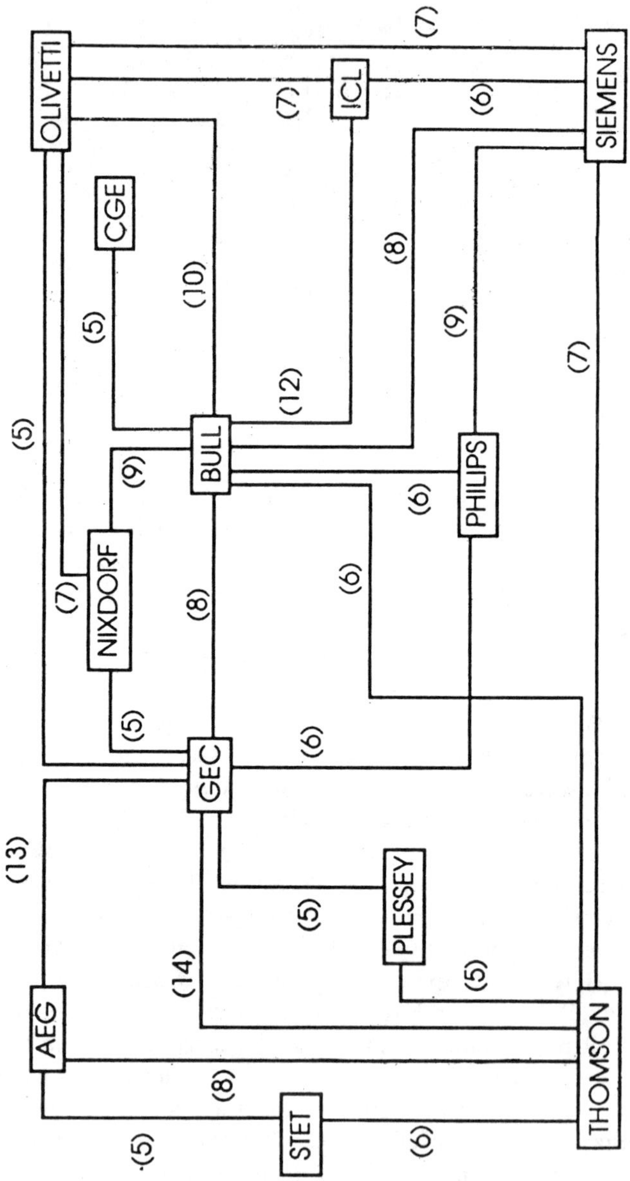

Figure 9.3 Linkages among Europe's major information technology firms through ESPRIT I

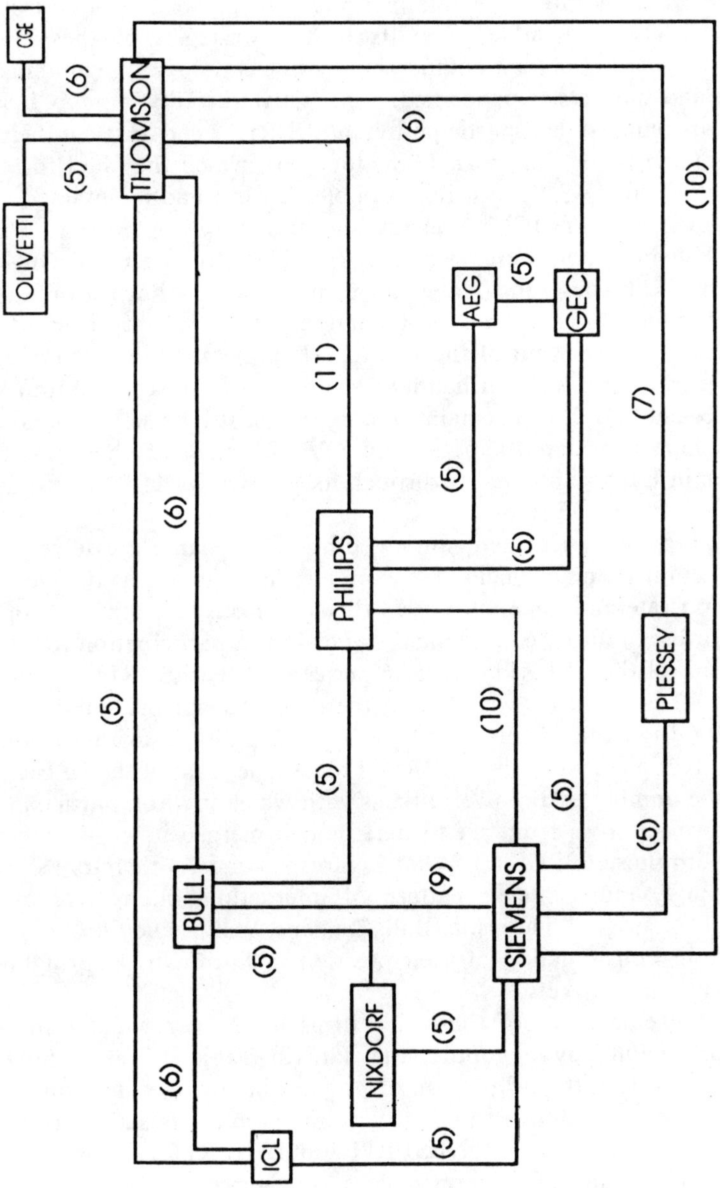

Figure 9.4 Linkages among Europe's major information technology firms through ESPRIT II

In part this reflects the shakeout currently underway in the European IT industry. Since the launching of ESPRIT, ICL has been bought by STC, AEG by Daimler-Benz, Plessey by an alliance of Siemens and GEC and most recently Nixdorf by Siemens.

But the division into core and periphery members of the European oligarchy is also indicative of shifts in the strategies of these firms, particularly in so far as their emphasis on core technologies, recombinative strategies and markets is concerned. Thus Olivetti, STET and ICL have substantially reduced their participation in ESPRIT 2 and have cut their ties to many of the other European IT majors with which they had formerly been linked. Under ESPRIT I, for example, Olivetti had maintained close ties to GEC, Nixdorf, ICL, Siemens and Bull (See Figure 9.3). Under ESPRIT II it has intense linkages only with Thomson. Stet and Olivetti's alliances with Japanese and American firms, however, have proliferated. GEC also reduced its overall participation from 18.2 per cent of the ESPRIT I to 10.5 per cent of the ESPRIT II projects (Table 9.6) and the number of firms with which it had intense linkages from seven to four (See Figures 9.3 and 9.4). But it remains among the most intensely active of the Big-twelve in its overall participation in ESPRIT I and II and has reinforced its position in European markets through its takeover of ITT's telecommunications activities in Europe.

A similar pattern is evident among other European Big-twelve firms. Thomson, Philips and Siemens, for example, have increased their overall participation rate and have intensified their linkages with other European major IT firms. In the case of Siemens, for example, participation rose from 11.1 per cent of the ESPRIT I to 17.6 per cent of the ESPRIT II projects and from intense linkages with five of the majors to intense linkages with seven of the Big-twelve firms. Thomson's participation also rose dramatically from 16.9 per cent of the ESPRIT I to 28.1 per cent of the ESPRIT II projects, the number of Big-twelve firms with which it was a participant in over five projects rose from six to nine, and it merged its semiconductor activities with those of SGS (I). What Figures 9.3 and 9.4 therefore show is an increasingly more intense pattern of interaction among five of the European IT majors — Thomson, Bull, Siemens, Philips and GEC — and a move towards consolidation of their position in Europe as a springboard into international markets.

Despite the emergence of these five firms at the core of a European information technology oligopoly, the data in Table 9.5 also show an impressive growth in the proportion of projects involving non-major firms in partnership with each other and/or with research organisations (type 3). More than one-third of both the ESPRIT I and ESPRIT II projects are of this type. While many of the non majors are themselves large firms, this group includes a growing number of SMEs.

Under the new rules of ESPRIT 2, many of these firms have opted for 'associate' or 'sub'-contractor status. The multiplier effect of access to all research results obtained in a project and the gains in knowledge accumulation that accrue to 'contractors' are thus likely to be far less significant for these firms in the future than they have been in the past. Within the context of broad networks (Table 9.5) involving both majors and non-majors (Type 2) that are the dominant form of networking within ESPRIT — 50.7 per cent of the ESPRIT I projects and 56.9 per cent of the ESPRIT II projects — SMEs that do not participate as 'contractors' find themselves increasingly linked to technological trajectories that they have not shaped.

While the growth of participation by SMEs through Types 2 and 3 projects appears to lend support to the argument that ESPRIT has fostered competition in the short run, the dominance of broad networks suggests that Europe's IT majors are positioning themselves so as to structure the pattern of intra-European competition in the future. Of considerable interest in this connection is the way in which several of the European majors have created 'private' networks of firms and research organizations through ESPRIT projects, a process that is concealed within the rising number of type-2 projects recorded in Table 9.5. For Philips, Olivetti and Thomson this has been a particularly important aspect of their partnering activity. Less intensely linked to other member of the Big-twelve during the first phase of ESPRIT (Figure 9.3), 28 per cent of the projects in which Philips was a partner involved no other major but linked Philips to a broad European network of smaller firms and research organisations. Olivetti engaged in this form of networking in 26 per cent of its projects, while for Thomson, 36 per cent of its ESPRIT-I projects fell into the category of 'private' networks.[9] Under ESPRIT II, as we saw above, Thomson has also been pursuing a strategy of intensifying its links to other members of the European IT oligopoly. In contrast, under ESPRIT II CGE has intensified its 'private' networking activities and some 42 per cent of its twenty projects are of this type.

Conclusion

The ESPRIT case nicely sums up many of the themes raised elsewhere in this volume. It points to the role that public agencies, in this case the European Communities, can play in strengthening the system of innovation and the regional technological base by providing financial support and linkage mechanisms for small and medium-sized enterprises, facilitating the movement of research results from research organizations into production, promoting trans-European collaboration and focusing that collaboration in a structured way. Smaller European firms have thus been able to pool scattered resources and achieve economies of scale in R & D.

Networking through ESPRIT has also enabled European firms to exploit the possibilities for combinative strategies, particularly in such critical new fields as computer-integrated-manufacturing systems. It has speeded up the process of technology 'catch-up' in those branches of the information technology industry in which Europe has been particularly weak, semiconductors for example, and has given a boost to those sectors where

European firms had a technological edge, as in information processing and software.

Participation in ESPRIT has enhanced the knowledge-accumulation possibilities of SMEs. Across firms it has demonstrated that distributed cooperation is a useful management technique in collaborative research projects. Within firms, ESPRIT appears to have led to a new openness with respect to new routines, partners and ways of looking at research and development.

With nearly eight years of positive experience in trans-European partnerships, the ESPRIT programme also suggests that collaboration and competition can coexist and indeed must coexist in the present context of uncertainty and rapid technological change. In this connection, networking through ESPRIT has enabled firms to window on the future shape of the market and thus be better positioned to take advantage of new developments. It has led to the establishment of standards that enhance the competitive advantage of combinative strategies through flexible technology-based partnerships and it has created supplier–client links that have opened new markets to large and small enterprises across Europe.

The networking behaviour among European firms which is the distinguishing feature of ESPRIT also addresses the larger issue of competition in the world economy. In particular it points to the way in which networks in R & D have emerged as partial substitutes for traditional forms of oligopoly as the barriers to entry in the industry became more permeable and the knowledge-intensity of production increased. The ability to access these networks and to ensure that membership in a network enhances knowledge accumulation and flexibility in a participating firm is thus of strategic importance not only for small and medium-sized enterprises in the information technology industry but, as concentration proceeds on a global scale, for the giants that dominate this industry as well.

Notes

1. I would like to thank Tom Hartley and Wayne Cox for their assistance in helping to create and update the ESPRIT data base on which much of the analysis contained in this chapter is based. A special thanks is also due to Jeff Gould whose help in guiding me through the use of his 'Mac'made possible the figures presented here.
2. There were, however, some differences between EC countries and across sectors. Applying an index of revealed technological advantage (RTA) that takes a given country's share of American patenting within a sector and divides it by that country's share of total American patents in the information technology industry, Luc Soete found considerable dynamism (RTA = >1) in the Japanese electronics and telecommunications industries and in the French telecommunications industry over the period 1963–81, but a major decline in the RTA index in both electronics and telecommunications for West Germany and the United Kingdom over the same period.
3. The most notable failure was the 1972 effort by Bull, Philips and Siemens to

pool their computing resources and form UNIDATA (Jublin and Quatrepoint, 1976).

4. The French study (Delapierre *et al.*, 1988) reports on a series of in-depth interviews with six research organizations and thirteen firms currently participating in ESPRIT projects. On the research side the study includes the three major publically funded research organizations the Commissariat a l'Energie Atomique (CEA), the Centre National d'Etudes des Télécommunications (CNET) and the Institute Nationale de Recherche en Informatique et Automatique (INRIA) — as well as the Institute National Polytechnique de Grenoble, Laboratoire de Genie Logiciel and the Ecole Nationale des Mines de Paris. From a total of sixty-four French firms that are participating in ESPRIT projects, thirteen were interviewed as part of this study. These included the three French 'majors' Bull, CGE and Thomson, — France's largest electronics and software engineering firms, MATRA and CAP GEMINI SOGETI; a major communications firm, SAGEM, three medium-sized firms, two in software and one in software and robotics TECSI, SYSECA, EUROSOFT — and four small companies in the software industry, SIMULOG, CRIL, ESI and CHORUS. These thirteen firms collectively account for 64 per cent of the 153 projects in which there is French participation. These projects span all five ESPRIT sub-programmes — twenty-seven in advanced microelectronics, twenty-four in software technology, sixteen in advanced information processing, twenty in Office Systems and eight in computer integrated manufacturing — and each of the programme years from the pilot-year 1983 through to the last call for projects in 1987. Of the thirty-three projects in which the six ROs were participants, only six did not include one of the thirteen French firms as well. The thirteen firms plus the six research organizations collectively accounted for 69 per cent of all French participation in ESPRIT projects. Finally, and for the purpose of reducing the possibility of idiosyncratic responses based on a single experience of cooperation, with the exception of CHORUS and ESI, all firms and research organizations interviewed for this study participate in more than one ESPRIT project and all have engaged in at least one technological cooperation agreement outside of ESPRIT.
5. Advanced medical and bio-informatics (AIM), Basic Research on Industrial Technologies (BRITE), European Research on Advanced Materials (EURAM), Transport Informatics (DRIVE), Telecommunications (RACE).
6. In practice, however, there is some evidence to suggest that this has also led to a large number of rather disparate projects which weaken the contribution of EUREKA to the building of a coherent and competitive industrial structure in Europe. More recently, therefore, the EC Commission itself has become a member of EUREKA projects that offer the potential for developing an integrated base through coordination with existing ESPRIT, RACE, DRIVE or other projects. With regard to administration, differences between the two programmes probably favour ESPRIT. Under ESPRIT, budget and project review procedures are centralized in DG XIII of the European Commission. EUREKA, however, is administered nationally and funding is provided by each member–state to the firms and research organizations located within it own national borders. Approval and financing procedures are thus multiples of the number of participating countries in a given project and this has lengthened the process of project approval and created difficulties when the proportion of a firm's total costs paid by the government varies across EUREKA member states.
7. Although the sample was biased toward universities and research organizations

(50 per cent of the respondants) as opposed to firms, some indication of the impact of ESPRIT mid-way through its first phase can be gained from these data.

8. Given that this ratio varies among these three firms, the networking multiplier effect cannot simply be attributed to the larger number of partners in ESPRIT-2 projects.
9. While standard setting tends to create barriers to entry, under certain circumstances, it may actually facilitate new entrants. Thus Alain Lipietz has suggested that the more international norms there are, the easier it will be for imitators to enter the market.
10. As large MNCs, all of the European IT majors have multiple strategic goals that they pursue simultaneously. Thomson, for example, has agreeements with GTE (US) to equip the United States' army with the RITA system, with Marconi (UK) and Selenia (I) to build new radar systems, with MBB (D) to modernize anti-aircraft defence systems and with National Semiconductor (US) for reciprocal second sourcing in integrated circuits for the telecommunications industry. It is a participant in thirty-eight ESPRIT 1 projects worth FF700 million, is engaged in discussions on ten EUREKA projects and has pursued more traditional strategies by taking over MOSTEK (US) in 1985 and merging its semiconductor activities with SGS (I) in 1987. Similar profiles can be constructed for each of the majors. What is interesting here is how their ESPRIT strategy complements these other activities. For additional details on Thomson's strategy see Chapter 5.

References

Abernathy, W. and Utterback, J. (1975), 'A Dynamic Model of Process and Product Innovation', Omega, **3**, No. 6, pp.639–56.

Arthur, B.W., (1985), 'Competing Technologies and Lock-in by Historical Small Events: The Dynamics of Allocation under Increasing Returns', Center for Economic Policy Research, Publication Number 43.

Bellon, B., 1986, *L'Interventionisme libéral la politique industrielle de l'Etat fédéral americain*, Paris, Economica.

Braendgaard, A. (1987), 'International Technology Programmes and National Systems of Production, ESPRIT and the Danish Electronics Industry' in C. Freeman and B.-A. Lundvall (eds), *Small Countries Facing the Technological Revolution*, London, Pinter Publishers, pp. 184–200.

Bull, 1987, *Annual Report 1986*, Paris.

Cainarca, G., Colombo, M. and Mariotti, S. (1988), 'Cooperative Agreements in the Information and Communications Industrial System', October.

Cadiou, J-M, 1986, 'Esprit, un premier bilan', *Bulletin de Liaison de la Recherche en Informatique et Automatique*, No. 105, pp. 36.

CAP GEMINI SOGETI, *Annual Report 1986*.

Carli, G.,1983, 'Investment and Technological Competitiveness' in A. Heertje (ed.). *Investing in Europe's Future*, UK, Basil Blackwell, pp.100–116.

Carpentier, M., 1984, 'Interview with Michel Carpentier, directeur général of DG XIII' in *La Féderation, des projets pour un grand marche les enjeux technologiques de l'Europe*, No. 464, Autumn.

Caty, G-F, (1984), 'Le programme ESPRIT', *Futuribles*, June, pp.26–36.

Chesnais, F., (1988), 'Technical Co-operation Agreements between Independent Firms, Novel Issues for Economic Analyses and the Formulation of National Technological Policies' *STI Revue*, No. 4, pp. 51–121.

Commission of the European Communities, 1983, *The Community IT Industry in Brief*, Brussels, June.

—, 1985, *Evaluation Intermediaire du Programme ESPRIT*, Brussels, 15 October.

—, 1986, *Communication from the Commission to the Council The Second Phase of Esprit*, Brussels, 21 May, COM, 86, 269 final.

—, (1987a), *Draft ESPRIT Workprogramme*, Brussels, D.G. XIII Telecommunications, Information Industries and Innovation, 22 July.

—, (1987b), *ESPRIT The First Phase, Progress and Results*, Brussels.

—, (1988), *ESPRIT 1987 Annual Report*, Brussels, D.G. III.

—, (1989a), *1989 ESPRIT Work Programme*, Brussels, D.G. III., 25 July.

—, (1989b), *ESPRIT, The Project Synopses*, Brussels, D.G. III. . . . and earlier years.

—, (1989c), *Research and Development in Advanced Communications Technologies in Europe, RACE '89*, Brussels, D.G. XIII, March.

—, (1989d), *The Review of ESPRIT 1984–1988*, The Report of the ESPRIT Review Board, Brussels, May.

—, (1989e), *ESPRIT Information Package*, Brussels, September.

Cowan, R., 1988, 'Backing the Wrong Horse, Sequential Choice Among Technologies of Unknown Merit', unpublished paper, February.

Cuneo, B., Gimenez, A.D. and Weinstein, O. (1988), *Recherche industrielle et cooperations europeennes dans l'industrie électronique*, Paris, GIP Mutations Industrielles.

Delapierre, M., Lermettre, J.F., Mytelka, L.K., Zimmemann, J-B., Vavakova, B. (1988). 'Cooperation between Firms and Research Institutes: The French Case' Background paper for an Eureka Conference on the Institutes and Industry, Milan, Bocconi University.

Dosi, Giovanni, (1982), 'Technological paradigms and technological trajectories, a suggested interpretation of the determinants and directions of technical change', *Research Policy*, **11**, pp.147–62.

Ergas, H., (1987), 'Does Technology Policy Matter?' in B. Guile and H. Brooks, (eds.), *Technology and Global Industry, Companies and Nations in the World Economy*, Washington, DC, National Academy Press.

Freeman, Christopher, (1987), 'The Challenge of New Technologies' in OECD, *Interdependence and Co-operation in Tomorrow's World*, Paris, OECD, pp.123–56.

Freeman, Christopher and Perez, Carlotta (1988), 'Structural crises of adjustment, business cycles and investment behaviour' in G. Dosi, C. Freeman, R. Nelson, G. Silverberg and Soete, L., (eds), Technical Change and Economic Theory, London, Pinter Publishers, pp.38–66.

Georghiou, L., Guy, K. *et al.*, (1987), *Evaluation of the Alvey Programme Interim Report*, London, Her Majesty's Stationery Office.

Hergert, M. and Morris, D. (1988), 'Trends in International Collaborative Agreements' in F. Contractor and P. Lorange, (eds.), *Cooperative Strategies in International Business*, Lexington, Lexington Books, pp. 99–110.

Jublin, J. and Quatrepoint, J.M., (1976), *French Ordinateurs*, Paris, A. Moreau.

LAREA/CEREM, (1986a), 'Le Trâitement de l'Information', Nanterre, Universite de Paris-X.

—, (1986b), *Les Strategies d'accords des groupes européens entre la cohesion et l'éclatement*, Nanterre, Universite de Paris-X.

Launet, E., (1988), 'Danemark, Petit Pays Industrialise Cherche Partenaires' *Science & Technologie*, No. 7, July-August, pp.12–17.

Mytelka, L.K. and Delapierre, M. (1987), 'The Alliance Strategies of European Firms and the Role of ESPRIT' in *Journal of Common Market Studies*, **XXVI**, No. 2, pp.231–54.

National Science Foundation, (1986), 'International Science and Technology Data Update 1986', Washington, D.C., Government Printing Office.

—, (1987), 'International Science and Technology Data Update 1987', Washington, DC, Government Printing Office.

Nelson, Richard R. and Winter, Sidney G., (1982), *An Evolutionary Theory of Economic Change*, Cambridge, Mass, The Belknap Press of Harvard University Press.

OECD, (1986), 'Technical Co-operation Agreements Between Firms, Some Initial Data and Analysis' Paris, OECD, Directorate for Science, Technology and Industry, 21 May, DSTI/SPR/86.20-Part 1.

Richonnier, M., (1984), 'Les hesitations offensives de l'Europe, le cas de l'electronique' Revue d'economie Industrielle, No. 27, pp.91–107.

Sciberras, E., (1987), 'Government sponsored programmes for international technological exchanges and applied collective research', *R & D Management*, No. 17, pp.15–33.

Sharp, M. and Holmes, P. (1989), 'Conclusions, Farewell to the National Champion' in M. Sharp and P. Holmes , (eds.), *Strategies for New Technologies, Case Studies from Britain and France*, Philip Allan, pp.212–233.

— and Shearman, C. (1987), *European Technological Collaboration*, London, Routledge & Kegan Paul.

Soete, L., (1985), 'Electronics' in L. Soete, (ed.), *Technological Trends and Employment, Electronics and Communications*, Aldershot, Gower.

von Tunzelmann, N. and Soete, L. (1987), 'Diffusion and Market Structure with Converging Technologies', paper prepared for the Conference on Technology and Government Policy in Computers and Communications' at the Brookings Institution, Washington DC, 4–5 June.

United Nations, (1988), *Transnational Corporations in World Development, Trends and Prospects*, New York, UN Centre on Transnational Corporations.

Vickery, G., (1987), 'Diffusing New Technologies Micro-electronics' in *STI Review*, No. 2 , pp.41–80.

Walsh, V., (1987), 'Technology Competitiveness and the Special Problems of Small Countries' *STI Review*, No. 2, September, pp.81–133.

Woods, S. (1987), *Western Europe: Technology and the Future*, U.K., Croom Helm.

Index of companies

Index of Partnerships and Programmes

General Index